Here's a look at the Toolbox; it's expanded so that you can see all its tools.

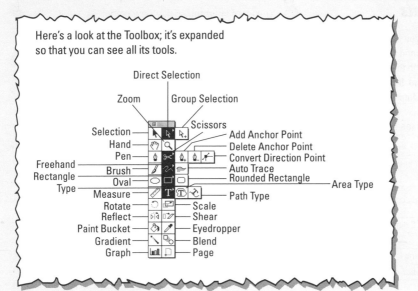

Zoom — Direct Selection — Group Selection — Scissors
Selection — Add Anchor Point
Hand — Delete Anchor Point
Pen — Convert Direction Point
Freehand — Auto Trace
Brush
Rectangle — Rounded Rectangle — Area Type
Oval
Type — Path Type
Measure
Rotate — Scale
Reflect — Shear
Paint Bucket — Eyedropper
Gradient — Blend
Graph — Page

You can use Illustrator's Paint palette to add color to your artwork. Here's a look at what's in the palette.

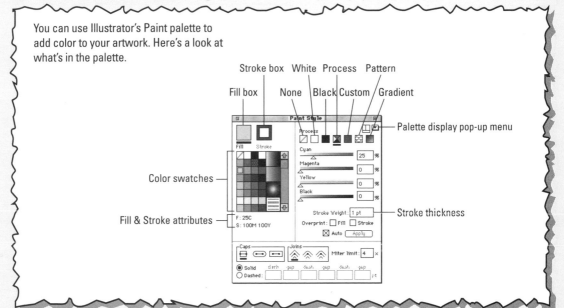

Fill box Stroke box None White Black Process Custom Pattern Gradient

Palette display pop-up menu

Color swatches

Fill & Stroke attributes

Stroke thickness

Paint Style

Process
Cyan   25 %
Magenta   0 %
Yellow   0 %
Black   0 %

Stroke Weight: 1 pt
Overprint: ☐ Fill ☐ Stroke
☒ Auto Apply

F: 25C
S: 100M 100Y

Caps   Joins   Miter limit: 4 x
○ Solid
○ Dashed: pt

...For Dummies: #1 Computer Book Series for Beginners

FOR DUMMIES®

COMPUTER
BOOK SERIES
FROM IDG

Illustrator™ 6 For Macs® For Dummies®

Cheat Sheet

Keyboard Shortcuts

By using keyboard shortcuts, you can work efficiently and quickly. If you use a command over and over again, you may want to pay attention to the keyboard shortcut (so that you can use it next time). If you forget some of the shortcuts, you can always look for them here.

Keyboard shortcuts in the File menu:

⌘+N	New File
⌘+Option+N	New File with Template
⌘+O	Open File
⌘+S	Save File
⌘+W	Close File
⌘+Shift+D	Document Setup
⌘+P	Print File
⌘+K	Open General Preference dialog box
⌘+Q	Quit Illustrator

Keyboard shortcuts in the Edit menu:

⌘+Z	Undo
⌘+Shift+Z	Redo
⌘+X	Cut
⌘+C	Copy
⌘+P	Paste
⌘+A	Select All
⌘+Shift+A	Select None
⌘+F	Paste In Front
⌘+B	Paste In Back

Keyboard shortcuts in the Arrange menu:

⌘+D	Repeat Transform
⌘+Shift+M	Open the Move dialog box
⌘+=	Bring to Front
⌘+-	Send to Back
⌘+G	Group
⌘+U	Ungroup
⌘+1	Lock selected objects
⌘+2	Unlock All
⌘+3	Hide selected objects
⌘+4	Show All

Keyboard shortcut in the Filter menu:

⌘+Shift+E	Apply Last Filter

Keyboard shortcuts in the View menu:

⌘+Y	Preview view
⌘+E	Artwork view
⌘+Option+Y	Preview Selection
⌘+Shift+W	Hide Template
⌘+R	Show Rulers
⌘+Shift+H	Hide edges of a selected object
⌘+]	Zoom In
⌘+[	Zoom Out
⌘+H	Actual Size
⌘+M	Fit in Window
⌘+Ctrl+V	Open the New View dialog box

Keyboard shortcuts in the Object menu:

⌘+I	Show/Hide Paint Style palette
⌘+Ctrl+A	Open Attribute dialog box
⌘+J	Join anchor points
⌘+L	Average anchor points
⌘+5	Make Guides
⌘+6	Release Guides
⌘+7	Lock/Unlock Guides
⌘+8	Make Compound
⌘+9	Release Compound

Keyboard shortcuts in the Type menu:

⌘+Shift+S	Type Size
⌘+ Shift+L	Left Alignment
⌘+ Shift+C	Center Alignment
⌘+ Shift+R	Right Alignment
⌘+Shift+J	Justify
⌘+ Shift+B	Justify Last Line
⌘+ Shift+K	Tracking/Kerning
⌘+ Shift+O	Type Spacing
⌘+ T	Show/Hide Character palette
⌘+ Shift+P	Show/Hide Paragraph palette
⌘+ Shift+G	Link Blocks
⌘+ Shift+U	Unlink Blocks

Keyboard shortcuts in the Window menu:

⌘+Ctrl+T	Show/Hide Toolbox
⌘+Ctrl+L	Show/Hide Layers palette
⌘+Ctrl+I	Show/Hide Info palette
⌘+Shift+T	Show/Hide Tab Ruler palette

References for the Rest of Us! ®

COMPUTER BOOK SERIES FROM IDG

Are you intimidated and confused by computers? Do you find that traditional manuals are overloaded with technical details you'll never use? Do your friends and family always call you to fix simple problems on their PCs? Then the *... For Dummies* computer book series from IDG Books Worldwide is for you.

... For Dummies books are written for those frustrated computer users who know they aren't really dumb but find that PC hardware, software, and indeed the unique vocabulary of computing make them feel helpless. *... For Dummies* books use a lighthearted approach, a down-to-earth style, and even cartoons and humorous icons to diffuse computer novices' fears and build their confidence. Lighthearted but not lightweight, these books are a perfect survival guide for anyone forced to use a computer.

> *"I like my copy so much I told friends; now they bought copies."*
>
> **Irene C., Orwell, Ohio**

> *"Quick, concise, nontechnical, and humorous."*
>
> **Jay A., Elburn, Illinois**

> *"Thanks, I needed this book. Now I can sleep at night."*
>
> **Robin F., British Columbia, Canada**

Already, hundreds of thousands of satisfied readers agree. They have made *... For Dummies* books the #1 introductory level computer book series and have written asking for more. So, if you're looking for the most fun and easy way to learn about computers, look to *... For Dummies* books to give you a helping hand.

ILLUSTRATOR™ 6

FOR MACS™ FOR

DUMMIES®

ILLUSTRATOR™ 6 FOR MACS™ FOR DUMMIES®

by Adele Droblas Greenberg
and Seth Greenberg

IDG Books Worldwide, Inc.
An International Data Group Company

Foster City, CA ♦ Chicago, IL ♦ Indianapolis, IN ♦ Braintree, MA ♦ Southlake, TX

Illustrator™ 6 For Macs™ For Dummies®

Published by
IDG Books Worldwide, Inc.
An International Data Group Company
919 E. Hillsdale Blvd.
Suite 400
Foster City, CA 94404

Library of Congress Catalog Card No.: 96-75119

ISBN: 1-56884-914-1

Printed in the United States of America

10 9 8 7 6 5 4 3 2 1

1E/RZ/QS/ZW/IN

Distributed in the United States by IDG Books Worldwide, Inc.

Distributed by Macmillan Canada for Canada; by Computer and Technical Books for the Caribbean Basin; by Contemporanea de Ediciones for Venezuela; by Distribuidora Cuspide for Argentina; by CITEC for Brazil; by Ediciones ZETA S.C.R. Ltda. for Peru; by Editorial Limusa SA for Mexico; by Transworld Publishers Limited in the United Kingdom and Europe; by Al-Maiman Publishers & Distributors for Saudi Arabia; by Simron Pty. Ltd. for South Africa; by IDG Communications (HK) Ltd. for Hong Kong; by Toppan Company Ltd. for Japan; by Addison Wesley Publishing Company for Korea; by Longman Singapore Publishers Ltd. for Singapore, Malaysia, Thailand, and Indonesia; by Unalis Corporation for Taiwan; by WS Computer Publishing Company, Inc. for the Philippines; by WoodsLane Pty. Ltd. for Australia; by WoodsLane Enterprises Ltd. for New Zealand.

For general information on IDG Books Worldwide's books in the U.S., please call our Consumer Customer Service department at 800-762-2974. For reseller information, including discounts and premium sales, please call our Reseller Customer Service department at 800-434-3422.

For information on where to purchase IDG Books Worldwide's books outside the U.S., contact IDG Books Worldwide at 415-655-3021 or fax 415-655-3295.

For information on translations, contact Marc Jeffrey Mikulich, Director, Foreign & Subsidiary Rights, at IDG Books Worldwide, 415-655-3018 or fax 415-655-3295.

For sales inquiries and special prices for bulk quantities, write to the address above or call IDG Books Worldwide at 415-655-3200.

For information on using IDG Books Worldwide's books in the classroom, or ordering examination copies, contact the Education Office at 800-434-2086 or fax 817-251-8174.

For authorization to photocopy items for corporate, personal, or educational use, please contact Copyright Clearance Center, 222 Rosewood Drive, Danvers, MA 01923, or fax 508-750-4470.

is a trademark under exclusive license to IDG Books Worldwide, Inc., from International Data Group, Inc.

About the Authors

Adele Droblas Greenberg

Adele Droblas Greenberg is a New York-based artist and desktop publishing/prepress consultant. She teaches at Pratt Institute in Manhattan and United Digital Artists at Apple Computer-NYC. She is also former training director at a New York City prepress house.

Seth Greenberg

Seth Greenberg is a member of the Apple Solution Professionals Network. He is a computer consultant, database/multimedia programmer, and freelance writer. He has worked as a television producer and script writer and has written for several computer magazines.

ABOUT IDG BOOKS WORLDWIDE

WINNER
*Eighth Annual
Computer Press
Awards ≥ 1992*

WINNER
*Ninth Annual
Computer Press
Awards ≥ 1993*

IDG BOOKS WORLDWIDE

Welcome to the world of IDG Books Worldwide.

IDG Books Worldwide, Inc., is a subsidiary of International Data Group, the world's largest publisher of computer-related information and the leading global provider of information services on information technology. IDG was founded more than 25 years ago and now employs more than 7,700 people worldwide. IDG publishes more than 250 computer publications in 67 countries (see listing below). More than 70 million people read one or more IDG publications each month.

Launched in 1990, IDG Books Worldwide is today the #1 publisher of best-selling computer books in the United States. We are proud to have received 8 awards from the Computer Press Association in recognition of editorial excellence and three from Computer Currents' First Annual Readers' Choice Awards, and our best-selling ...*For Dummies*® series has more than 19 million copies in print with translations in 28 languages. IDG Books Worldwide, through a joint venture with IDG's Hi-Tech Beijing, became the first U.S. publisher to publish a computer book in the People's Republic of China. In record time, IDG Books Worldwide has become the first choice for millions of readers around the world who want to learn how to better manage their businesses.

Our mission is simple: Every one of our books is designed to bring extra value and skill-building instructions to the reader. Our books are written by experts who understand and care about our readers. The knowledge base of our editorial staff comes from years of experience in publishing, education, and journalism — experience which we use to produce books for the '90s. In short, we care about books, so we attract the best people. We devote special attention to details such as audience, interior design, use of icons, and illustrations. And because we use an efficient process of authoring, editing, and desktop publishing our books electronically, we can spend more time ensuring superior content and spend less time on the technicalities of making books.

You can count on our commitment to deliver high-quality books at competitive prices on topics you want to read about. At IDG Books Worldwide, we continue in the IDG tradition of delivering quality for more than 25 years. You'll find no better book on a subject than one from IDG Books Worldwide.

John J. Kilcullen

John Kilcullen
President and CEO
IDG Books Worldwide, Inc.

IDG Books Worldwide, Inc., is a subsidiary of International Data Group, the world's largest publisher of computer-related information and the leading global provider of information services on information technology. International Data Group publishes over 250 computer publications in 67 countries. Seventy million people read one or more International Data Group publications each month. International Data Group's publications include: **ARGENTINA:** Computerworld Argentina, GamePro, Infoworld, PC World Argentina; **AUSTRALIA:** Australian Macworld, Client/Server Journal, Computer Living, Computerworld, Digital News, Network World, PC World, Publishing Essentials, Reseller; **AUSTRIA:** Computerwelt, PC TEST; **BELARUS:** PC World Belarus; **BELGIUM:** Data News; **BRAZIL:** Annuário de Informática, Computerworld Brazil, Connections, Super Game Power, Macworld, PC World Brazil, Publish Brazil, SUPERGAME; **BULGARIA:** Computerworld Bulgaria, Networkworld/Bulgaria, PC & MacWorld Bulgaria; **CANADA:** CIO Canada, ComputerWorld Canada, InfoCanada, Network World Canada, Reseller World; **CHILE:** Computerworld Chile, GamePro, PC World Chile; **COLUMBIA:** Computerworld Colombia, GamePro, PC World Colombia; **COSTA RICA:** PC World Costa Rica/Nicaragua; **THE CZECH AND SLOVAK REPUBLICS:** Computerworld Czechoslovakia, Elektronika Czechoslovakia, PC World Czechoslovakia; **DENMARK:** Communications World, Computerworld Danmark, Macworld Danmark, PC World Danmark, PC World Danmark Supplements, TECH World; **DOMINICAN REPUBLIC:** PC World Republica Dominicana; **ECUADOR:** PC World Ecuador, GamePro; **EGYPT:** Computerworld Middle East, PC World Middle East; **EL SALVADOR:** PC World Centro America; **FINLAND:** MikroPC, Tietoverkko, Tietoviikko; **FRANCE:** Distributique, Golden, Info PC, Le Guide du Monde Informatique, Le Monde Informatique, Reseaux & Telecoms; **GERMANY:** Computer Business, Computerwoche, Computerwoche Extra, Computerwoche Focus, Electronic Entertainment, GamePro, I/M Information Management, Macwelt, PC Welt; **GREECE:** GamePro, Macworld & Publish; **GUATEMALA:** PC World Centro America; **HONDURAS:** PC World Centro America; **HONG KONG:** Computerworld Hong Kong, PCWorld Hong Kong, Publish in Asia; **HUNGARY:** ABCD CD-ROM, Computerworld Szamitastechnika, PC & Mac World Hungary, PC-X Magazine; **INDIA:** Computerworld India, PC World India, Publish in Asia; **INDONESIA:** InfoKomputer PC World, Komputek Computerworld, Publish in Asia; **IRELAND:** ComputerScope, PC Live!; **ISRAEL:** PC World 32 BIT, People & Computers; **ITALY:** Computerworld Italia, Computerworld Italia Special Editions, Lotus Italia, Macworld Italia, Networking Italia, PC Shopping, PC World Italia, PC World/Walt Disney; **JAPAN:** Macworld Japan, Nikkei Personal Computing, SunWorld Japan, Windows World Japan; **KENYA:** East African Computer News; **KOREA:** Hi-Tech Information/Computerworld, Macworld Korea, PC World Korea; **MACEDONIA:** PC World Macedonia; **MALAYSIA:** Computerworld Malaysia, PC World Malaysia, Publish in Asia; **MEXICO:** Computerworld Mexico, GamePro, Macworld, PC World Mexico; **MYANMAR:** PC World Myanmar; **NETHERLANDS:** Computable, Computer! Totaal, LAN Magazine, Macworld, Net Magazine; **NEW ZEALAND:** Computer Buyer, Computerworld New Zealand, MTB, Network World, PC World New Zealand; **NICARAGUA:** PC World Costa Rica/Nicaragua; **NIGERIA:** PC World Africa; **NORWAY:** Computerworld Norge, Computerworld Privat, CW Rapport Klient/Tjener, CW Rapport Nettverk & Telecom, CW Rapport Offentlig Sektor, IDG's KURSGUIDE, Macworld Norge, Multimedia World, PC World Ekspress, PC World Nettverk, PC World Norge, PC World's Produktguide, Windows Spesial; **PAKISTAN:** Computerworld Pakistan, PC World Pakistan; **PANAMA:** GamePro, PC World Panama; **PARAGUAY:** PC World Paraguay; **P. R. OF CHINA:** China Computerworld, China Infoworld, Computer & Communication, Electronic Product World, Electronics Today, Game Camp, PC World China, Popular Computer Week, Software World, Telecom Product World; **PERU:** Computerworld Peru, GamePro, PC World Profesional Peru, PC World Peru; **POLAND:** Computerworld Poland, Computerworld Special Report, Macworld, Networld, PC World Komputer; **PHILIPPINES:** Computerworld Philippines, PC Digest, Publish in Asia; **PORTUGAL:** Cerebro/PC World, Correio Informático/Computerworld, Mac•In/PC•In Portugal; **PUERTO RICO:** PC World Puerto Rico; **ROMANIA:** Computerworld Romania, PC World Romania, Telecom Romania; **RUSSIA:** Computerworld Rossiya, Network World Russia, PC World Russia; **SINGAPORE:** Computerworld Singapore, PC World Singapore, Publish in Asia; **SLOVENIA:** MONITOR; **SOUTH AFRICA:** Computing S.A., Network World S.A., Software World; **SPAIN:** Computerworld España, COMUNICACIONES WORLD, Dealer World, Macworld España, PC World España; **SWEDEN:** CAP&Design, Computer Sweden, Corporate Computing, MacWorld, Maxi Data, MikroDatorn, Nätverk & Kommunikation, PC/Aktiv, PC World, Windows World; **SWITZERLAND:** Computerworld Schweiz, Macworld Schweiz, PCtip; **TAIWAN:** Computerworld Taiwan, Macworld Taiwan, PC World Taiwan, Publish Taiwan, Windows World; **THAILAND:** Thai Computerworld, Publish in Asia; **TURKEY:** Computerworld Monitôr, MACWORLD Turkiye, PC WORLD Turkiye; **UKRAINE:** Computerworld Kiev, Computers & Software Magazine, PC World Ukraine; **UNITED KINGDOM:** Acorn User, Amiga Action, Amiga Computing, Amiga, Appletalk, CD Powerplay, CD-ROM Now, Computing, Connexion, GamePro, Lotus Magazine, Macaction, Macworld, Open Computing, Parents and Computers, PC Home, PC Works, The WEB; **UNITED STATES:** Cable in the Classroom, CD Review, CIO Magazine, Computerworld, Computerworld Client/Server Journal, Digital Video Magazine, DOS World, Electronic, InfoWorld, I-Way, Macworld, Maximize, MULTIMEDIA WORLD, Network World, PC World, PUBLISH, SWATPro Magazine, Video Event, WebMaster; **URUGUAY:** PC World Uruguay; **VENEZUELA:** Computerworld Venezuela, GamePro, PC World Venezuela; and **VIETNAM:** PC World Vietnam   10/17/95

Dedication

To our family for their love and support.

Acknowledgments

We want to give a special thanks to the many people at IDG Books Worldwide, Inc., who helped to make this book a reality, particularly Diane Graves Steele, Jennifer Wallis, Diane Giangrossi, Leah Cameron, Kelly Ewing, Suzanne Packer, Gail Scott, Megg Bonar, and technical editor Tim Warner. Their conscientiousness and enthusiasm made the *Illustrator 6 For Macs For Dummies* path smooth going.

We especially would like to thank Patricia Pane and Sean McKenna of Adobe Systems for their assistance.

We also want to thank Nancy Carr at Apple Computer, who helped see to it that we could slip away from the cold weather for a few days to the warm weather in Florida and still continue working — with a spiffy Apple PowerPC Powerbook 5300c.

We'd like to thank all of the artists who contributed their excellent work and the companies who sent us stock images on CD-ROMs to use in the book.

Thanks also to everyone else who helped us along the way.

(The Publisher would like to give special thanks to Patrick J. McGovern, without whom this book would not have been possible.)

Credits

Contents at a Glance

Cartoons at a Glance

By Rich Tennant

Page 134

Page 268

Page 189

Page 233

Page 77

Page 55

Page 164

Page 297

Page 5

Page 331

Table of Contents

Introduction

Why Illustrator 6 For Macs For Dummies?

If you've been using a Mac for any length of time, you know that most Mac programs are pretty intuitive. You probably know people who say that they can learn a Mac program without a manual and without a book. But when you ask one of these people to help you do something in Adobe Illustrator, they suddenly become afraid of mice.

Illustrator requires a little more preflight training than most Macintosh programs. When you use Adobe Illustrator, you can't put your brain on autopilot and expect to taxi down your mouse pad without a few complications. So what's the solution? You guessed it: an *Illustrator 6 For Macs For Dummies* book.

We wrote this book to help you get safely off the ground when you use Illustrator. This book not only gives you the preflight and in-flight training that you need to successfully work with Illustrator but it also introduces you to some show-stopping special effects.

Keep reading and you'll find that this book is your passport to a whole new world of artistic possibilities. *Illustrator 6 For Macs For Dummies* is filled with easy-to-follow examples and step-by-step exercises. You don't need to be a computer genius or a master artist to get the most from this book. All you need to do is grab your mouse and read on — you'll find that a smooth, fun journey lies ahead. And we assure you that you don't need a parachute.

How to Use This Book

Following are conventions used in this book.

Menu commands look like this:

File➪Preferences➪General

When you see this format, you start by clicking on File to get the File pull-down menu. When you click (and see the menu), keep the mouse button pressed and choose Preferences from the list of items in the File menu. With the mouse button *still* pressed, choose General from the Preferences submenu — then and *only* then release the mouse to execute the command.

Keyboard shortcuts look like this:

⌘+S

When you see this format, you press and hold the Command key on the keyboard. With the Command key down, press S to execute the command. (By the way, this keyboard shortcut saves your work.) For more keyboard short-cuts, see the Cheat Sheet (at the very beginning of this book) and Chapter 22.

How This Book Is Organized

This book covers the features in Illustrator 6 for Macintosh and PowerMac users.

We wrote this book so that you can read it from beginning to end or just jump around from topic to topic. That is, you don't have to read the whole book to learn how to use Illustrator. Just find the topic you want to know more about, and start reading. To make it easier for you to find what you are looking for, we divided this book into six main parts: Illustrator 101, Drawing and Coloring, All About Working with Text, More Amazing Illustrator Stuff, Advanced Topics, and The Parts of Ten.

Part I: Illustrator 101

This part helps get you off the ground with Illustrator. You'll see how Illustrator works and what you can do with it. You'll find out what Illustrator's tools do and start creating basic shapes. Also, you'll discover how to print your first works of Illustrator art.

Part II: Drawing and Coloring

In this part, we show you how to use Illustrator's Pen tool to begin creating sophisticated art. This part also covers how Illustrator's Paint Style palette helps to create gradations and patterns.

Part III: All About Working with Text

This part covers how to use text in Illustrator and how to create text tricks. You'll see how to bend text along a curve, create text within shapes, and link objects with text in them.

Part IV: More Amazing Illustrator Stuff

In this part, you'll use Illustrator's magical filters. You'll be amazed at how they transform your simple artwork into complex shapes. This part also shows you how to create special effects with blends and compound paths. The last chapter in this part shows you all the great things that you can do with graphs.

Part V: Advanced Topics

This part shows you how the pros work. You'll see how professional artists work with Illustrator and other programs to create artwork for newspapers and magazines. The final chapter covers advanced outputting techniques for color publishing.

Part VI: The Part of Tens

This part shows you the top ten Path and top ten Type keyboard shortcuts, and it provides you with a list of top ten Drawing and Type tips.

Icons Used in This Book

We've used several icons in this book to help you find things quickly and easily.

This icon indicates that we're revealing a shortcut or helpful point to add to your ever-growing bag of Illustrator tricks and techniques.

When you see this icon, be prepared for some impressive technical information about Illustrator, computers, or publishing. Knowing this kind of information may impress your friends. Of course, you probably have other ways of impressing them, so you only need to read the technical stuff if the topic interests you.

Watch out for this icon; it cautions you when turbulence may be lurking ahead! Heed the advice provided by these warnings and you'll keep yourself from taking any wrong turns on your flight path.

We use this icon to remind you about techniques or aspects of Illustrator that are helpful to keep in mind while you are using the program.

This icon points you to some pretty important stuff. The information here may get you out of some sticky situations during your encounters with Illustrator.

Part I
Illustrator 101

The 5th Wave   By Rich Tennant

I HAVEN'T LOCATED THE PROBLEM YET.

In this part . . .

*B*efore you can get up and running in any graphics program, you need to make yourself at home and get adjusted to your new surroundings. We designed the next five chapters to introduce you gradually to the world of Illustrator. After making your acquaintance with Illustrator's screens, menus, and palettes, you can take your first steps at creating your own works of Illustrator art.

Chapter 1

Your First Steps

*B*efore the world's first artists began to create the world's first cave art, the first thing they probably did was take a tour of their caves. Once they knew how to make their way around the nooks and crannies of the caves and lost their fear of the dark, they could pick up their prehistoric pens, apply them to the stone walls, and begin to express their creativity.

A lot has changed since the days of cavemen and cavewomen, but people haven't. Everyone likes to feel comfortable and get used to his or her surroundings before embarking on anything new. Here's your chance to explore some nooks and crannies of Illustrator and examine the tools you'll use to create art.

What Is Adobe Illustrator?

A decade ago, the first drawing programs available on the Mac were quite simple and easy to use. If you needed to create circles, squares, and lines, these programs were perfect — perfect for playing tic-tac-toe. However, the most popular pastime for many drawing program users was creating organization charts. Once managers realized how easy it was to create and edit organization charts, they ordered up organization charts on a weekly basis. Strangely enough, all the managers who asked artists to create organization charts were eventually removed from those organization charts.

Soon managers began to ask artists to create more sophisticated work, maybe a logo that had one or two curves in it. Unfortunately, curves proved beyond the power of many of the first drawing programs.

Fortunately, along came Adobe Illustrator, which provides artists with the power to create not only circles, squares, and lines, but perfectly smooth curves as well. With Illustrator, virtually any illustration that can be created by hand can be created on the computer. Illustrator even allows users to import scanned logos and other images and trace over them to create a new, digital version on the computer. Once the traced image is created on the computer, it can be enlarged or shrunk without any loss in quality.

Fortunately Illustrator lets you do all of this and more. Illustrator is one of the most powerful tools for creating art on the computer, primarily because everything is created from something called a *path*. If working with paths is unfamiliar to you, you'll undoubtedly have to spend some time getting acquainted with them. However, once you understand how paths work, you can become a master at Illustrator. And you can start right here.

Going down the Illustrator path

In Illustrator, all shapes and objects are created from paths. Now, to most people, a path is something that you wander down. It's usually associated with nice spring days, verdant meadows, trees, and possibly a crystal-clear, babbling brook.

Illustrator's paths are quite a different beast. In Illustrator, a path is a collection of *segments* that can be straight or curved. The segments in the path are connected by *anchor points*. Sprouting from the anchor points of curve segments are lines called *direction lines*. Figure 1-1 shows how paths are joined together to create a football. (Don't worry too much about anchor points and direction lines now. You'll find out more about them in Chapters 3, 6, and 7.)

Think of paths as wires that you can bend and twist in any direction to make any shape you want. In Illustrator, paths appear somewhat like shapes made from wireframes. These wireframe shapes appear on-screen but won't print unless you add color to them.

Why use a program that uses paths? Because paths allow you to precisely manipulate the path segments by dragging the anchor points on-screen and by clicking and dragging on the direction lines.

For example, in Figure 1-1, you can make the football wider or narrower by clicking and dragging on its top and bottom anchor points. You can make the bump in the curve of the football smoother by clicking and dragging the direction lines. See Chapters 3, 6, and 7 for more information on paths.

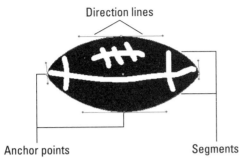

Direction lines

Anchor points   Segments

Figure 1-1:
Illustrator
paths
combine to
create a
football.

Why use Illustrator?

Let's be honest. To most people, it's simpler to sketch an image with pen and paper than to take the time to learn Illustrator and try to figure out which way to click a direction line to smooth out bumpy curves. Why use Illustrator when you can draw the same things with pen or pencil?

Consider something as simple as drawing a flower. To draw a flower by hand, you may start by drawing one petal. Then you may create more petals around the center of the flower. But how do you make the curved shapes of the flowers perfect? What happens if you make a mistake, particularly if you're working with pen and ink? You may even need to throw out the work you did and start from scratch.

With Illustrator, the drawing is a snap. You create a path to represent the petal. You then adjust the path to perfection by manipulating the path's anchor points and direction lines. Then you duplicate the petal as you rotate it around the flower's stem. The flower is perfectly drawn. You can also easily edit it and quickly color it. If you wish to create the flower at a smaller or larger size, you simply enlarge or reduce it using the Scale tool. Using the Rotate and Scale tool to create objects is covered in Chapter 8.

Once you create your art in Illustrator, you can save it, and then you can import it into a page layout program for inclusion in an advertisement, book, or magazine. You can also import it into an image-editing program such as Adobe Photoshop, where you can integrate your artwork into photo montages. Just think of all the other cool things, (like creating Web pages) that you can do with the art you create in Illustrator.

In Chapter 20, you see how to save in different file formats so that you can import Illustrator art into other programs. In Chapter 3, you see how to copy and paste and "drag and drop" images between Illustrator and Photoshop files.

Vexing over vectors and biting into bitmaps

Computer graphics programs are generally broken down into two main families: *bitmap* programs and *vector* programs. In general, you use bitmap programs for displaying and editing digitized images (such as scanned photographs), while you use vector programs for creating illustrations and working with type. Illustrator is considered a vector program. Vector programs create graphics from curves and lines that are described mathematically. Bitmap programs, on the other hand, are based upon the tiny individual picture elements, called *pixels,* that compose the image. Paint programs and image-editing programs — like Photoshop — are bitmap programs (to confuse matters, bitmap programs are sometimes called *raster* programs).

The differences between the two types of programs are significant. In a *vector program,* such as Illustrator, the paths you create are objects that are based on mathematical formulas. The math determines the position, the shape, and the size of an object. When you enlarge an object, the computer simply does the math to compute the new object. A great advantage that you have with vector programs is that when you double the size of an object on-screen, the file size doesn't double — in general, it doesn't even change. When you move an image around on-screen, you can just click and drag it around because the computer mathematically recalculates the object's new position. When you print the image, the number of dots per inch (dpi) that the printer outputs determines image quality. All

of this is true because the images that you see on-screen are simply mathematical representations of your work, rather than a grid of pixels that make up the image.

In *bitmap programs,* the greater the number of image elements, or pixels per inch, the finer the image and the larger its file size. When you enlarge a bitmap image, you often decrease the number of pixels per inch. Because of this, the quality of the image can suffer when you print it because there are not enough pixels per inch to truly represent the image. So, even if you print an image at a high resolution (large number of dots per inch), the quality of the image won't necessarily improve. In order to ensure that resized images are output properly, you may even need to use your calculator to determine the proper number of pixels you need to output your image.

What does this mean for you Illustrator users? You're lucky. There's much less to worry about when using a vector program. For example, in Illustrator you don't have to worry about setting up an image with the correct number of pixels, nor do you need to worry that an image's file size is going to grow or that the image's quality will suffer when you enlarge the image. Now you can brag to all your friends about what a wise purchase you made and impress them with your brilliant discourse on the differences between vector programs and bitmap programs (aren't you glad you decided to read this sidebar?).

It's not as difficult as you think

Although we don't like to admit it, it is true: Illustrator has a reputation as being a program that is somewhat difficult to learn. The fact is, though, that Illustrator only *seems* difficult because you need to create your artwork using tools that are unfamiliar to many artists. For example, the Pen tool in Illustrator just doesn't work like the pen on your desk (or the one that recently fell behind your desk). Once you get used to the tools that Illustrator provides, you'll be amazed at how a program that once seemed difficult becomes quite easy to use.

So, as you embark down the digital drawing path, don't worry. There are no crocodiles hidden in dialog boxes, no booby-trapped tools waiting to spring at you when you open the Toolbox. At the end of the path, however, there is a pot of gold. You'll have new marketable skills. You'll be able to create and color art in ways you never before thought possible. So stick around.

Launching Illustrator

Adobe Illustrator 6.0

Ready to get started? Your first step is to open Illustrator. You open Illustrator just like you open all Macintosh programs: Move the mouse pointer to the Illustrator icon, and double-click.

Where's the Illustrator icon? If you've installed Illustrator by following the program's installation instructions, you have an Illustrator folder on your hard disk. Open the Illustrator folder by double-clicking it, and inside you should see the Illustrator icon. Figure 1-2 shows the Adobe Illustrator folder.

Figure 1-2:
The Adobe
Illustrator
folder; just
double-click
on the
Illustrator
icon to run
Illustrator.

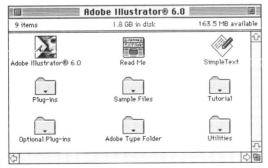

Exploring the Illustrator Screen

When you open Illustrator, a new document is automatically created, and the document opens into a standard and familiar Macintosh document window. On-screen you see the title bar, close box, zoom box, scroll bars, resize box, Illustrator's Toolbox, and many other — perhaps unfamiliar — elements, as shown in Figure 1-3. But don't worry. Keep reading and you'll be as familiar with them as you are with your favorite pair of faded jeans.

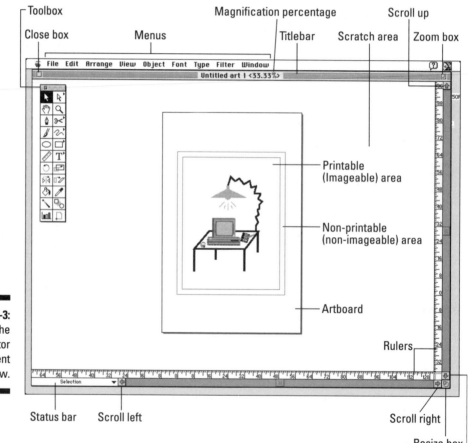

Figure 1-3: The Illustrator document window.

Examining the document window

Here's a review of Illustrator's document window: The *close box* in the upper-left corner allows you to close the current active document window by clicking it. Click the *zoom box* in the upper-right corner to change the size of the current window back and forth from full size to a size you set with the *resize box* in the lower-right corner.

The name of the current document appears in the *title bar.* If the current document hasn't been saved, the words `Untitled Art` appear there instead. (Illustrator is a very positive program. It assumes that everything you create is art.) Next to the title is the current magnification percentage. Documents normally open at a 66.67 percent magnification, which means that everything viewed on-screen is about $^2/_3$ of its actual size.

The Illustrator window also includes several other features that you should take a moment to examine.

- ✔ The *printable* (also called *imageable*) area is the portion of the screen that prints on your printer. This area is bordered by dotted lines.

- ✔ The *non-printable* (also called *non-imageable*) areas are the page margins. This is the area beyond the dotted lines and bordered by solid lines.

- ✔ The *Artboard* is the area composed of both the printable and non-printable areas. It's the rectangular area on-screen defined by the solid lines. By default, the Artboard appears as a standard letter-sized page, $8^1/_2 \times 11$ inches. If desired, the area of the Artboard can be expanded to 120×120 inches. You see how to change the Artboard's size in Chapter 2.

- ✔ The *scratch area* is the area to go to if you're itching to experiment. The scratch area is the vast space that extends beyond the Artboard. It's handy for creating and testing design ideas. You can also use the scratch area as a holding space for objects that you will later place on the Artboard.

- ✔ The *status bar* keeps you informed about what's going on on-screen — just in case you forget. By default, the status bar tells you the name of the currently selected tool. In Figure 1-3, the status bar shows that the Selection tool is selected. You can make the status bar tell you the current date and time, how much memory is free, or how many undos and redos you have left. (Undoing and redoing are covered in Chapter 3.) To change the status bar display, simply click the status bar area. This click opens a pop-up menu, shown in Figure 1-4, where you can select exactly what you want to appear in the status bar.

For some unusual and entertaining status bar options, Option+click the status bar.

Figure 1-4:
The status
bar pop-up
menu.

| ✓ Current Tool |
| Date and Time |
| Free Memory |
| Number of Undos |

Touring the menus

When faced with a new program, the first thing most Mac users do is head for the menu bar and start clicking through the menus. It's sort of like thumbing through the table of contents of a book before you buy it. Examining a program's menus gives you an idea of the lay of the land, whether the path that lies ahead is going to be bumpy or smooth.

Taking a few moments to examine each of Illustrator's eight menus helps orient you to the program. It can also prove helpful when you're searching for a command and just can't remember where it's hidden.

Before diving into the menus, though, take a look at Figure 1-5, which shows Illustrator's File menu. Notice that some of the menu commands are followed by three dots, some are followed by arrows, and some are followed by that funny "four leaf clover" symbol that you see on your keyboard (called the Command symbol). What do all of these things mean?

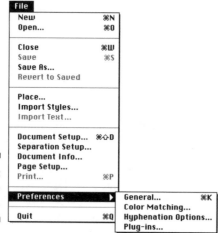

Figure 1-5:
The File
menu.

Occasionally you'll see other funny symbols next to the clover leaf command key character in a menu. The keys and symbols are shown here in the following Funny Symbol Table. If you see more than one of these symbols in the table it means you need to hold down the keys for the symbols while pressing the letter designated in the menu. If you don't have enough fingers free to press all of these keys at once and can't grab a coworker's hand to help you out, just execute the menu command with the mouse.

Table 1-1	Funny Symbol Table
What It Looks Like	*What It Means*
⌘⇧	Command+Shift
⌘⌃	Command+Control
⌘⌥	Command+Option

✔ When you see three dots in a menu (the three dots are called an *ellipsis*), the menu command that you choose will not be executed immediately. Instead, a window called a *dialog box* appears. The dialog box allows you to choose different options before proceeding. After choosing from the options, you complete the command by clicking the OK button or pressing Enter. To dismiss the dialog box without executing the command, either click Cancel or press Esc.

✔ The arrows to the right of a menu command indicate that the menu choice opens up a submenu of other commands. Figure 1-5 shows the Preferences submenu, which appears when you click the Preferences choice. For software designers, submenus are an efficient way of adding lots of commands to menus. To users, though, submenus can be quite annoying because you must keep the mouse pressed while you drag from the menu command to the submenu choice.

✔ The command symbol followed by a letter of the alphabet or number indicates a keyboard shortcut. For example, in Figure 1-5 the Save command is followed by the command symbol followed by an S. That means that in order to quickly save your work, you can hold the command key down while you press the S key, and then release them both. Now how's *that* for speed!

Whenever you see a grayed-out menu command, you might as well not click it. A grayed-out command means that you cannot access the menu item. Why? Usually because you didn't execute the right step before trying to execute the menu command. How do you know what the right steps are? Keep reading this book.

Here's a brief preview of what you'll find in each menu. Don't try to memorize what command is where, because the menu commands are covered throughout the book. Use the following preview to orient yourself and get a sense of how Illustrator divides up its power.

File: The File menu's main concern is your hard disk. Use the File menu, shown back in Figure 1-5, to do things such as open, close, save, and print files. One of the most helpful features found in the File menu is the Document Info command. When you choose Document Info, Illustrator opens a dialog box that shows you an encyclopedia of information about what's in your document. Using the pop-up menu in the Document Info dialog box, you can see what objects, custom colors, patterns, gradients, fonts, placed EPS, and Raster Art images you are using. You can also save this information, print it out and/or give it to a service bureau. Another helpful feature is the Place command. This command allows you to load digitized images or images created in other programs so they can be integrated into your Illustrator artwork. Using the Place command is covered in Chapters 9 and 20.

Edit: The Edit menu, shown in Figure 1-6, includes the Mac's standard Cut, Copy, and Paste commands. The Copy and Paste commands allow you to copy objects and then paste them elsewhere on-screen. The Cut and Paste commands can be used to remove objects from one document and paste them into another. You can also use the Edit menu to paste an object in front of or behind another object.

Figure 1-6:
The Edit menu includes standard Mac Cut, Copy, and Paste commands.

Edit	
Undo Move	⌘Z
Redo	⌘⇧Z
Cut	⌘H
Copy	⌘C
Paste	⌘U
Clear	
Select All	⌘A
Select None	⌘⇧A
Paste In Front	⌘F
Paste In Back	⌘B
Publishing	▶
Show Clipboard	

NOTE

Every time you copy or cut an object, Illustrator stores that object in the Clipboard so that you can later paste the object into your artwork. The Clipboard can only hold one item at a time. Therefore, the next time you cut or copy an object, you replace the previous object in the Clipboard with the new object.

Arrange: As you may have guessed, the Arrange menu, shown in Figure 1-7, allows you to rearrange objects on-screen. If one object is in front of another, you can rearrange the objects so that the object in front moves to the back. The Repeat Transform command is a quick way to repeat the last transformation command that you executed.

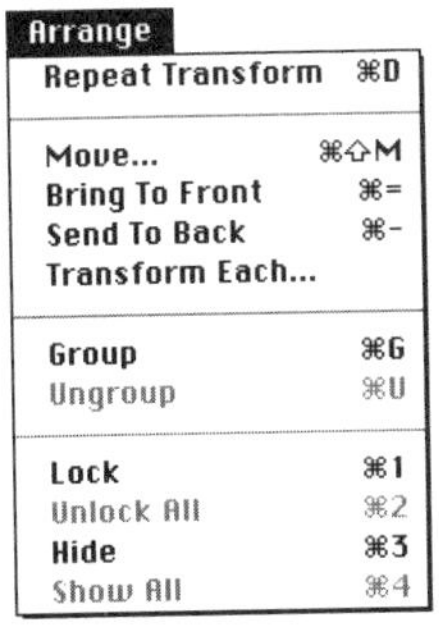

Arrange

Repeat Transform	⌘D
Move...	⌘⇧M
Bring To Front	⌘=
Send To Back	⌘-
Transform Each...	
Group	⌘G
Ungroup	⌘U
Lock	⌘1
Unlock All	⌘2
Hide	⌘3
Show All	⌘4

Figure 1-7:
The Arrange menu allows you to reposition objects.

What is a transformation? Anytime you change an object's shape or rotate it with a command, you've transformed it. You'll be using transformation commands such as Scale, Rotate, Reflect, and Shear throughout this book.

View: The View menu, shown in Figure 1-8, allows you to change how things look on-screen. The Zoom In command allows you to magnify different areas of your work. You can use the Artwork command to see only the object paths — the outlines of your artwork — without the colors. This option can be helpful when you wish to fine-tune the outlines of objects that you've created.

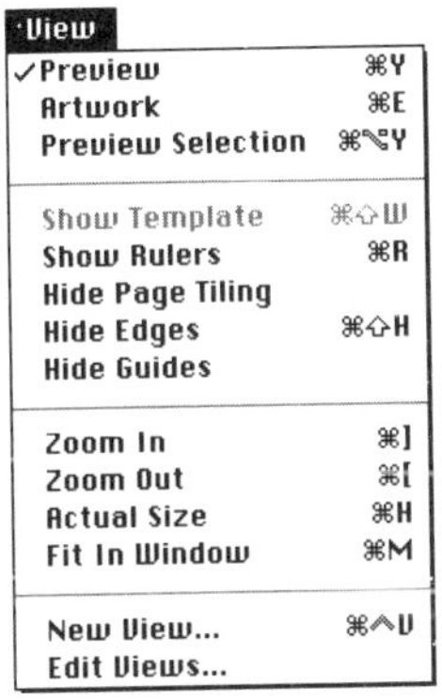

View

✓Preview	⌘Y
Artwork	⌘E
Preview Selection	⌘⌥Y
Show Template	⌘⇧W
Show Rulers	⌘R
Hide Page Tiling	
Hide Edges	⌘⇧H
Hide Guides	
Zoom In	⌘]
Zoom Out	⌘[
Actual Size	⌘H
Fit In Window	⌘M
New View...	⌘⌃V
Edit Views...	

Figure 1-8:
The View menu allows you to change how you view objects.

Object: The Object menu, shown in Figure 1-9, allows you to edit objects on-screen. Use the Paint Style command to open the Paint Style palette, which allows you to fill objects with colors and change an object's colors. Use the Custom Color command to add or delete custom colors. Down on the lower part of the menu, things get a bit more sophisticated. For example, the Mask command allows you to use one object as a mask for another. Assume that you created a fish. Also assume that you've created a coral design. You can use the Mask command to make the coral appear only within the silhouette of the fish. Need to create graphs? The lower part of the Object menu is where you find Illustrator's powerful charting commands. In Chapter 19, you'll see how to create graphs and enhance them with the artwork that you create.

```
Object
Paint Style...        ⌘I
Custom Color...
Pattern...
Gradient...
Attributes...         ⌘⌃A

Join...                ⌘J
Average...             ⌘L
Expand...
Apply Knife
Rasterize...

Guides              ▶
Masks               ▶
Compound Paths      ▶
Cropmarks           ▶
Graphs              ▶
```

Figure 1-9:
The Object
menu can
help you
edit objects.

Font: There's so much you can do with type in Illustrator that the folks at Adobe needed to divide everything up into two menus that handle text: Use the Font menu, shown in Figure 1-10, to choose a typeface. All other commands for using type are found in the Type menu.

```
Font
Bellevue
Carta
Castellar MT
Chicago
Courier                      ▶
Dorchester Script MT
Frutiger                     ▶
Futura                       ▶
Geneva
✓Helvetica                   ▶
Helvetica Narrow             ▶
Isadora                      ▶
Monaco
New York
Officina Sans                ▶
Palatino                     ▶
Pepita MT
Present
Regular Joe
Rosewood                     ▶
Snell Roundhand Script       ▶
Symbol
Times                        ▶
Woodtype Ornaments Two
Zapf Chancery Medium Italic
Zapf Dingbats
```

Figure 1-10:
The Font
menu
displays the
fonts
installed in
your system.

Type: Use the Type menu, shown in Figure 1-11, to choose the size and the spacing between letters. The linking commands in the menu allow you to create type effects, such as wrapping type around objects or flowing it into columns. Linking text is covered in Chapter 14. The Create Outlines command changes type into paths. After you execute this command, you'll be able to bend type in your bare hands. See Chapter 15 for more information on creating crafty type tricks. Using commands in the Type menu, you can also find a word or a font in your document, change case and punctuation, and export text to other programs.

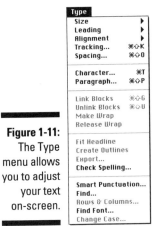

Figure 1-11:
The Type
menu allows
you to adjust
your text
on-screen.

Filter: You're going to love using this menu. The Filter menu, shown in Figure 1-12, allows you to access *plug-in filters.* These are separate program modules that are accessed from within Illustrator. Filters can create unusual special effects, change color, and select and adjust objects. You can also use filters to create different shapes by combining and subtracting different images on-screen. For example, you can lay a circle over a square and call upon a filter to create a shape from the intersecting areas of the two objects.

Figure 1-12:
The Filter
menu allows
you to
create
special
effects and
select and
adjust
objects.

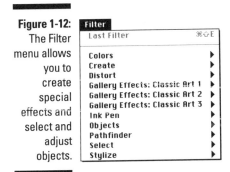

Window: You can use the Window menu, shown in Figure 1-13, to open and close Illustrator's floating palettes. Each palette is described in the next section.

Figure 1-13:
The Window
menu allows
you to open
and close
Illustrator's
palettes.

```
Window
New Window

Hide Toolbox        ⌘⌃T
Show Layers         ⌘⌃L
Show Info           ⌘⌃I
Hide Paint Style
Show Gradient
Show Character
Show Paragraph
Show Tab Ruler      ⌘⇧T
Show Align
Show Plug-in Tools
Show Control Palette

✓Untitled art 1 <66.67%>
```

A peek at Illustrator's palettes

You'll quickly find that Illustrator's floating palettes are great pals to have. The floating palettes stay floating on-screen, never dipping out of view behind other windows. The palettes provide quick and easy access to commonly used commands and features. All palettes can be opened and closed by using the Window menu or by pressing the keyboard commands that are listed in the Window menu. For example, to open the Paint Style palette, you simply choose Window⇨Show Paint Style. To close the Palette, select Window⇨Hide Paint Style. You can close each palette by clicking its close box.

You can also open the Paint Style and Gradient palettes from the Object menu. You can open the Type and Character palettes from the Type menu.

Toolbox tour

Of all the palettes, the Toolbox is the one you'll probably use the most. Just as every craftsperson needs the right tool for the right job, when you work with Illustrator, you'll get the job done better and more efficiently when you use the right tool. Illustrator's tools are accessed from the Toolbox. Figure 1-14 shows the Toolbox, and each specific tool is discussed further later in the chapter.

Figure 1-14:
The Toolbox.

Using tools in the Toolbox is quite simple. You click a tool to activate it. Illustrator responds by highlighting the tool. Notice that some tools have tiny arrows in their Toolbox cubbyhole. The arrows indicate that one or two related tools will pop up when you press and hold down the mouse button on a specific tool. These related tools are shown in Figure 1-15. To select the tool, keep the mouse button pressed while you drag the mouse over the related tool that you want to select. When you release the mouse, you activate the tool, and its icon appears in the main palette area of the Toolbox.

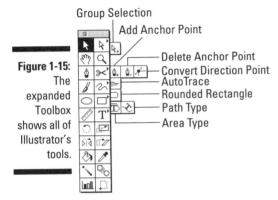

Group Selection
Add Anchor Point
Delete Anchor Point
Convert Direction Point
AutoTrace
Rounded Rectangle
Path Type
Area Type

Figure 1-15: The expanded Toolbox shows all of Illustrator's tools.

After you choose a tool, you can change the default Toolbox icon back to its default settings by double-clicking the tool in the Toolbox. If you've been working with several tools and want to change all the tools in the Toolbox back to their defaults, press ⌘+Shift while you double-click any tool.

Here's a brief discussion of the features of each tool. You get a chance to practice using them in the upcoming chapters of this book.

Selection: The Selection tool selects entire paths. Once a path is selected, you can move it, change its color, copy it, and paste it.

You can temporarily change any tool to the Selection tool by pressing the Command key.

Direct Selection: A path is a series of segments and connected points, called *anchor points*. The Direct Selection tool selects the individual points on a path one at a time. Once an individual point on the path is selected, you can click and drag to edit a portion of the entire path. If a path, such as a rectangle or square, is filled with color, clicking the filled area with the Direct Selection tool selects the entire path.

The Selection tool arrow is a black arrow while Direct Selection is a hollow arrow.

Group Selection: When you create complicated objects in Illustrator, you can group sections of a path together. The Group Selection tool allows you to select all the objects in any group by selecting one object in the group. If you select another object in another group, that entire group is added to the selection. If this all sounds very cozy, it is — and it's very helpful. You can read all about grouping objects in Chapter 9.

Hand: Shake hands with the Hand tool, which allows you to scroll on-screen. When you click and drag with the Hand tool, the screen scrolls in the direction that you drag the tool. The Hand tool is particularly helpful when you want to scroll diagonally.

TIP

With any tool selected, you can access the Hand tool by pressing and holding the Spacebar.

Zoom: No, this icon isn't a tennis racket (although it certainly looks like one). It is a magnifying glass, representing the Zoom tool. It allows you to magnify or minimize how objects are viewed on-screen. Just click the screen or click and drag over an area to magnify an object. Press and hold the Option key, while you click on-screen to zoom out (reduce the magnification).

Pen: No pen in the real world is as powerful as Illustrator's Pen tool, which allows you to create straight and curved paths. If you want to become an Illustrator superstar, you must master the intricacies of using the Pen tool. Step-by-step instructions for using the Pen tool to draw lines and curves are provided in Chapter 7.

Scissors: Use the Scissors tool to split a path. After the path is split, the endpoints of the two fragments overlap, so you usually need to click and drag with the Direct Selection tool to separate the points. You see how to use the Scissors tool in Chapter 7.

Add Anchor Point: Use the Add Anchor Point tool to add an anchor point to a path. Adding an anchor point is often the first step in changing the shape of a path. You see how to use this tool in Chapter 7.

Delete Anchor Point: Use this tool to delete anchor points. You see how to use this tool in Chapter 7.

Convert Direction Point: This tool changes smooth points into corner points and corner points into smooth points. You see how to use this tool to edit paths in Chapter 7.

Brush: You may wonder what a brush is doing in a drawing program. Usually, Brush tools are found only in painting programs. Illustrator's Brush tool allows you to draw long, thin, cylindrical paths at different widths. If you're using a pressure-sensitive graphics tablet and a stylus pen (instead of a mouse), you can change the width of the brush stroke by varying the pressure that you apply to the pen. Press hard, and you produce a thicker brush stroke. Press lightly, and you draw a thinner brush stroke. If you don't have a pressure-sensitive graphics tablet and a stylus pen, you can only set the width of the brush stroke before you paint. You get a chance to try out the Brush tool in Chapter 6.

Freehand: The Freehand tool allows you to draw as if you picked up a real pencil to create shapes and lines. Many artists turn to the Freehand tool only when they want to provide an informal, sketchy look. You get a chance to try out the Freehand tool in Chapter 6.

Auto Trace: Illustrator allows you to import graphic objects and trace over them. After you activate Auto Trace, you can click the mouse to have Illustrator automatically trace over an image on-screen. At first, you may think that this is a cheater's tool. Many artists actually pencil-sketch their ideas, scan them, load the scanned image into Illustrator, and then trace over them. The tool works best with simple shapes. Intricate shapes should be traced with the Pen tool. You can test drive the Auto Trace tool in Chapter 9.

Oval: Use the Oval tool to create circular shapes on-screen. With the tool selected, just click and drag to create an oval. You'll have a chance to create some ovals in Chapter 3.

Rectangle: Use the Rectangle tool to create rectangles on-screen. With the tool selected, just click and drag to create a rectangle. You'll have a chance to create some rectangles in Chapter 3.

Rounded Rectangle: Use the Rounded Rectangle tool to create rectangles with rounded corners. With the tool selected, just click and drag to create an oval. You'll have a chance to create some Rounded Rectangles in Chapter 3.

Measure: This one is Illustrator's electronic tape measure. Use it to measure the distance between objects on-screen. You can see how this tool measures up in Chapter 4.

Type: Use the Type tool to create type on-screen. You'll have lots of opportunities to use the Type tool in Chapters 13, 14, and 15.

Path Type: Use this tool for creating type along a path. The Path Type tool is commonly used to create type along a curve. See how to do this in Chapter 15.

Area Type: Use this tool to fill a path with type. Using this tool, you can fill a circle or any other object with text. Try it out in Chapter 15.

Rotate: The Rotate tool allows you to turn objects along a 360-degree axis. Assume that you created a picture of a painting on a wall. If you want to tilt the painting, you can do it with the Rotate tool. You can use the Rotate tool to turn it completely upside down. Turning objects upside down is covered in Chapter 8.

Scale: Use the Scale tool to enlarge or shrink the objects you create. This is a handy tool for shrinking logos so that they'll fit on envelopes and in letterheads. Shrinking and enlarging objects is covered in Chapter 8.

Reflect: When you use this tool, think of a mirror. The Reflect tool allows you to create an image that is like a reflected image of the object you just created. See Chapter 8 for more information on reflecting images.

Shear: Use the Shear tool to slant objects, thereby distorting them. Shearing objects is covered in Chapter 8.

Paint Bucket: The Paint Bucket tool is used for filling objects on-screen with color. The Paint Bucket uses the color that is currently selected in the Paint Style palette. Try out this tool in Chapter 10.

Eyedropper: The Eyedropper tool allows you to sample a color on-screen by clicking on an object's color. Sampling a color pops its color components' percentages into the Paint Style palette. Once the colors are in the palette, they are readily accessible so that you can use that color again. See Chapter 10 for more information about the Eyedropper tool.

Gradient Vector: The Gradient Vector tool is used to edit gradients. *Gradients* are transitions from one color to another. The Gradient Vector tool can be used to change the angle and start and end points of a gradient. The tool can also be used to change the center point of a radial gradient (a circular gradient that changes colors from its center out to its circumference). See Chapter 11 for more information about creating gradients and the Gradient Vector tool.

Blend: The Blend tool creates effects by transforming the color and shape of one selected object into another. It can be used to create many of the same effects as those produced by the Gradient Vector tool. Why use one tool instead of another? The Gradient Vector tool is easier to use, but the Blend tool allows you to create certain effects that are not possible with the Gradient Vector tool. See Chapter 17 for more information about using the Blend tool.

Graph: The Graph tool is used for creating graphs. To start creating a graph in Illustrator you don't need to do much more than click and drag the mouse with the Graph tool activated. Using Illustrator's graphing features, you can integrate your artwork into graphs Illustrator creates. See Chapter 19 for more information about creating graphs and integrating art into graphs.

Page: The Page tool tells Illustrator which portion of your images to print on what page. You may be wondering why Illustrator doesn't know enough to print the entire image on a page. Actually, Illustrator does; the Page tool is needed when you create images that are larger than the paper you are printing on. In Illustrator , you can *tile* when you print, which means that you can divide your artwork up so that different sections print on different pages. Using the Page tool, you control where each section begins and ends. See Chapter 5 for more information about using the Page tool.

More palettes

Following is a brief preview of Illustrator's other floating palettes, each of which is accessed through the Window menu. For example, to open the Plug-in Tools palette, you simply choose Window⇨Show Plug-in Tools. To close the Palette, select Window⇨Hide Plug-in Tools.

Paint Style: The Paint Style palette, shown in Figure 1-16, allows you to quickly *fill* or *stroke* an object with a color, gradient, or pattern. When you fill an object, you fill the interior of the object with color. When you stroke an object, you create an outline color for the object. You can access this palette by choosing Object⇨Paint Style. The long bars in the palette are called *sliders*. By clicking and dragging on the triangular slider controls, you can change an object's color in terms of its CMYK color components. (CMYK stands for **C**yan, **M**agenta, **Y**ellow and blac**K**.)

The Paint Style palette is actually divided into three sections. By clicking the panel pop-up menu, you can choose to view one section or several sections of the palette at one time. Using the Paint Style palette is covered in Chapters 3 and 10.

Figure 1-16:
The Paint
Style palette
allows you
to choose
colors and
select a
gradient or
pattern.

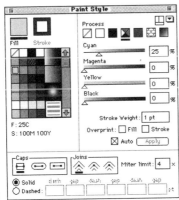

Info: The Info palette, shown in Figure 1-17, provides vital information about the position and size of objects on-screen. This palette can also be used to measure the distance between objects and the angle from one point on-screen to another. As you work with different tools, the readouts in the Info palette change. For example, when you work with the Type tool, the palette tells you the name of the font you are using. When you work with the Scale tool, the Info palette shows the scaling percentage. See Chapter 4 for more information about using the Info palette.

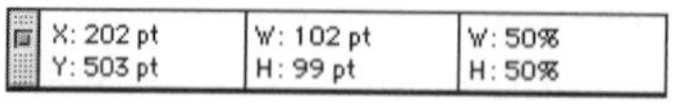

Figure 1-17:
The Info
palette.

Character: The Character palette, shown in Figure 1-18, is like a floating type dialog box. Use it to change type size and spacing between letters. See Chapter 13 for more information about using the Character palette.

Figure 1-18:
The
Character
palette
allows you
to pick a
font and
size.

Layers: Illustrator's Layers palette, shown in Figure 1-19, allows you to create objects and work with them as if some of your artwork were floating in different levels above or below other artwork. You can work with one layer independent of the other layers — and you can work in one layer without viewing the other layers. See Chapter 9 for more information about using the Layers palette.

Figure 1-19:
The Layers
palette
allows you
to create
and edit
objects in
different
layers.

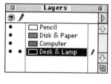

Gradient: The Gradient palette, shown in Figure 1-20, allows you to create and adjust gradients. A *gradient* is a gradual transition from one color to another. See Chapter 11 for more information about using the Gradient palette.

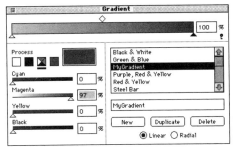

Paragraph: The Paragraph palette, shown in Figure 1-21, allows you to quickly change the indents of a paragraph of text. You can also make a paragraph of text centered, flush right, or flush left by clicking an icon in the palette. See Chapter 14 for more information about using the Paragraph palette.

Figure 1-21:
The
Paragraph
palette
allows you to
change
alignment
and
indentation
of para-
graphs.

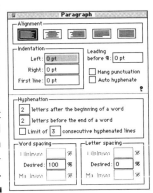

Tabs: The Tabs palette, shown in Figure 1-22, allows you to set tabs in your text. You can find out more about how to use this palette in Chapter 13.

Figure 1-22:
The Tabs
palette.

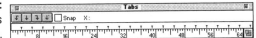

Align: The Align palette, shown in Figure 1-23, can save you lots of clicking and dragging and measuring time. You can use the Align palette to line objects up vertically or horizontally at the click of a button. You can also use the palette to distribute objects equidistantly from one another. You can find out more about the Align palette in Chapter 4.

Figure 1-23: The Align palette allows you to align and distribute objects.

Control: The Control palette, shown in Figure 1-24, provides a fast way to resize, move, scale, and rotate objects. To learn more about the Control palette, see in Chapter 4.

Figure 1-24: The Control palette allows you to resize, move, scale, and rotate objects.

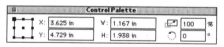

Plug-in Tools: If you need to create spirals, stars, and polygons, you've come to the right palette. All you need to do is select either the spiral (the second tool in the first row), star, or polygon in the palette. Then, click and drag to create the object. The object is created in whatever color is set in the Paint Style palette. If you want, you can change its color using the Paint Style palette.

The Plug-in Tools palette, shown in Figure 1-25, not only provides a quick way of creating simple shapes, but it also allows you to transform them into twirling objects with the Twirl tool and slice them up into pieces with the Knife tool. If you press and hold the Option key while you click a tool, the tool's name appears. The Plug-in Tools palette is covered in Chapter 6.

Figure 1-25:
The Plug-in Tools palette allows you to quickly create spirals, stars, and polygons.

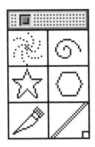

Saving and Reverting

Once you start creating art in Illustrator, you're going to want to save it on disk. When you work with Illustrator, save your work frequently. Artwork is not something that you want to recreate after you've patiently labored for hours.

Illustrator's File commands are quite easy to use. They're virtually identical to most Mac programs. Save your file by choosing File⇨Save or File⇨Save As. In the Save dialog box, shown in Figure 1-26, name your file. If you're only going to be creating, loading, and saving your artwork in Illustrator, make sure that the Format pop-up menu is set to Illustrator 6.0. If you are saving your work so that you can load it into QuarkXPress, Adobe PageMaker, or Adobe FrameMaker, you need to save it in Encapsulated PostScript (EPS) format. EPS is a file format that can read many drawing and page layout programs. To save in EPS format, click the Format pop-up menu and choose EPS. Then click OK. Working with different programs and saving in different file formats is covered in Chapters 9 and 20.

Figure 1-26:
The Save dialog box allows you to save your documents in various formats.

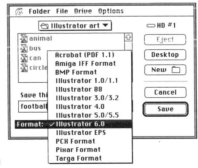

If you make additional changes in your work, you can simply choose File⇨Save, and Illustrator resaves your work. If you saved your work and want to return to the previously saved version, choose File⇨Revert to Saved. If you want to save your work and create a new version under a new filename, choose File⇨Save As and then enter a new filename in the Save dialog box.

Opening Files, Closing Files, Creating New Files, and Quitting

Opening files, closing files, creating new files, and quitting in Illustrator follow standard Macintosh conventions. If you haven't been using the Mac much, here's a brief review of basic file operations:

- ✔ To open an existing file, choose File⇨Open and then double-click the file you want to load.

  If the file you want doesn't appear, you may need to double-click a folder icon. After you double-click, the contents of the folder appear in the file list and you can find the correct file. Also, if all the names of all the files don't fit on the screen, click the scroll bar down-arrow to scroll down to see more files.

- ✔ To close a file, you can click the close box or choose File⇨Close from the menu bar.

- ✔ To create a new file, choose File⇨New from the menu bar.

- ✔ To quit Illustrator, choose File⇨Quit from the menu bar.

Save any work that you want to keep before closing a document.

Chapter 2

Changing Your Point of View

- -

In This Chapter

▶ Changing the document setup

▶ Using Artwork, Preview, and Preview Selection modes

▶ Using the Zoom tool

▶ Creating custom views

- -

*O*ften it's a good idea to take a look at things from different perspectives. Looking at things from different points of view can be very helpful, particularly if you've got a meeting to show a prospective client your new portfolio and you can't find your wallet, your keys — or even your portfolio.

Creating a Portrait or a Landscape

When you create a new document, Illustrator normally slaps a vertical page on-screen. If you want to create artwork that is oriented horizontally, you can change the orientation of the page. You can also change the size of your work area and the size of your page. Most commands for controlling the page view are found in the Document Setup dialog box, shown in Figure 2-1. To access the dialog box, choose File⇨Document Setup. Here are some pointers about using the Document Setup dialog box:

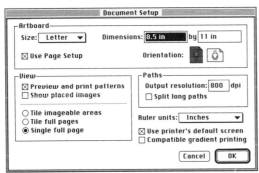

Figure 2-1: The Document Setup dialog box allows you to change the Artboard and page dimensions.

✔ Changing the size of the Artboard changes the size of your work area. To change the Artboard size, click the Size pop-up menu to choose a page size. To create a custom size, choose Custom in the pop-up menu and then enter the dimensions in the Dimensions field.

✔ If you want to view and print the patterns that you create on-screen, choose the Preview and print patterns option, which is in the View area of the Document Setup dialog box. See Chapter 12 for more information on how to create patterns.

✔ If you want to show scanned images on-screen that were placed in Illustrator using the File⇨Place command, select the Show placed images option in the View area of the Document Setup dialog box. You can find out about placing images in Illustrator in Chapter 8.

The Show placed images option can slow Illustrator down because of the time it takes your computer to redraw the placed images on-screen.

✔ The tiling options in the Document Setup dialog box deal with how the image on-screen fits on printed pages. To view one page in the Artboard, choose the Single full page option. If multiple pages can fit on your Artboard, choose either Tile full pages or Tile imageable areas. These options are important when you need to print your Illustrator artwork, and they're covered in Chapter 5.

✔ Click one of the orientation icons to specify whether you want your page to be portrait (vertical) or landscape (horizontal). Figure 2-2 shows how portrait and landscape orientations appear on-screen.

You can also set page orientation in the Page Setup dialog box, accessed by choosing File⇨Page Setup. If you want the Artboard to match the settings in the Page Setup dialog box, select the Use Page Setup option in the Document Setup dialog box.

Figure 2-2:
A page with portrait orientation (left) and one with landscape orientation (right).

A Preview of Three Views

Illustrator allows you to view images on-screen in three viewing modes. You can view your images as they appear when printed, or you can view them as wireframe images on-screen — without any frills. The third viewing mode allows you to view part of your image as wireframes and part of the image as it appears when printed. Following is a description of the options, each of which is accessible from the View menu.

Preview

Preview allows you to view all images as they appear when you print them. In this mode, images appear on-screen filled or stroked with their assigned colors. If you place scanned images or other artwork on-screen, you won't be able to see them unless you're in Preview mode. Most artists like to work in Preview mode because it provides immediate feedback for all coloring and shading commands. The keyboard shortcut for Preview mode is ⌘+Y. Figure 2-3 shows an image in Preview mode.

Figure 2-3:
An image in
Preview
mode.

Artwork

In Artwork mode, images appear as wireframe shapes without color. If you place artwork created in other programs or digitized images (such as photographs) on-screen, you won't see the artwork on-screen. Instead, a box with an X inside appears as a placeholder for the art. Artwork mode is handy when you wish to fine-tune paths. Colors and placed images do not appear on-screen, so you can usually work faster in Artwork mode. Figure 2-4 shows an image in Artwork mode.

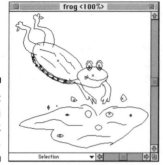

Figure 2-4:
An image in
Artwork
mode.

Preview Selection

The Preview Selection mode allows you to see selected objects in Preview mode. Images that you've selected appear as they would when printed; anything that's not selected appears as it would in Artwork mode. For the image in Figure 2-5, we selected the water and then chose Preview Selection. The keyboard shortcut for this mode is ⌘+Option+Y.

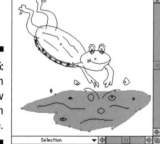

Figure 2-5:
An image in
Preview
Selection
mode.

Zooming Around

Assume that your next artwork assignment requires you to illustrate a picnic scene. Everything is fine until you need to start drawing the smiles on the faces of the happy ants. How do you work with such tiny creatures? One solution is to magnify your image so that your ants are as large as ham sandwiches.

In Illustrator, you can magnify any object up to 1600 percent — meaning 16 times its normal size. Or if you prefer to view things from a bird's-eye view, you can back up and zoom out to 6$^1/_4$ percent.

Illustrator provides a variety of tools to change the magnification of your image on-screen. You can use the View menu commands, keyboard shortcuts, or the Zoom tool. No matter how you zoom, the zoom percentage is always indicated in the title bar at the top of your document window.

When you magnify your image, you are only creating a new way of looking at it — you aren't actually changing the size of your image. When you print your image, it prints at 100 percent of its size, no matter what the magnification percentage.

Using the Zoom tool

The easiest way to magnify your image is to use the Zoom tool. After you select the Zoom tool from the Toolbox, you can zoom in simply by clicking your image. After you click, the area that you clicked will be magnified. The more you click, the more you zoom.

If you wish to zoom in on a specific area, you can select the Zoom tool and then click and drag over that area. As you drag, a dotted marquee appears, indicating the zoom area, as shown in Figure 2-6. When you release the mouse, Illustrator zooms in on that area, as shown in Figure 2-7. (The smaller the area you drag over, the larger the magnification.)

Figure 2-6:
With the Zoom tool selected, click and drag over the area that you want to magnify.

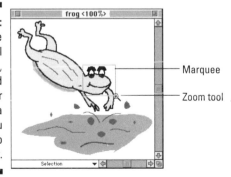

Marquee

Zoom tool

Figure 2-7: The area that you click and drag over becomes magnified.

Using the View commands

You can also magnify the document window by choosing Zoom In or Zoom Out from the View menu. The keyboard shortcuts are ⌘+] for zooming in and ⌘+[for zooming out. However, if you choose these commands, you can't pinpoint the exact area on-screen that you zoom in to or zoom out from.

Two other View menu commands can be quite handy. To make your image fit in the current window, you can choose Fit In Window from the View menu or press ⌘+M. To set the screen display to actual size (100 percent), choose View⇨Actual Size or press ⌘+H.

TIP

Zoomin' like a pro

Here are a few Zoom tool pointers:

- To zoom *out* instead of *in,* press and hold Option while you click with the Zoom tool selected.

- Double-click the Zoom tool in the Toolbox to set the display to actual size (100 percent).

- Double-click the Hand tool in the Toolbox to set the display to Fit to Windows.

- To zoom in when you're working with another tool, press and hold ⌘ and the spacebar and then click in the area that you want to magnify.

- To zoom out while you're working with another tool, press and hold ⌘+ Option+spacebar and then click in the area that you want to zoom out from.

Take me by the hand

The Hand tool works hand-in-hand with the Zoom tool. Once you've zoomed in, you may need to scroll to exactly the point on-screen that you want to see. Instead of using the scroll bars, you can use the Hand tool. Simply select the Hand tool, and then click and drag over your image. Your image scrolls in the direction in which you're clicking and dragging. As you work with the Hand tool, you'll find that it's most helpful when you need to scroll diagonally.

Here are a few Hand tool pointers:

- To temporarily activate the Hand tool while working with another tool, press the spacebar.

- If you scroll too far afield and want to see the entire Artboard within the document window, double-click the Hand tool in the Toolbox.

I've grown accustomed to your view

Once you know how to zoom in and out and switch between Preview and Artwork modes, you may want to speed up the process of changing views and magnification settings by creating a custom view. Using Illustrator's New View command, you can set up a view in Preview, Artwork, or Preview Selection mode at a specific magnification and give it a name. Here's how:

1. **Set the desired magnification by using the Zoom tool, keyboard commands, or Zoom commands in the View menu.**

2. **Choose Preview or Artwork from the View menu.**

3. **From the View menu, choose New View.**

4. **Enter a name in the Name field or enter a percentage for a name, as shown in Figure 2-8.**

5. **Click OK.**

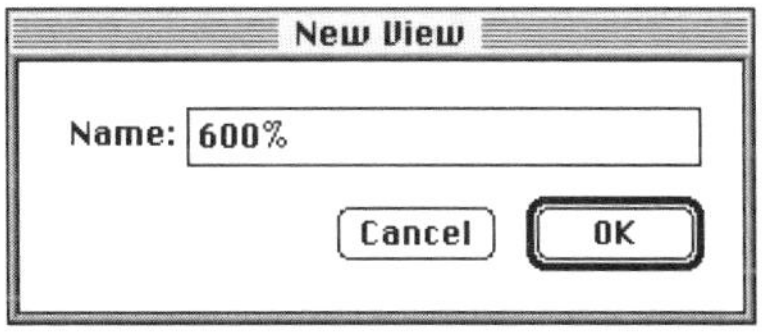

Figure 2-8:
The New
View
dialog box.

```
╔═══════════════ New View ═══════════════╗
║                                         ║
║  Name: │600%                         │  ║
║                                         ║
║              ( Cancel )  ╔════ OK ════╗ ║
╚═════════════════════════════════════════╝
```

Using a custom view

After you've created a custom view, Illustrator conveniently adds the new view to the View menu and assigns it a keyboard shortcut. Illustrator assigns ⌘+Ctrl+1 to the first view you create, ⌘+Ctrl+2 to the next view, and so on up until you reach ⌘+Ctrl+25 (see Figure 2-9). To use your custom view, simply choose it from the View menu or press the keyboard shortcut keys: the Command key, the Control key, and the number Illustrator assigns to it. For a review of what all the funny icons in the menus mean, see Chapter 1.

Figure 2-9:
The View menu.

View	
✓Preview	⌘Y
Artwork	⌘E
Preview Selection	⌘⌥Y
Show Template	⌘⇧W
Show Rulers	⌘R
Hide Page Tiling	
Hide Edges	⌘⇧H
Hide Guides	
Zoom In	⌘]
Zoom Out	⌘[
Actual Size	⌘H
Fit In Window	⌘M
New View...	⌘⌃V
Edit Views...	
600%	⌘⌃1
400%	⌘⌃2

Deleting or renaming a custom view

Tired of the same old view? You can delete or rename a view by choosing the Edit Views command from the View menu. This command opens the Edit Views dialog box, shown in Figure 2-10. In the dialog box, select the view that you want to delete or rename by clicking it. To delete the view, simply click the Delete button. If you wish to rename the view, enter a new name in the name field and then click OK.

Figure 2-10:
The Edit Views dialog box.

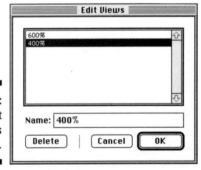

Edit Views

600%
400%

Name: 400%

Delete   Cancel   OK

Chapter 3
Getting Your Feet Wet

. . . .

In This Chapter

▶ Creating rectangular and oval shapes

▶ Selecting with the selection tools

▶ Filling and stroking with color

▶ Moving and editing objects

▶ Using the Send To Back and Bring To Front commands

. . . .

*B*efore Michelangelo tackled the Sistine chapel ceiling, he must have started with smaller stuff: probably a wall here or there or maybe a few cabinets.

Instead of diving head first into Illustrator, do yourself a favor: Start small. Start creating some basic shapes, and then move on to the big stuff. That's the best way to gradually become an expert. Then maybe someday a client will come and ask you to create an illustration for the ceiling of his or her office. But don't turn down the job just because you don't have a monitor that's as big as a ceiling.

Creating Your First Shapes

If you take a look around, you will find that many objects can be recreated on your screen using simple rectangular and circular shapes. For example, you can draw that bagel sitting next to your computer with two simple click-and-drags using Illustrator's Oval tool. You can also recreate a bowling ball, Easter egg, snowman, bulls-eye, CD, and so on. Using Illustrator's Rectangle tool, you can easily create images of filing cabinets, computer desks, piano keys, or boxes. Using the Rounded Rectangle tool, you can create pop cans, computers, briefcases, and that cup of coffee you're drinking with your bagel. Figure 3-1 shows an illustration created primarily with the Oval and Rectangle tools. To create the Illustration, Artist Daniel Pelavin also used the Compound Paths command, covered in Chapter 18. The image was created for *Crains New York Business Magazine* (Ann McGettigan, Art Director).

Figure 3-1:
Objects
created
primarily
using the
Oval and
Rectangle
tools.
Artwork by
Daniel
Pelavin.

Before you get started creating your first shapes using the Oval and Rectangle tools, here are a few basic facts about creating ovals and rectangles (and circles and squares) in Illustrator.

✔ To create an oval, rectangle, and/or rounded rectangle, select the appropriate tool from the Toolbox and then click and drag in your document window to create the desired shape.

✔ If a + appears in the middle of the selected tool in the Toolbox, the shape will be drawn from the center out. After you select the tool, the mouse pointer also has a frame around it when the tool is in this "center out" mode. If there is no plus sign and frame, the shape will be drawn from where you click to where you drag to.

✔ To make the plus signs appear in the Rectangle and Oval tool, double-click either tool in the Toolbox. Double-click either tool again to make the plus signs disappear.

✔ If you want to draw a shape from the center out and the tool's icon in the Toolbox doesn't show the plus sign, you can just press and hold the Option key when you create the shape.

✔ To constrain a shape so that it draws perfect circles or perfect squares, press and hold the Shift key as you click and drag.

Creating an oval manually

The Oval tool draws elliptical shapes. You can use it to create anything from perfect circles to long, cylindrical cigar shapes and flying saucers. Here's how to create an oval with the Oval tool:

1. **Select the Oval tool in the Toolbox.**

2. **Move the mouse pointer into the document window.**

   When the pointer reaches the document window, it changes to a crosshair icon.

3. **Click and drag diagonally down and to the right, as shown in Figure 3-2. Or you can drag down and to the left, or diagonally up and to the right or left.**

Figure 3-2:
Click and drag to create an oval.

If you select Fill or Stroke in the Paint Style palette, the object you draw is filled or stroked with whatever color you select. If you see a diagonal line through the Fill or Stroke box in the Paint Style palette, no fill or stroke is selected. When no fill or stroke is selected, you will see the wireframe path created by the Oval tool. Remember that the path prints only if it's stroked or filled. More on how to fill and stroke is coming up later in this chapter.

Creating rectangles and rounded rectangles manually

The Rectangle tool shares its cubbyhole in the Toolbox with the Rounded Rectangle tool. By default, the Rectangle tool is what the Toolbox displays.

The Rectangle tool draws your common, everyday rectangle. The Rounded Rectangle tool creates rectangles with rounded corners. To create a rounded rectangle, follow these steps (to create a regular rectangle, just select the Rectangle tool and skip to Step 4):

1. **Position the mouse pointer over the Rectangle tool in the Toolbox.**

2. **Press and don't release the mouse button.**

   The Rounded Rectangle tool pops up to the right of the Rectangle tool.

3. **With the mouse button still pressed, drag the mouse pointer over the Rounded Rectangle tool. Once the Rounded Rectangle tool is selected, release the mouse.**

   Note that the active tool in the Toolbox is now the Rounded Rectangle tool.

4. **Move the mouse pointer into the document window, position it where you want to start creating your shape, and click and drag diagonally down and to the right, as shown in Figure 3-3.**

   You can also drag down and to the left, or up and then left or right.

Figure 3-3:
Click and drag diagonally to create a rounded rectangle or regular rectangle.

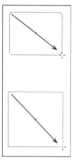

The default setting for the *radius* of rounded rectangles is 12 points ($^1/_6$ of an inch). The best way to understand the concept of a radius in a rectangle is to imagine four tiny circles each with a radius of $^1/_6$-inch. Take the four circles and place them so they touch the corners of the rectangle . Now imagine the rectangle as one object with four rounded corners instead of sharp corners. You can change the default radius setting by choosing File⇨Preferences⇨ General. In the General Preferences dialog box, enter a new radius value in the Corner radius field. The larger the value, the rounder your rectangle will be.

Creating an oval or rectangle by the numbers

If you know the width and height of the rectangle or oval that you wish to create, you can open a dialog box to enter the exact measurements of the shape you are creating.

To create a rectangle or oval using specified measurements, simply activate either the Oval or Rectangle tool and click in the document where you want the oval or rectangle to appear. In the dialog box that appears after you click, enter the measurements desired and then click OK. The dialog boxes are shown in Figure 3-4.

Figure 3-4:
The Oval
and
Rectangle
dialog
boxes.

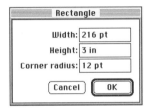

Notice that the measurement units in the dialog box shown in Figure 3-4 are not inches. The abbreviation *pt* stands for *points,* a measurement unit used by typographers. An inch consists of 72 points. If you want, you can enter values in inches: Simply type the number of inches followed by a space and the letters **in**. You can also enter values using picas (a pica consists of 12 points): Enter the number, a space, and the letter **p**.

Adobe Illustrator uses 72 points in every inch. Most graphic arts rulers that measure points and picas use 72.27 points per inch. So don't be surprised if you measure something on-screen and it doesn't match your measurements with a pica ruler.

If you enter **0** in the Corner radius box of the Rectangle dialog box, the rectangle will have sharp corners. If you enter a radius value greater than 0, the rectangle will be drawn with rounded corners.

What Do These Dots on the Screen Mean?

You may have noticed those tiny dots along the edges of and inside your Illustrator images. Figure 3-5 shows several objects spotted with a few of these dots. The little dot in the center of your object is called the *center point*. What's it good for? If you click and drag on the center point, you can move an object. Many artists also use the center point as an alignment mark to line up groups of objects at their centers.

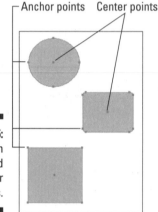

Anchor points   Center points

Figure 3-5:
Objects with
center and
anchor
points.

If you don't like seeing the center point on-screen, you can hide it by deselecting the Show center point check box in the Attributes dialog box. To access the Attributes dialog box, choose Object⇨Attributes.

The dots along the edges of the objects are *anchor points*. The anchor points show where path segments begin and end. In a rectangle, four straight path segments create the object. In an oval, four curved segments create the object.

Is this path open or closed?

A path is either *closed* or *open*. If a path ends at the point where it begins (sort of like a round trip), it's closed. That is, the closed path's end-point overlaps its starting point. If the path ends anywhere other than exactly where it began, then it's open. All ovals and rectangles are closed paths. When you fill a closed path with color, it is completely filled with the filling color. An open path is filled from the first end-point of the path to the last end-point of a path.

Some Important Points: What's Selected and What's Not

The anchor points in an object not only help reveal how the shape is created but tell you whether the object is selected or if any individual anchor points are selected. Only when you select an entire object, a path segment, or anchor point of an object can you fill, stroke (color its edges), or move it. If an individual anchor point is selected and no other part of an object is selected, you can click and drag that point to edit the object. How do you know what's selected?

✔ Selected anchor points are blue. Unselected anchor points are hollow. (They're called *hollow* because you can see through the unselected point.)

✔ An entire object is selected if all its anchor points are selected (solid blue, rather than hollow).

✔ If only a segment of a path is selected, the path's anchor points are hollow. Once a path segment is selected, it can be moved or reshaped.

Although a path's segment is selected, the two anchor points of the segment remain hollow. In some graphic programs, selecting a line segment also selects the line's handles. Illustrator does not work this way. A segment can be selected without its anchor points being selected.

✔ If no anchor points of a path are selected and the object is not filled or stroked, it will not appear on-screen in Preview mode. If you are in Artwork mode, all paths appear on-screen whether they are selected or not.

✔ If you want to see a selected object that is filled or stroked without its path and anchor points, choose View➪Hide Edges. To see the path and anchor points, choose View➪Unhide Edges.

✔ You can hide any object on-screen by choosing Arrange➪Hide. To make hidden objects reappear, choose Arrange➪Show All.

Figure 3-6 shows selected and unselected anchor points.

Unselected anchor points

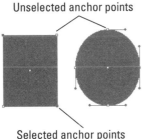

Figure 3-6:
Selected
and
unselected
anchor
points.

Selected anchor points

Using the Selection Tool

Before you can begin to put a nice, colored frame around an object or fill it with color, you must select it. When you select an object, Illustrator says, "Aha, now I know what object you want to deal with." So your first step before stroking (that is, framing) an object or filling it is to select it, and the easiest way to do that is with the Selection tool.

Here are a few important facts to remember about selecting with the Selection tool:

- If the object you are selecting is already filled with a color, you can click anywhere inside the shape to select it.

- To select an object that is not filled with a color, click the edge of the object with the Selection tool.

- To select several objects, first select one object with the Selection tool. Then press and hold Shift while you select the other objects by clicking them with the Selection tool.

  When an object is selected, its anchor points are blue, not hollow.

  Or you can click and drag with the Selection tool to create a *marquee* (a dotted rectangle that encloses an object or group of objects) over the objects that you want selected. If the marquee touches part of the object, the entire object is selected when you release the mouse button.

- To deselect all objects, click in the document window away from the selected object. Or you can choose Edit⇨Select None.

- You can also select items using the Filter⇨Select submenus. Filters are covered in Chapter 16.

Using the Direct Selection Tool

The Direct Selection tool selects only one point on a path. If one point on a path is selected, you can click and drag the point to edit the path. For example, Figure 3-7 shows the steps of changing an oval into a banana. In part (a) of the figure, one anchor point has been selected and dragged to change the shape to what appears in part (b). In part (c), we have stroked the banana and used the Brush tool to add some detail. For more information on using the Brush tool, see Chapter 6.

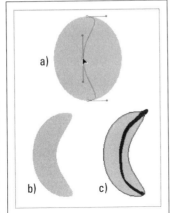

Figure 3-7:
An oval
being
converted
into a
banana.

✔ To use the Direct Selection tool, click the path that is not selected. This click selects a segment and makes the anchor points visible. Next, click any anchor point with the Direct Selection tool.

✔ If an object is filled, the Direct Selection tool selects the entire object when you click inside the object.

✔ You can also use the Direct Selection tool to deselect one anchor point when other anchor points are selected — just press and hold Shift while you click with the Direct Selection tool on the anchor point you want to deselect.

This Would Look Better Framed

Previously we've described how to create very simple shapes. Any shape you create is like a wireframe skeleton that won't print unless you fill it with color or stroke it to outline it with color. If you are working in Preview mode, you may be in for a surprise if you deselect an object that isn't filled or stroked. Remember that Preview mode is the mode that shows how objects print. For this reason, shapes that are not filled or stroked disappear in Preview mode. If you want to see the object in Preview mode or if you just want to add some pinache to it, then either stroke or fill the shape with color using the Paint Style palette.

"Stroking" an object is like putting a colored frame around it. Here's how to stroke an object with color.

1. **Select the object by clicking it with the Selection tool.**

2. **If the Paint Style palette isn't open, open it by choosing Object⇨Paint Style.**

Depending upon the task at hand, you may not want to see the entire Paint Style palette. You can control which part of the palette is in view, with the Paint Style pop-up menu.

Figure 3-8 shows the Paint Style palette with the Panel pop-up menu opened. If the color swatches (the tiny colored squares) aren't in view, use the Panel pop-up menu to change palette views so you can see the swatches. To open the Panel pop-up menu, click and hold down the mouse on the tiny down-arrow in the top-right corner of the palette. To view the swatches, you can pick any of the first three choices in the Panel pop-up menu. For more information about using the Paint Style palette, see Chapter 10.

3. **Click the Stroke box at the top left-hand corner (next to the Fill box), and pick a color from the swatches below.**

   Instantly, your object is framed!

4. **To change the thickness of the stroke, type a number in the Stroke Weight field.**

   Values in the Stroke Weight field are measured in points.

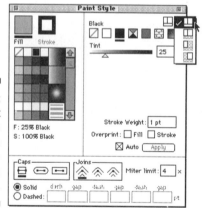

Figure 3-8:
The Paint Style palette with the Panel pop-up menu open.

If you want to fill the object with color, click the Fill box in the top left-hand corner of the palette and pick a color from the swatches below. Instantly, your object is filled with color.

Once you set the colors and fill and stroke options, they are applied to all new objects you create. If you click on an object, the colors, fill and stroke option in the Paint Style change to show you the settings of the object you clicked.

See Chapter 7 for information on creating dashed strokes.

To change the color of everything on-screen, first choose Select All from the Edit menu and then choose a color in the Paint Style palette.

By default, Illustrator selects the Auto button in the Paint Style palette. When Auto is selected, all fills and strokes appear as you create paths on-screen. If you turn Auto off, you must click the Apply button to apply color to selected paths — you can also press Enter or Return to apply strokes and fills.

Fill 'er up with nothing

Illustrator allows you to create transparent objects. When you move a transparent object over another object, you can see the underlying object through the one on top of it.

To create an outlined, transparent object, first select the object. In the Paint Style palette, click the Fill box (in the top left-hand corner of the dialog box). Then click the small square with the diagonal line, just below the Fill box in the group of small colored boxes, called swatches. Notice that below the swatches area, the word None replaces the color percentage next to the letter F (that's the readout for the Fill color) and a diagonal line appears in the Fill box.

See Chapter 11 for information on filling objects with gradients, Chapter 12 for filling objects with patterns, and Chapter 10 for filling objects with process and spot colors.

Moving and Editing Shapes

When you create objects on-screen, you often need to reposition them as you fine-tune your work. Fortunately, objects in Illustrator don't lock themselves down onto the electronic drawing board as they do in many painting programs. You can easily move any selected object by clicking and dragging with the mouse or by using the Move command.

Moving using the Selection tool

To move an object with the Selection tool, first select the tool by clicking it. Next move the mouse pointer over the object you want to move. If the object is filled with a color, you can click anywhere within the object. Then click and drag the object to where you want to position it. If the object isn't filled with a color, click the edge of the object or its center point and then drag to reposition it.

Here are some tips for selecting and moving objects:

  ✔ You can temporarily turn any tool into the Selection tool by pressing and holding the Command key.

> ✔ If you press and hold the Option key as you drag, you create a duplicate of the object that you're dragging.
>
> ✔ To constrain an object so that it moves at a 45-degree angle, press and hold the Shift key as you drag.

Moving using the keyboard arrow keys

Sometimes you need to move an object just a hair to the left or right, or a hair up or down (or maybe a few hairs). In these delicate moments, the mouse just doesn't cut it. It just isn't precise enough. Fortunately, Illustrator allows you to nudge in increments as small as a point at a time.

To move an object using the keyboard keys, just select it with the Selection tool and then press the up-, down-, right-, or left-arrow key on your keyboard.

By default, Illustrator moves objects one point (about $1/72$ of an inch) at a time anytime you press an arrow key on the keyboard. The amount of space an object moves can be changed by typing a value in the Cursor Key field of the General Preferences dialog box. To access the dialog box, choose File⇨Preferences⇨General.

Moving using the Move command

If you know how far you want to move an object, you can use the Move command to tell the object exactly where to go. Here's how:

1. **Select the object that you want to move.**

2. **Choose Arrange⇨Move. In the Move dialog box, shown in Figure 3-9, enter the distance that you want to move the object.**

   Your choices are divided into two sections.

   • The top section allows you to move an object horizontally or vertically. Positive values entered into the Vertical field move the object up; negative values move the object down. Positive values entered into the Horizontal field move the object to the right; negative values move it left.

   • The bottom section of the dialog box allows you to move an object at an angle. Simply enter the distance you want to move the object in the Distance field, and then enter the angle (measured in degrees) you want to move the object in the Angle field.

To copy an object and move it at the same time, click the Copy button in the Move dialog box after you fill in the other dialog box options.

Figure 3-9:
The Move
dialog box.

If you use the Measure tool, the distance that you measure automatically appears in the Move dialog box. For more on the Measure tool, see Chapter 4.

Moving art from one document to another

You can use the Copy or Cut and Paste commands to move an object or objects within one document or from one Illustrator document to another. Here's how to cut an object from one document and paste it in another.

1. **Select the object you want to move.**

2. **Choose Edit⇨Cut.**

   This command places the object in the area of the Macintosh's memory called the Clipboard.

3. **Activate or open the document that you want to move the object to.**

4. **To copy the contents of the Clipboard into the document, choose Edit⇨Paste.**

To see the contents of the Clipboard, choose Edit⇨Show Clipboard.

Dragging and Dropping to Photoshop

If you're an Adobe Photoshop user, you'll be happy to know you can copy and paste your Illustrator images directly into Photoshop. You can also copy and paste Photoshop images into Illustrator. Or you can "drag and drop."

Now, to most people the term "drag and drop" sounds like something that happens when you've done too much Christmas or Hanukkah shopping. To others, "drag and drop" means a vacation with the kids. To the Illustrator/Photoshop user, "drag and drop" means you can quickly copy and paste images between the two programs without touching a menu.

Here's how to drag an image from Adobe Photoshop and drop it into Adobe Illustrator:

1. **Open both Adobe Photoshop and Adobe Illustrator.**

2. **Open or create an image in Photoshop, and make sure you have a new document open in Illustrator.**

   Be sure to position the Photoshop and Illustrator document windows so you can see both programs' document windows on-screen. If you have a small monitor, you may want to make the document windows smaller and/ or you may want to overlap the two windows.

3. **Activate Photoshop's Move tool (the cross with the arrows), and then click the image in Photoshop while keeping the mouse button pressed.**

4. **Drag the image from the Photoshop document window into the Illustrator document window.**

   If you want to drag and drop from Illustrator, use the Selection tool.

5. **When you see a frame around the Illustrator document window, release the mouse.**

For more information about importing and exporting to and from Illustrator, see Chapter 20.

From the Back to the Front, and Back Again

When you paste objects from one document to another or when you paste into the same document, it's sometimes helpful to paste the new object behind the objects already on-screen. Doing so saves you the trouble of disassembling a group of objects on-screen and then dragging a bunch of objects on top of another object.

Pasting in back and in front

Sometimes when you've got one or more objects placed on top of other objects, you may want to change the stacking order of the objects. You may want to place an object in front of or behind other objects in a stack of objects. (For more information about stacking objects, see Chapter 9.)

To paste an object behind other objects that are stacked on top of each other, first select the object that should appear behind the others. Then choose Edit⇨Cut or Edit⇨Copy to place it into the Clipboard. Next, select the objects that you want to be on top of the object you are pasting. Finally, choose Edit⇨Paste in Back. The object in the Clipboard is then pasted behind the selected objects.

To paste an object in a stack of objects from the Clipboard over selected objects, choose Edit⇨Paste In Front.

Sending to front and sending to back

If you just want to send an object to the back or front of a stack of objects, you don't need to copy and paste. You can move any selected object to the back of the shapes it appears in front of by choosing Arrange⇨Send To Back. To move any object in front of the objects that appear above it, select the object and then choose Arrange⇨Bring To Front.

Editing Shapes

If you're getting tired of creating simple rectangles and ovals, you can spice them up a bit by changing their shapes. The easiest way to do this is to use the Direct Selection tool. Select a portion of an object using the Direct Selection tool, and then move just that area with the Direct Selection tool, the Move command, or the keyboard arrows.

For example, to create the exclamation mark in Figure 3-10 we first created a rectangle, part (a) of Figure 3-10. Next we used the Direct Selection tool to select and move the bottom anchor points closer together to create part (b). To create the final exclamation mark, we created a circle and added some text as shown in part (c).

If you're looking for some fascinating techniques for editing paths, check out the Pathfinder filters described in Chapter 16.

If you make a mistake when editing a shape or object, you can undo it by choosing Undo from the Edit menu or by pressing ⌘+Z. To set the levels of undo, choose File⇨Preferences⇨General. In the General dialog box, set the number of Undo Levels in the Edit Behavior group. When you set an Undo level, you tell Illustrator how many commands you want it to keep in memory just in case you mess things up. For example, assume you set the Undo Levels to 5. Now assume you just executed five different commands, and you decide that you want to go back to where you were before you executed the five different commands. To do this, execute the Edit⇨Undo five different times — and you're right back where you started. Now, if only undoing other things in life were this easy!

(a)

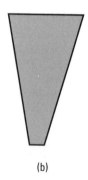

(b)

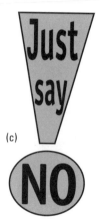

(c)

Figure 3-10:
A rectangle
converted
into an
exclamation
mark.

Gone but Not Forgotten

Every artist grows attached to his or her own creations. But sometimes for the good of the entire work of art, you need to remove something from the screen. As you may expect, getting rid of something is much easier than creating it.

To delete an object, you need to first select it. Then you can press Delete on your keyboard. You can also delete an object by choosing Edit➪Cut, which, unlike the Delete key, places the object on the Clipboard so that it can later be pasted into any open document. But it's not there forever. It's replaced the next time you copy or cut. To save clips of your Illustrator artwork, use a separate Illustrator document or copy your objects into the Mac's Scrapbook.

As long as you are using System 7.5 or greater, you can drag and drop Illustrator files to and from the Mac's Scrapbook.

The 5th Wave By Rich Tennant

"I SAID I WANTED A NEW MONITOR FOR MY BIRTHDAY! MONITOR! MONITOR!"

Chapter 4

How You Measure Up

*H*ave you ever tried to pick up a tape measure or ruler and measure something precisely? Maybe it was a few pieces of wood to make shelves; maybe it was fabric to make a dress or curtains. Often, no matter how hard you try, your measurements just aren't precise enough. The shelves or dress doesn't fit. If your measurements aren't too far off, you sometimes can fix the problem; otherwise, you have to start your work all over again from scratch. Fortunately, you won't have these problems with Illustrator. When it comes to measuring and lining objects up exactly the way you want them, Illustrator proves as precise as can be.

Take Me to Your Ruler

One of the easiest ways to keep track of where you are and how large things are on-screen is to measure them with the help of Illustrator's rulers. To view the rulers, choose View⇨Show Rulers. Immediately, Illustrator's vertical ruler appears across the bottom of the screen, and its horizontal ruler appears along the right side of the screen.

With the rulers on-screen, a tiny tick mark slides along both rulers as you move the mouse. By keeping an eye on the tick mark, you can keep track of where you are at all times and easily pinpoint the precise place on-screen where you want to start creating an object.

Understanding ruler readings

If you're hunting for the one-, two-, or three-inch mark on Illustrator's rulers, you may be searching in vain. By default, Illustrator's standard units of measure are points and picas. As mentioned in Chapter 2, points and picas are the standard measurement unit used in graphic design.

When Illustrator's rulers are set to points and picas, the large tick marks are picas. For example, when you see the numbers 8, 16, and 24, the ruler is indicating distances of 8 picas, 16 picas, and 24 picas. Each smaller tick mark is half of a pica (36 points). If you zoom in or out, the ruler changes accordingly: When you zoom in, the distance between the numbers on the ruler grows; zoom out, and the distance shrinks.

If you are going to do a lot of work with type, you'll probably prefer to keep your measurement units in points and picas. However, if you want to change the measurement units on the ruler, follow these steps:

1. **Choose File⇨Document Setup.**

2. **In the Document Setup dialog box, choose a measurement unit from the Ruler units pop-up menu.**

   Choose from Picas/Points, Inches, and Millimeters.

3. **Click OK.**

Alternatively, you can choose File⇨Preferences⇨General and change the measurement units in the General Preferences dialog box.

If you change the measurement units to inches, the values in the Move dialog box change to inches. However, type-related dialog boxes such as those in the Type and Paragraph menus are always measured in points and picas.

Changing the zero point

One of the advantages of using a traditional ruler to measure is that you can pick up the ruler, place the zero point of the ruler up against an object, and simply read a number on the ruler to tell you how large an object really is.

Although you can't pick up and move Illustrator's electronic rulers, you can reset the origin or *zero point* of the rulers so that you can measure any object starting at zero.

By default, the zero point of Illustrator's rulers is at the bottom far left of your screen. What if you want to measure an object that you created in the middle of the screen? You change the zero point of the ruler so that it lines up with the object that you want to measure.

Here's how to change the zero point on the ruler:

1. **Move the mouse pointer to the lower-right corner of the document window, positioning the mouse pointer where the vertical and horizontal rulers intersect.**

2. **Click and keep the mouse button pressed while you drag to where you want the new zero point to be.**

   As you drag, two intersecting dotted lines appear — as shown in Figure 4-1 — indicating where the new zero point will be when you release the mouse button.

New zero point

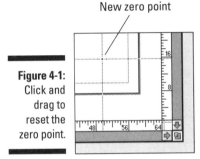

Figure 4-1:
Click and
drag to
reset the
zero point.

3. **Release the mouse.**

   The zero point of both the horizontal and vertical rulers is set at the position where you release the mouse.

Now you can place an object at the zero point and easily measure how large it is by examining the rulers.

Where Am I? Understanding the Info Palette

Illustrator's Info palette is another handy aid in measuring. To open the Info palette (shown in Figure 4-2), choose Window⇨Show Info.

Figure 4-2:
The Info
palette.

X: 224 pt	W: 24 pt	D: 44.9444 pt
Y: 526 pt	H: 38 pt	∠ 57.725°

When you move the mouse, the Info palette reads your screen position. The X readout is your horizontal position, and the Y readout is your vertical position. If you are creating an object using the Rectangle or Oval tool, the W readout indicates the width of the object, and the H readout indicates the height of the object. If you are creating objects using the Pen tool, the D readout indicates the distance your current position is from the origin of the object to the tool.

The first time you click on-screen, the Info palette indicates the point where you clicked. As you drag the mouse, the D readout indicates the distance from your original click. The angle readout (next to the angle icon) indicates your drawing angle.

Using the Measure Tool

 The closest thing to an electronic tape measure that you get with Illustrator is the Measure tool. The Measure tool is used in two ways. First, you can click the beginning of an object that you want to measure and drag to the end of that object. Or you can click where you want to begin measuring and then click again at the end of the object that you want to measure. The distance is displayed in the Info palette, even after you release the mouse — which means that you can always refer back to the measurement, at least until you click the mouse again. The distances are also copied into the Move dialog box, so you can conveniently move an object without typing in lots of numbers.

 If you want to drag the Measure tool in 90-degree increments, press and hold the Shift key while you click and drag.

Taking Control with the Control Palette

If you're the type of person who likes to control everything in sight, you'll want to get acquainted with the Control palette which allows you to move and edit objects without measuring anything.

To open the Control palette, choose Window⇨Show Control Palette. The Control palette, shown in Figure 4-3, not only allows you to move objects, but it allows you to scale and rotate them as well. Before you start using the Control palette, it's important to understand that the palette is divided into four sections: the Reference Point options, the X and Y axis fields, the W (width) and H (height) fields, and the Rotate and Scale fields.

Figure 4-3:
The Control
palette
allows you
to quickly
move,
resize, and
rotate
an object.

You can change the field measurement unit to Points/Picas, Inches, or Millimeters by choosing File⇨Preferences⇨General. In the General Preferences dialog box, click the Ruler units pop-up menu and make a selection.

Even if the default measurement is set to Points/Picas, you can still enter measurements in inches into Control palette fields: Just type a number followed by the letters **in**. However, if the default measurement is set to Inches, just type a number followed by the letters **pt** for points or **p** for picas. Following is a description of the major features of the Control palette. Before reading through the explanations, select an object on-screen, and then try out the Control panel by typing numbers into the palette's fields.

Reference point square: Before using the Control palette, set a reference point for the selected object by clicking one of the dots on the square on the far left of the palette. Click any of the dots on the square to tell Illustrator what part of the object that you want it to use as a point to measure, rotate, or scale from. For example, if you click one of the left dots of the square and then use the Control palette to move the object to the 5-inch mark on the horizontal ruler, the left side of the object will line up on the 5-inch mark of the ruler. If you click the center dot of the square and use the Control palette to move it to the 5-inch mark, the center point of the object lines up with the 5-inch mark of the ruler.

After you click, the dot in the reference square that you click becomes bold, indicating that it has been selected.

X field: To move a selected object horizontally, enter a number in the X field and press Tab or Enter. The value you enter should correspond to where you want the object to move along the horizontal ruler on-screen. For instance, if you enter the number **5** in the X field, the object jumps to the left or right and stops when the object's reference point (specified in the palette's reference point square) lines up with the 5-inch mark on the horizontal ruler.

Y field: To move a selected object vertically, enter a value in the Y field and press Tab or Enter. The value you enter should correspond to where you want the object to move along the vertical ruler on-screen. For example, if you enter the number **2** in the Y field, the object jumps up or down and stops when the object's reference point lines up with the 2-inch mark on the vertical ruler.

W field: To change the width of a selected object, enter a value into the Width field and press Tab or Enter. The object grows in size relative to the selected reference point. For example, if you click the center reference point and enter the number **4** in the width field, the object grows two inches to the left and two inches to the right.

H field: To change the height of a selected object, enter a value into the Height field and press Tab or Enter. The object grows in size relative to the selected reference point. For example, if you click the top reference point of the rectangle and enter the number **2** in the height field, the top of the object grows two inches high.

Scale field: To enlarge or shrink a selected object, enter a percentage into the Scale field and then press Tab or Enter. When you enter a value that is less than 100 percent, the object gets smaller; when you enter a value that is greater than 100 percent, the object gets larger. If you click the center dot in the reference point rectangle, the object is scaled from its center point.

Rotate field: To rotate a selected object, enter an angle value in the rotate field and press Tab or Enter. When the object rotates, its axis is based upon the selected reference point. For instance, if you click the center reference point, the object rotates around its center point. If you choose the bottom-left corner as the reference point, the object rotates around the bottom-left corner.

You can also use the Arrange➪Transform Each command to move, scale, and rotate one or several selected objects. Turn to Chapter 8 for more information about the Transform Each dialog box.

Guiding the Way

When you need to line things up on a piece of paper, you normally take out a ruler and draw a straight line to use as your guide. Illustrator provides non-printing electronic guides that serve the same purpose. These guides appear as dotted lines on the Artboard. Not only do they help you visually line objects up on-screen, but they actually do some of the alignment work for you. When the Snap to Point check box in General Preferences is selected and you move an object within two pixels of a guide, the object jumps to the guide.

You may want to use guides to create a grid for a layout design.

Now that you know why you need guides, you're probably wondering where you get them. Illustrator houses its guides in its vertical and horizontal rulers. When you want a guide, you need to coax it out of the ruler. Here's how to create guides:

1. **If the rulers aren't on-screen, choose View⇨Rulers.**

2. **Position the mouse pointer just to the right of the vertical ruler line (to start creating a vertical guide) or just below the horizontal ruler line (to start creating a horizontal guide) in the ruler area.**

3. **Click the mouse, and drag inward toward the document window. As you drag, a guide appears. Release the mouse when the guide is in the desired position, as shown in Figure 4-4.**

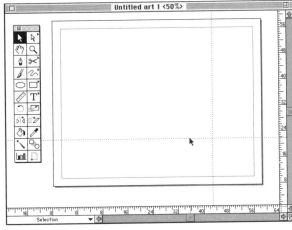

Figure 4-4:
Guides are
created by
clicking
and
dragging
from the
ruler.

To automatically create a guide at a specific point on the ruler, press Option while you click the ruler. Pressing Option and clicking the vertical ruler creates a horizontal guide at the point where you click. Pressing Option and clicking the horizontal ruler creates a vertical guide at the point where you click.

When you start creating layers, it's very handy to place all guides in one layer (layers allow you to work as if different objects are floating in different levels on-screen). When you need to change a guide, you'll always know where to find it. See Chapter 9 for more information about working with layers.

I want my guide to be a square, or a circle

Just when you're saying to yourself how great guides are and how you're going to use them in your next project, Illustrator comes along and tops the feature with something better. Illustrator allows you to create a guide out of any graphic object.

What a great idea! Why should guides be only horizontal and vertical lines? What if you want to use a rectangular or circular path as a guide so you can line up objects around a circle or square? You simply turn the rectangle or circle into a guide. Figure 4-5 shows a thank-you card created with the help of a semicircle guide. When creating the image, we also used the Oval tool, the Type tool, and a digitized texture from Artbeats Marble Paper Texture CD-ROM.

To create the semicircle guide, we created an oval path with the Oval tool. Then we deleted the bottom anchor point of the oval path to make it an open semicircle path. Next, we made the open path a guide with the Object➪Guides➪Make command.

Figure 4-5: An illustration created with the help of a semicircle guide.

Here's how to turn an object into a guide:

1. Select the path or paths that you want to use as your guide.

To select more than one path, click and drag over the paths with the Selection tool or Shift-click different paths.

2. Choose Object⇨Guides⇨Make, as shown on the left of Figure 4-6.

The selected paths turn into dotted lines, indicating that they are now guides. The guide is shown on the right of Figure 4-6.

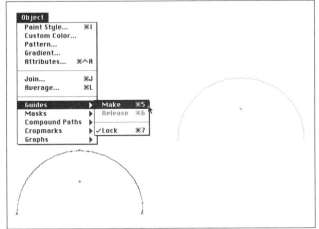

Figure 4-6:
Making a
guide out of
a path (left);
a guide
created out
of a path
(right).

To release an object guide, you need to first unlock it (if it is locked) by choosing Object⇨Guides⇨Lock. With the object guide selected, choose Object⇨Guides⇨Release. The object is now printable.

Locking and unlocking guides

If you spend the time to carefully place your guides in exactly the right place, you want to be sure that you don't inadvertently move them as you click and drag to create and edit your artwork.

The solution is to lock your guides. Illustrator features two commands for locking guides. To lock all guides on-screen, choose Object⇨Guides⇨Lock. Illustrator then places a check mark next to the menu command to indicate that the guides are locked.

To lock an individual guide, first make sure that the Object⇨Guides⇨Lock command is off. Then select the guide that you want to lock. Choose Arrange⇨Lock.

If you want to lock the actual objects on your screen, and not just the guides, then select the object and choose Arrange⇨Lock. This command is especially useful when you have spent lots of time carefully lining up objects on-screen and you don't want to inadvertently move something.

Once you've created a guide out of an object or locked a guide, you may want to unlock it or turn it back into an object. If all guides are locked, first unlock them by choosing Object⇨Guides⇨Lock, which removes the check mark next to the Lock command. If you locked an individual guide or object (with Arrange⇨Lock), unlock it by choosing Arrange⇨Unlock All.

You can hide all guides on-screen by choosing View⇨Hide Guides. To see the guides again, choose View⇨Show Guides.

If you have locked a guide with Object⇨Guides⇨Lock, you can move it by pressing Control+Shift and clicking and dragging the guide.

Deleting guides

Once you've finished working with a guide, you'll probably want to remove it from the screen to reduce screen clutter. You can delete any unlocked guide by selecting it with the Selection or Direct Selection tool and then pressing Delete.

Snapping to it

Having your artwork "snap to" the guides that you create can often be handy. When you enable Illustrator's Snap to Point option, guides work as tiny magnets. If you drag an object within two pixels of the guide, the object jumps onto the guide. To turn on this feature, choose File⇨Preferences in the General Preferences dialog box and select the Snap to Point check box (if it is deselected).

If you will be using the Snap to Point feature, it's important to understand that this magnetizing power works not only for guides but for anchor points as well. With Snap to Point on, if you drag an object near another object, the anchor points of the two objects snap together.

Here's how to use Snap to Point:

1. **Make sure that the Snap to Point check box in the General Preferences dialog box is selected, as described earlier.**

2. **If you wish to snap an anchor point to a guide, position the mouse pointer over that anchor point.**

   If you wish to snap a segment to an anchor point, position the mouse pointer over the segment.

3. **Click the path segment or anchor point, and drag the object toward the guide.**

   As you near the guide, the mouse pointer changes to a hollow arrowhead, as shown in Figure 4-7.

4. **Drag the object until it snaps to the guide.**

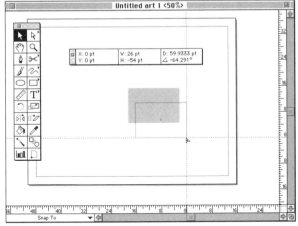

Figure 4-7:
Drag the object toward the guide, and the mouse pointer changes to a hollow arrowhead.

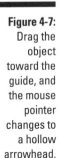

When Snap to Point is on, Illustrator saves the setting in the Illustrator Preferences file in your system folder. Illustrator reads this setting and turns on the Snap to Point feature for all future documents until you turn the option off.

Lining Things Up with the Align Palette

If you're looking for the absolutely, positively fastest way to line up a group of objects, look into the Align palette, shown in Figure 4-8. Just looking at the palette gives you some idea of how it works. You simply select the objects that need to be lined up and click the appropriate icon. For example, if you were lining up a drawing of flags on a flag pole, you could select the flags and then click the top-left icon in the align section of the palette. If you were creating a hot new sports car, you can make sure that all of the wheels touch the highway by selecting each wheel and then clicking on the bottom-right icon in the Align section of the palette.

Figure 4-8:
The Align palette allows you to distribute objects.

The lower section of the Align palette allows you to distribute objects so that they are the same distance away from one another. The icons in the palette show you which part of the object Illustrator uses as its distribution point.

Step and Repeat by Moving, Measuring, and Copying

Some graphics and page layout programs feature "step and repeat" commands. Using step and repeat, you can copy an object a specific number of times and move it a specified distance. This option is a great time-saver when you need to copy an object several times and position each the same distance away from the last one. Unfortunately, Illustrator has no step and repeat command. But you have ways of getting around this. You can use the Move dialog boxes, the copy function, and the Arrange⇨Repeat Transform command to accomplish a "step and repeat."

Figure 4-9 shows how this capability can save you time. The left side of Figure 4-9 shows the selected object (spiral binding) ready to be copied. We created the spiral binding using the Rectangle and Oval tools. With the rectangle and oval (spiral binding), we used the Move command to copy and move the selected objects to the right. The Repeat Transform command was used two more times to create two more spirals. The final image appears on the right side of Figure 4-9.

Here's how you can use the Move and Repeat Transform commands to "step and repeat":

1. Select the object or objects that you wish to copy and move.

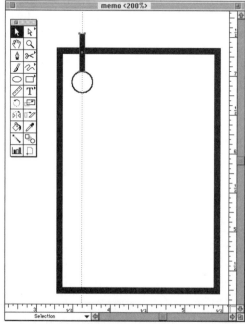
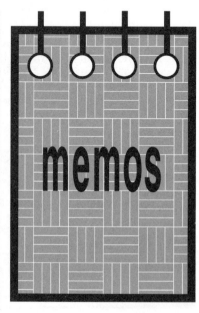

Figure 4-9:
Original image with guide (left) and Image after using the Move command with the copy function and the Repeat Transform command (right).

2. Choose Arrange⇨Move.

This command opens the Move dialog box, shown in Figure 4-10.

Figure 4-10:
The Move
dialog box.

3. In the Move dialog box, enter the distance that you want to move the object.

The distance is measured from the left side of the selected object.

4. Click the Copy button.

This action copies the object and moves it once.

5. Choose Arrange⇨Repeat Transform.

If you are repeating the transformation several times, you may want to use the keyboard shortcut: ⌘+D, to save time.

This command copies and moves the object one more time.

6. Choose Arrange⇨Repeat Transform to copy and move the object as many times as necessary.

You can move an object by using the keyboard arrow keys, and you can change the distance the object is moved by adjusting the Cursor Key field in the General Preferences dialog box. To access the General Preferences dialog box, choose File⇨Preferences General.

Creating a School Bus Using Illustrator's Measuring Features

We created the school bus, shown in Figure 4-11, with the help of the Align palette, the Info palette, the Measure tool, ruler, and guides, the Arrange⇨Move command (keyboard shortcut: ⌘+Shift+M), and the Arrange⇨Repeat Transform (keyboard shortcut: ⌘+D).

Figure 4-11:
School bus
created
using
various
measuring
features.

We used the Rounded Rectangle tool to create the body of the bus and the driver's window. Next, we used the Rectangle tool to create the other windows, door, headlight, and bumper. As we worked, we kept an eye on the Info palette which provided readouts of the size of the objects we created. To plan the location for the door, we used the ruler, Info palette, and guides. We used the Move command's Copy option to copy one window and move it into place. Then we executed Repeat Transform to copy and align the other windows. To create the wheels, we created one oval, filled and stroked it; then duplicated it and lined the two wheels up using the Align palette. (To review how to fill and stroke, see Chapter 3 or turn to Chapter 10.)

If you click on-screen with the Oval or Rectangle tool activated, a dialog box appears, allowing you to type in the dimensions of the object you are creating.

Even if the default measurement is set to Points/Picas, you can still enter measurements in inches into dialog boxes: Just type a number followed by the letters **in**.

After the bus was complete, we placed a digitized photograph behind the bus. Notice that you can see the background photograph through the windows of the bus. To create this effect, we used the Compound Path command. For more information on Compound Paths, see Chapter 18.

Chapter 5

The Proof Is in the Printing

*W*hen you want to show off your artwork, you can't always drag people into your studio so that they can view your portfolio on your computer monitor. And you're most likely not going to want to travel around with a Mac on your back to show people your artwork in their offices. The obvious solution is to print out your work (or spend a few thousand dollars to buy a new PowerBook). This chapter covers the basics of printing and setting up your documents to print. Sophisticated printing issues are discussed in Chapter 21.

Using the Page Setup Dialog Box

Before you print, you may need to tell Illustrator the page size that your printer is using. You do this in the standard Mac way: Choose File⇨Page Setup. In the Page Setup dialog box, pick your page size from the choices. The size that you choose in the Page Setup dialog box determines the size of the page that you see in the Illustrator document window. The Page Setup dialog box also enables you to choose orientation (whether you want to print vertically or horizontally) and whether you want to reduce or enlarge your image when you print.

To Tile or Not to Tile

Before you start to print, you need to set up your document so that your work appears on the right page. You set up your document by using the Document Setup dialog box. Using the options in the Document Setup dialog box, you can control what prints on what page. Normally, you set up the Artboard size and orientation in the Document Setup dialog box when you create your new document. (See Chapter 2 for more information on how to use the Size pop-up menu to change the Artboard size.)

If you select the Use Page Setup option in the Document Setup dialog box, the Artboard is set to the size of the page specified in the Page Setup dialog box.

If your art fits within the default $8^{1}/_{2}$ by 11 dotted page boundaries of the Artboard, life is easy. The simplest option to choose is Single full page. This tells Illustrator to print one page with your artwork on it. If, however, your image extends beyond the dotted lines on the page, selecting this option causes the image area beyond the margins to be cut off on the printout. That's when you need to use the tile options of the Document Setup dialog box.

If you have a printer that prints on legal or tabloid paper, you can set the Artboard size to Legal or Tabloid. Choose Single full page option, and all artwork that fits within the dotted page boundaries prints on the legal- or tabloid-size page.

Illustrator's tiling commands enable you to print images that don't fit on a single page. The Tile full pages and Tile imageable areas options handle the situation by dividing your image into sections and then printing out the sections on different pages. Following is a review of the Tiling section of the Document Setup dialog box:

Single full page: When this option is chosen, one page is displayed on the Artboard. The dotted margins on the page indicate the borders of the imageable (printable) area. If an image area extends beyond the dotted margin lines on the page, that part of the image isn't printed. When you select this option, only one page prints. Figure 5-1 shows how the Artboard looks when you select Single full page. (The background in this figure is from ColorBytes Sampler Two CD-ROM; photograph by Eric Wunrow.)

Figure 5-1:
A document
window with
Single full
page option
selected.

Tile full pages: When you select this option, you can see multiple pages on the Artboard as long as you made the Artboard size large enough to hold multiple pages. Figure 5-2 shows an Artboard with multiple pages. If an area of an image extends over the dotted margin lines, that part of the image does not print. The page numbers in Figure 5-2 do not print either. You can adjust the printable areas by moving the page borders with the Page tool. (See "Using the Page Tool," coming up next.)

Figure 5-2:
A document window with Tile full pages option selected.

Tile imageable areas: When you select this option, multiple pages appear on-screen. Image areas that extend over the dotted lines print on other pages. Only pages with objects on them print. Figure 5-3 shows the Artboard with the Tile imageable areas option selected. The truck in the figure is from Image Club's *Object Gear, Vol. 2* CD-ROM. Any portion of an image that spills onto another page prints on the page that it spills onto. When this image prints, the different sections of the truck print on different pages, and no blank pages print. The page numbers in Figure 5-3 do not print. As with the other options, you can specify exactly what prints on each page by adjusting the page borders with the Page tool.

Figure 5-3:
A document window with Tile imageable areas option selected.

Using the Page Tool

If you need to adjust what part of your artwork appears on what page, you can move the page borders on-screen. Whatever falls within the page borders prints on the page.

Here's how you use the Page tool to adjust the page:

1. **Select the Page tool in the Toolbox.**

2. **Move the mouse pointer into the active document area.**

   As the pointer reaches the document area, the tool changes into a crosshair.

3. **Click and drag the page to the desired location.**

If you want patterns to print, make sure that the Preview and print patterns check box is selected in the Document Setup dialog box. Patterns are covered in Chapter 12. For more information on some of the other options in the Document Setup dialog box, see Chapter 2.

Creating Crop Marks

Cropmarks are thin, perpendicular lines that print on the edges of your document. They're used by commercial printers as a guide for cutting the borders of the printed page. Here's how to create cropmarks:

1. **If you set the Single full page option in the Document Setup dialog box and if your Artboard is larger than the page size, you can skip this step; otherwise, use the Rectangle tool to create a border around your image.**

   The corners of the rectangle that you create define the cropping area.

2. **Choose Object⇨Cropmarks⇨Make, as shown on the left of Figure 5-4.**

   If you created a rectangle in Step 1, Illustrator immediately places crop marks around the corners of the rectangle, as shown on the right of Figure 5-4. If you did not create a rectangle, Illustrator places the cropmarks at the corners of the page borders. (The background in Figure 5-4 is from Digital Stock™'s *Oceans & Coasts* CD-ROM. Image courtesy of Digital Stock™.)

If you want to remove the crop marks from the page, choose Object⇨Cropmarks⇨Release.

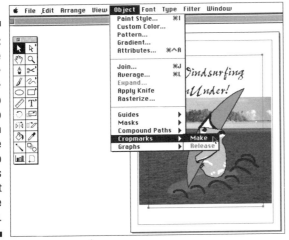

Figure 5-4:
Choose
Object⇨
Cropmarks⇨
Make to
create crop
marks from
a rectangle
(left); crop
marks
created at
rectangle
corners.

Used with express permission. Adobe® and Image Club Graphics Inc.™ are trademarks of Adobe Systems Incorporated.

Printing Your Illustrator Art

After you have your on-screen page or pages set up in the proper page boundary area, you're ready to output your image. Printing in Illustrator is not much different than printing in any other Macintosh program.

To print, choose File⇨Print. In the Print dialog box, as shown in Figure 5-5, specify how many copies of the document you want printed. You can also specify exactly which pages you want to print. If you want to print just a selected area, choose the Selection Only option. The Output Postscript and Data pop-up menus are covered in Chapter 22. If you are printing to a laser printer, you don't have to change these options. To output your Illustrator file to your printer, click OK.

If you are printing to a Postscript Level 2 printer, make sure that the Postscript pop-up menu is set to Level 2. This setting helps ensure that Illustrator can print complex patterns.

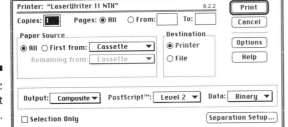

Figure 5-5:
The Print
dialog box.

If you're printing on a color printer or if you have different shades of gray in your document, make sure that the Color/Grayscale option is selected. This option can be found by clicking the Options button in the Print dialog box. To print your document, click the OK button.

Part II
Drawing and Coloring

The 5th Wave   By Rich Tennant

"Hold on, that's not a brushstroke, it's just a booger on the screen."

In this part . . .

This is the part that you've all been waiting for. You'll soon see how to create and edit paths using Illustrator's powerful Pen tool. After you begin using the Pen tool, you can start creating sophisticated images with precision. With Illustrator's Pen in hand, you can explore how to transform the objects you create: make them smaller, larger, rotate them, or even distort them. The last three chapters in this part explain the ins and outs of Illustrator's Paint Style palette. After you've read this part, you'll know not only how to create sophisticated art but how to embellish it with sophisticated color effects, too!

Chapter 6

Going Down the Right Path

*Y*ou usually use Illustrator as a precise illustration tool to create sophisticated and intricate drawings. But sometimes you may just want to take a break, doodle a bit, maybe draw a few sketches. When you want to take a break from the pressure of precision drawing, try your hand at Illustrator's freewheeling tools: the Freehand and Brush tools. These tools are also great for beginners who want to get started with some quick illustrations and practice editing paths. As you work, you may also want to use the Plug-in Tools palette to quickly create shapes such as stars, polygons, and spirals.

The Path to Freedom

 Now and then, most computer artists nostalgically long for the good old days when they would create an old-fashioned drawing with real pencils and pens. Illustrator can (almost) meet this desire with its Freehand tool. Drawing with the Freehand tool is the closest thing in Illustrator to actually picking up a pencil and starting to sketch. It's also a good way to start exploring some of the more sophisticated details of creating and editing paths. The pears shown in Figure 6-1 were created with the Freehand tool.

 If you use the Freehand tool to create an object out of several open paths, you can't use the Paint Style's Fill option to fill the entire image. You need to use the Join command to close the path. See Chapter 7 for more information about using the Join command. See Chapter 3 for more information on open and closed paths.

Here's how to draw with the Freehand tool:

1. **If you want to see the colors of the strokes and fills as you draw, choose View➪Preview from the menu bar. If you want to see the path only, choose View➪Artwork.**

   See Chapter 2 for more on the different viewing modes.

2. **Set the stroke and fill in the Paint Style palette, if desired.**

   Turn to the end of this chapter for more information on creating dashed lines. See Chapters 3 and 10 for more information on strokes, fills, and the Paint Style palette.

3. **Select the Freehand tool and move the mouse pointer into the document window.**

   As you move the mouse, the pointer changes to a pencil icon.

4. **Click and drag to create the desired object or shape.**

   As you draw the shape, Illustrator creates it with dotted lines, as shown in Figure 6-2.

5. Release the mouse.

A path is created from the Freehand stroke. If you are in Preview mode, the stroke that you created is filled or stroked according to the settings in the Paint Style palette. If you are in Artwork mode, only the path appears on-screen.

 If you want to completely fill your object with color, you should create a closed path. If you click and drag without releasing the mouse button and then you return the pencil pointer back to the starting anchor point, Illustrator tells you that you are creating a closed path — a tiny circle appears next to the pencil, and the top of the pencil turns black. Release the mouse button after you see the tiny circle, and you can be sure that the path you created is a closed path.

 If you are in Preview mode and deselect a path that isn't filled or stroked, the path disappears from the screen. The easiest way to reselect a path that you can't see on-screen is to choose Edit⇨Select All.

Erasing with the Freehand tool

As you work with the Freehand tool, you can change the pencil into an eraser and erase parts of the line that you just created. To erase while using the Freehand tool, do not release the mouse. With the mouse button held down, press the Command key, which changes the mouse pointer into an eraser. With the eraser on-screen, drag over any part of the line to erase it.

Adding to a path with the Freehand tool

After you are finished creating a sketch with the Freehand tool, you may want to return and add to an existing line or anchor point. If so, position the Freehand tool's pencil icon over either of the object's end-points. When the mouse is directly over an end-point, the pencil's tip turns white and its eraser turns black. After you see the white tip, click and drag from the end-point to continue drawing.

You can also use the Join command to connect lines. See Chapter 7 for more information about the Join command.

How tolerant are your paths?

When you draw objects, Illustrator creates a path from anchor points and segments. The more anchor points the path has, the more complicated and jagged the object is. The fewer the anchor points, the smoother your path is. When you output your images, you're less likely to have printing problems with smoother paths.

When using the Freehand tool, the number of anchor points created in a path is based on the Freehand tolerance setting in the General Preferences dialog box. If you want to change the complexity of your paths, you can change the tolerance setting.

To change the tolerance settings, choose File⇨Preferences. In the submenu that appears, choose General. In the General Preferences dialog box, shown in this sidebar, enter a value in the Freehand tolerance field. You can enter values between 0 and 10. A value of 0 creates paths with many anchor points. When this option is set to 0, Illustrator draws in its most precise mode. A value of 10 creates the fewest anchor points and the smoothest curves.

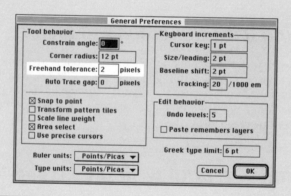

Editing Freehand paths

You edit a pencil sketch on paper by erasing and redrawing. In Illustrator, you edit a Freehand path by dragging the path's selected anchor points and/or segments. You fine-tune curves by clicking and dragging the end points of direction lines. Figure 6-3 shows a Freehand path with anchor points — the dots — and direction lines — the straight lines that run off the anchor points along the curves.

Here are the steps for editing Freehand paths:

1. **Deselect the path by clicking away from it or by choosing Edit⇨Select None.**

2. **Select a segment of the path by clicking its edge with the Direct Selection tool.**

   This makes the anchor points and direction lines appear.

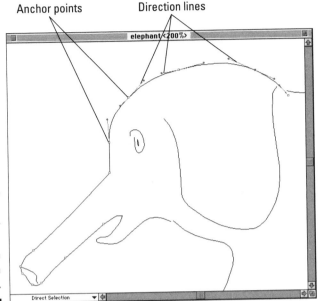

Anchor points   Direction lines

Figure 6-3:
Anchor
points and
direction
lines on a
path.

3. To edit part of the path, click and drag an anchor point with the Direct Selection tool.

4. To edit a curve, click an endpoint of the direction line and then drag.

As you drag the direction line down, the opposite end of the curve bends up, as shown on the left of Figure 6-4. As you drag the direction line up, the opposite end of the curve bends down, as shown on the right of Figure 6-4.

You can also edit a path segment by clicking and dragging on the segment with the Direct Selection tool.

Figure 6-4:
Dragging a
direction
line down
(left).
Dragging a
direction
line up
(right).

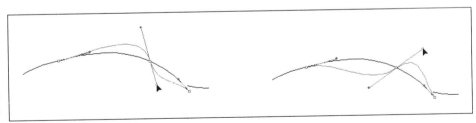

Dashing through the path

After you create a Freehand path, you may want to stroke it with dashed lines. Many artists fill a path and then stroke it with dashed lines or create a dashed line over a wider background path that is filled with another color. For example, you can create a set of dashed, white lines over a thick, black path to create a highway. You can use dashed lines to create interesting patterns or effects. To create dashes, you use the Paint Style palette's line attributes options, which enable you to create dot patterns and dashed strokes. Figure 6-5 shows you how dashed strokes can easily create unusual objects. In this figure, artist Daniel Pelavin used the Paint Style palette's dashed stroke options to create the accordion-style hoses for the tractors. The image was created for *Datamation* magazine (art director, Dave Gordon).

Figure 6-5:
The accordion hoses on each tractor were created by Daniel Pelavin, using the Paint Style palette's dashed stroke options.

To create different dash patterns, you need to access the bottom panel of the Paint Style palette. If the Paint Style palette is not open, open it by choosing Window⇨Paint Style. By default, the panel of the Paint Style palette that controls line attributes is hidden. To access this panel, click the Panel pop-up menu (in the upper-right corner of the Paint Style palette), as shown in Figure 6-6, and choose the first item in the menu.

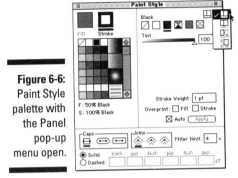

Figure 6-6:
Paint Style
palette with
the Panel
pop-up
menu open.

When you use the line attributes, you have several choices that determine exactly how dashed strokes can be created. The Caps section determines how stroked path end-points and the ends of dashed strokes appear. The Joins section determines how the corners of stroked paths are joined together. Figure 6-7 shows a collection of L-shaped paths illustrating the different Caps and Joins options. See the sections coming up for explanations of the terms used in the figure.

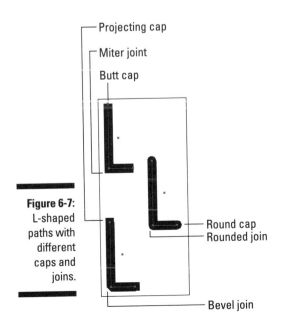

— Projecting cap

— Miter joint

Butt cap

Figure 6-7:
L-shaped
paths with
different
caps and
joins.

— Round cap
— Rounded join

— Bevel join

Firing off some caps

When you create stroked lines or dashes, the shapes of their end-points are determined by the Caps options in the Paint Style palette. As you read through the following descriptions, refer back to Figure 6-7.

 **Butt cap:** Produces flat ends with sharp corners.

Round cap: Produces round ends.

Projecting cap: Produces caps with flat ends and sharp corners. The end of the cap extends out beyond the end of the line. The distance beyond the line is half the strike width of the line. (Stroke width is also set in the Paint Style palette.)

Would you like to join us?

The Joins options enable you to control how a corner point appears when two stroked line segments meet to form a corner. The icons in the Paint Style palette provide an indication of how the joins look.

Miter join: Produces a sharp corner.

 Why miter, you may ask? The term is used in architecture and construction to refer to a joint created when two surfaces are joined together to form a sharp corner. To create the joint, the two surfaces are often beveled at a 45-degree angle. Now, after you've completed an Illustrator masterpiece, you can take out a hammer and saw and create a picture frame with miter joints to produce the four corners of the frame.

Rounded join: Produces a rounded corner.

Bevel join: Produces a flat edge.

 Illustrator enables you to create a *miter limit* from 1 to 500 for sharp joins. What's a miter limit? Even if you have a sharp mind, trying to understand the miter limit concept can dull the senses. Anyway, here goes: By setting a miter limit, you can specify when Illustrator automatically changes from a sharp join (miter) to a flat edge (bevel). Choosing a miter limit gets confusing because it involves the relationship between the length of the corner point of a join and the stroke width (which is measured in points).

The miter limit setting determines when the join switches from a sharp join to a flat edge join. The switch is determined by the length of the corner point and the stroke width.

For example, assume that you have two lines that intersect at a corner point. If you set the Miter Limit to 3, the sharp point switches to a flat edge if the length of the corner point reaches 3 times the stroke weight of the line. In other words, if the stroke setting is 1 point and the length of the corner point is 3 points, the corner automatically switches to a flat-edged join.

Dashed options

If you click the Dashed radio button in the Paint Style palette, you can create dashed lines by entering numbers in the dash and gap fields. These fields enable you to control the size and the spacing of the dashes. For example, if you enter **5** in the first dash field and **2** in the first gap field, the dashes are five points long with a two-point gap in between. (You don't need to fill in every dash and gap field.) The caps in the dashed lines are the caps specified in the Paint Style palette. You can create assorted patterns by entering different combinations into the dialog box fields. Figure 6-8 shows some of the dashed line possibilities. The settings for each line are displayed above the line. Each line has a different dash and gap value. Notice also that the Caps option varies. Each line has a 20-point black stroke.

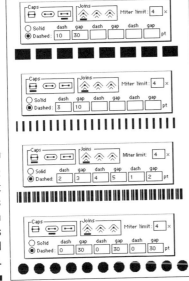

Figure 6-8:
Different dashed lines created with various dash and gap values.

Here are the steps for creating a dashed line with joins and end-caps:

1. **Use the Selection tool to select the path that you want to stroke.**

2. **If the Paint style palette isn't open, open it by choosing Window⇨Paint Style.**

3. **In the Paint Style palette, click the Stroke box to tell Illustrator that you want to stroke the line.**

4. **Enter a value for the stroke weight.**

   If you set a stroke weight of zero, Illustrator prints and displays a one-pixel-wide, hairline stroke. To better see the effects of line style options, set a stroke weight of at least 3 points.

5. **Choose a caps style by clicking a Caps icon.**

6. **If your path has corners, choose a join style by clicking a Join icon.**

7. **Set a Miter limit, if desired.**

8. **To create dashed lines, select the Dashed option at the bottom of the Paint Style palette and then enter values in the dash and gap fields.**

   If you're having a hard time seeing the effect of the Paint Style line options, zoom in to your artwork by using the Zoom tool and set the fill in the Paint Style palette to None.

Brushing Things Aside

You might be wondering what a Brush tool is doing in a drawing program. Illustrator's Brush tool is really a clever path-drawing tool that creates long, closed paths that look like brush strokes. The Brush tool can be used to create a sketchy, brush-type drawing or calligraphy. If you have a pressure-sensitive drawing tablet, you can change the brush stroke width by adjusting the pressure that you apply to the stylus pen when you create your brush strokes.

 Using the Brush tool is quite simple. You select it from the Toolbox and then click and drag in your document window. When you release the mouse, you see a thick path dotted with anchor points. If the Fill option is set in the Paint Style palette, the path is filled with the color specified.

Width pleasure

 How the brush paints depends upon the settings in the Brush dialog box. To open the dialog box shown in Figure 6-9, double-click the Brush tool. The first options in the dialog box are available only if you have a stylus pen. If you select the Variable check box, the width of the brush stroke varies as you apply more or less pressure to the stylus pen. The harder you press, the thicker the line becomes; if you ease up on the pressure, you produce a thinner line. The size of the variation is determined by the number that you enter into the minimum and maximum fields.

Figure 6-9:
The Brush
dialog box.

Creating with style

Figure 6-10 gives you an example of the types of strokes that the Brush tool can create with a stylus pen. We created the round shapes in the image with the Oval tool. Next, we created the rays of the sun with the Brush tool. The Variable setting was 4 points. The photo of evergreens is from ColorBytes' *Sampler One* CD-ROM (photograph by Eric Wunrow).

Figure 6-10:
Brush
strokes
drawn with
a stylus pen
with a
Variable
setting of 4
points.

Setting the Caps and Joins

The Caps option enables you to select sharp or round-cornered edges. The Joins options control how two segments are joined. You can pick a round or flat-edge (bevel) corner.

Using the Calligraphic Brush

The Calligraphic Brush style enables you to simulate the effect of creating brush strokes with a calligraphic pen. Figure 6-11 shows a bit of calligraphy created with the Calligraphic Brush options. The background image of a balloon and confetti is from MetaTool's KPT *Power Photos II* CD-ROM. So the next time you need to make an invitation, try creating the letters with Illustrator's Calligraphic Brush strokes.

Why create calligraphy with Illustrator rather than with the traditional calligraphy pen and ink? If you make a mistake with pen and ink, you throw out the invitation. If you make a mistake when creating calligraphy with Illustrator, you simply edit the path. To edit the path, you use the same procedures used to edit the anchor points and direction lines created by the Freehand tool. The steps for editing paths are described in the "Editing Freehand Paths" section.

To turn on this brush stroke, click the Calligraphic option in the Brush dialog box. (Double-click the Brush tool to get to the dialog box.) When you draw with the Calligraphic option selected, the width of the stroke changes depending on whether you are stroking or downstroking with the Brush tool. When you click the Calligraphic option, a Constrained Angle field appears on-screen. Entering a value in the field changes the effect of the Calligraphic Brush. The angle simulates turning the pen at a specific angle in relation to a piece of paper. For example, if you enter **30**, the brush stroke simulates the pen being held at a 30-degree angle to the paper.

Figure 6-11:
An invitation drawn with the Calligraphic Brush.

Creating and Editing Objects with the Plug-in Tools

If you want to create some simple shapes in no time flat or need to add a Star Spangled look to your artwork, you may want to take a trip to Illustrator's Plug-in Tools palette. The tools in the palette enable you to create polygons, spirals, and stars. You can also cut shapes into pieces by using the palette's Knife tool and twirl them by using its Twirl tool.

Creating polygons, spirals, and stars

To start using the Plug-in Tools, you need to first open the Plug-in Tools palette by choosing Window⇨Show Plug-in Tools. Figure 6-12 shows the Plug-in Tools palette and each of its tools.

Figure 6-12:
The Plug-in Tools palette enables you to quickly create and edit shapes.

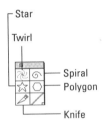

Star
Twirl
Spiral
Polygon
Knife

Here's how to use the Plug-in Tools palette to create a polygon, spiral, or star:

To use the Polygon, Spiral, or Star tools, select the tool and then click and drag where you want the object to appear. The object is created and filled with and/or stroked with the settings in the Paint Style palette. If you want the object to be a specific color, you can set the fill and stroke color before creating the object. You can also change the stroke and/or fill after you create the object.

You can also create a polygon, spiral, and/or star by entering specific numbers into each tool's dialog box. Select the tool and then press and hold Option as you click in your document with the tool selected. When the tool's dialog box appears, as shown in Figure 6-13, you can specify exactly how you want each object created. Click OK to create the object.

Figure 6-13
The
Polygon,
Spiral, and
Star dialog
boxes.

If you are creating polygons and spirals, the Radius value in the dialog box determines the distance from the shape's centerpoint to the farthest point of the shape.

If you are creating stars with the Star Plug-in Tool's dialog box, the Radius 1 field controls the distance from the center of the star to the shortest point in the star. The Radius 2 field determines the distance from the center of the star to the farthest point on the star.

If you are creating spirals, enter the number of path segments you want in the spiral into the Segments field. A full turn of the spiral is made up of four segments. The Decay field in the Spirals dialog box determines the proportion of one spiral turn to the next spiral turn. For example, if you enter 80 percent in the Decay field, each turn of the spiral is 80 percent of the previous spiral turn in size. The two spiral icons in the dialog box enable you to specify whether you want the spiral to turn clockwise or counter-clockwise.

If you change the setting in a tool's dialog box, those settings are used the next time you work with the tool.

Here are some tips for creating Polygons, Spirals, and Stars:

✔ To move the shape after you start creating it, press and hold the Spacebar while you drag with the mouse (with the Plug-in Tool selected).

✔ To increase the number of points on the star, sides on the polygon, or spirals on the spiral, press and hold the up-arrow key as you drag (with the Plug-in Tool selected).

✔ To decrease the number of sides on the star or polygon or spiral, press and hold the down-arrow key as you drag (with the Plug-in Tool selected).

✔ You can change the shape of the star so that every other segment is parallel to each other by pressing Control as you drag (with the Star tool selected).

✔ If you want to create a triangle, open the Polygon dialog box and enter **3** in the sides field.

✔ If you want, you can edit the object with one of the transformation tools to scale, rotate, reflect, or shear the object. For more information about the transformation tools, see Chapter 8. You may want to use the Object↷Join command to join one spiral with another. To find out how to join objects, see Chapter 7. You can also use one of the Area Type or Path Type tools to add text either inside or along the object's path. For more information on using the Area or Path Type tools, see Chapter 15.

Editing objects by using the Twirl tool, Knife tool, and Apply Knife command

The Plug-in Tools palette's Twirl and Knife are handy tools that enable you to quickly edit any path. The Twirl tool can transform an object to make it look as though you dropped it into a blender. The Knife tool enables you to surgically cut any path into pieces.

Give it a Twirl

You can use the Twirl tool to twirl any selected object. Twirling an object can completely transform its shape. For example, if you twirl a star-shaped object, you can turn it into something that looks like a round blade for a power saw. This effect is shown in Figure 6-14. The star on the left was created with the Star Plug-in Tool; the twirling effect was created with the Twirl tool. If you twirl a long thin rectangle, you can transform it into an S shape.

Here's how to use the Twirl tool:

1. **Select the object that you want to twirl.**

2. **Select the Twirl tool in the Toolbox.**

Figure 6-14: Star created with the Star Plug-in Tool (left); star twirled with the Twirl Plug-in Tool (right).

3. **Position the mouse pointer over the object you want to twirl and then click and drag in the direction you want the object to twirl.**

As you drag, the object begins to twirl.

4. **Release the mouse after you attain the desired twirling effect.**

You can specify the exact angle that you want to twirl a selected object by selecting the Twirl tool and then Option + clicking on-screen. This opens the Twirl dialog box, where you can enter the number of degrees that you want to twirl an object.

Any way you slice it

Illustrator's Knife tool enables you to cut your images down to size. It's almost like having an electronic Exacto knife. You click and drag over an object, and the object is sliced into pieces. Using the Knife tool is easy: Simply select the Knife tool, and then click and drag over an object or objects that you want to slice. To move the sliced pieces away from one another, deselect the object by clicking away from it. Then select the Selection tool. Use the Selection tool to drag one piece of the object away from the others. After the pieces are separated, they remain distinct objects.

The Knife tool cuts all objects beneath it. If you use the Knife tool to cut one path that is on top of other paths, all paths are sliced.

The Knife tool's cousin in Illustrator's cupboard is the Object➪Apply Knife command. The Apply Knife command is more like an electronic cookie cutter than a knife. Instead of merely slicing, the Apply Knife command uses an overlapping object as a stencil that cuts into underlying paths.

Here's how to use the Apply Knife command:

1. **Create a path to use as the cookie cutter object (the object that you want to cut out of another path).**

You can use the Freehand, Pen, Star, Spiral, Polygon, or any other of Illustrator's shape creation tools.

2. **If you didn't create the cookie cutter over the object you want to cut, position the cookie cutter object over that object, as shown on the left of Figure 6-15.**

3. **With the cookie cutter object still selected, choose Object➪Apply Knife.**

The color attributes of both paths changed to those of the background path. The areas where the cookie cutter overlaps the underlying object are cut into a separate path or separate paths.

After the Apply Knife command is executed, Illustrator deletes those parts of the cookie cutter objects that do not overlap the underlying object.

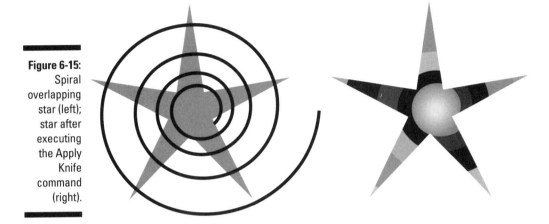

Figure 6-15:
Spiral
overlapping
star (left);
star after
executing
the Apply
Knife
command
(right).

4. **You can also fill the separate pieces with different colors, or you can move the separate pieces away. To fill the separate sliced objects, deselect the original object, select the piece you want to fill with the Direct Selection tool, and fill it. To move one of the sliced objects, deselect the original object and then click and drag the piece you want to move with the Direct Selection tool.**

In Figure 6-15, on the right, we filled the separated pieces with different colors.

Now that you know how to slice, dice, and twirl, you're ready to create more sophisticated paths and transformations of objects. Turn to Chapter 7 for more information about creating paths with the Pen tool. Turn to Chapter 8 for more about transforming objects.

Chapter 7

With Pen in Hand

*H*ave you ever tried to draw a perfect curve with a real pencil or pen on real paper?

Unless you've got the steadiest of steady hands, you probably ended up with less than a perfect curve — one with a few bumps or dents in it. How do you smooth out the curve that you draw on paper? Get out the old art gum eraser, start rubbing away the imperfections, and then try to redraw the rough spots. Unfortunately, unless you have a bagful of different-sized orange juice cans to trace around, your curve is always going to suffer from the unsteadiness of your all-too-human hand. What's the solution? The Pen tool, truly the most valuable player in the team of powerful tools in Illustrator's Toolbox.

To many new Illustrator users, the Pen tool is their nemesis. Instead of working together with the Pen as a team, they fight it every click and drag along the way. If you ever get near one of these Pen haters, you'll know it. Curves will be flying in so many directions that you'll feel like you need a helmet to protect yourself.

If you want to truly master Illustrator, you need to be a Pen pal rather than a Pen hater. If you start simple and follow the right steps, you'll soon find that it's easy to work with the Pen tool — and you'll soon appreciate the power that it puts in your hand. So get ready to pick up the Pen tool and enter a new world of artistic possibilities.

What the Pen Tool Can Do for You

 The Pen tool allows you to draw straight lines and perfect curves. It is a drawing tool that allows you to precisely control the objects you create. Take a look at Figure 7-1. Each creature was drawn with the Pen tool (background courtesy of Digital Stock™'s *Oceans & Coasts* CD-ROM and *Undersea Life* CD-ROM). The precise curves and lines on the penguin, fishes, and shark could not have been drawn using the Freehand tool or the Brush tool. In fact, such precision is easier to attain with the Pen tool than the Brush or Freehand tool.

TIP If you need art in a hurry, many clip art collections include paths created by the Pen tool in Adobe Illustrator. Most of these collections allow you to use the images royalty-free. Once you understand how to use the Pen tool, you may even want to get an image started with the Pen tool, add clip art, and edit the clip art paths to embellish your own images.

Connecting the Dots

If you're ready to get going, don't fall into the trap of trying to do too much too soon. Remember that the *Mona Lisa* wasn't created in a day. Before you can master the Pen tool, you must know how to create basic shapes with the Pen tool. You must know how to create simple straight lines and curves and how to attach a curve to a straight line. At first, you may think that such topics are child's play. When you use a real pen, you just create curves by drawing an arc on a piece of paper. To create a line, you draw from point A to point B. Not so when using the Pen tool. When you work with the Pen tool, it's more of a connect-the-dots type of operation than freehand drawing from one point on paper to another.

The Pen tool doesn't work like a real pen. When you use the Pen tool, you click one point (and often drag the mouse) and then click another point (and often drag the mouse). Illustrator then connects the lines with a straight or curved segment. Using the Pen tool, you can create both open and closed paths (for more information about open and closed paths, see Chapter 3). Once the paths are created, they can easily be edited, using standard path-editing techniques. As we discuss later in this chapter, paths can also be edited by adding and removing anchor points.

Before you get started drawing curves with Illustrator, it's best to get accustomed to the feel of the Pen tool by drawing straight-path segments.

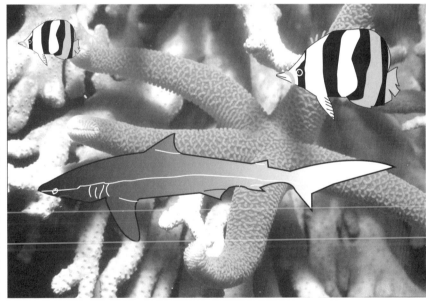

Figure 7-1:
With the Pen tool, you can put a penguin on a tropical island or some marine life in front of giant starfish.

Following the Straight and Narrow Path

The easiest way to get started with the Pen tool is to create the simplest paths possible: straight paths. In many drawing programs, you create straight lines by activating a line tool and then clicking and dragging across the screen. In Illustrator, you create straight lines by clicking once with the Pen tool to establish an *anchor point,* moving the mouse, and clicking again to create another anchor point. After you click, Illustrator connects the two anchor points with a straight line.

You can use this technique of connecting anchor points to draw straight lines or to connect lines to create closed paths, such as the diamond shape shown in Figure 7-2.

TIP If you're a stickler for precision, you may want to create vertically spaced guides on-screen to help you draw your diamond shape. If you create three equally spaced horizontal guides and three vertical guides, you'll be able to draw a perfect diamond shape. To review how to create guides, see Chapter 4.

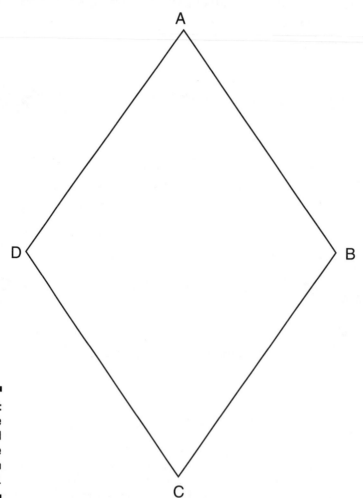

Figure 7-2:
A precise
diamond
shape
created with
the Pen tool.

We created the diamond shape in Figure 7-2 by selecting the Pen tool. We then clicked at Points A, B, C, and D. Next we moved the mouse pointer over Point A. At this point a tiny circle appeared next to the Pen tool, indicating that the path would be closed when we clicked the mouse. Our last step was to click the mouse to create the closed path.

Deleting and moving path segments

After you create a few path segments with the Pen tool, you may wish to move the path or fine-tune the path by editing it. Most of the techniques for moving and editing are the same for editing any path.

Here are a few helpful editing tips to keep in mind when creating simple paths:

- To delete the last segment after you create it, press Delete. The Delete key removes whatever is currently selected — and the last segment that you create is always the one that's selected.

- To delete any segment that is not selected, first click it with the Direct Selection tool and then press Delete.

- You can move any path by selecting it with the Selection tool and then dragging it. To move filled objects, click the middle of the object and drag.

Every open or closed path has a center point. When you work with the Pen tool, Illustrator does not show the center point on-screen. To view the center point, choose Objects⇨Attributes and then click the Show Center Point option. You can then move any path by selecting the Selection tool, clicking its center point, and dragging. The center point of a straight-path segment also can be used to tell you where its midpoint is.

Editing segments

Editing segments is quite an easy task. To enlarge or shrink an unselected straight-path segment, select an anchor point with the Direct Selection tool and then click and drag. You can also edit a segment by selecting it with the Direct Selection tool and then move the segment by dragging it or by pressing the arrow keys on your keyboard.

Coming Unglued

In many respects, using the Pen tool is like pulling taffy. As you click, the path segment stretches from the last point that you clicked to the next point that you click. If you create a closed path (like the diamond in the previous section), the Pen tool turns off its connecting option, which means that you can go off and create another path as soon as you finish creating a closed path. However, if you don't close the path, the Pen tool keeps creating connecting lines at every point you click on-screen. This behavior often drives beginners crazy. Imagine this scenario: You simply want to create one line segment at the top of the screen and another line segment at the bottom of the screen. If you try it, you'll see that the Pen connects the top line to the bottom line segment. This situation brings up an important point: If you create an open path and then want to create another path, you must do something to tell the Pen to stop connecting every last anchor point of one open path to the first anchor point of another open path.

Here are four ways to tell the Pen tool to stop connecting anchor points:

 ✔ The easiest way is to click the Pen tool in the Toolbox.

 ✔ The second easiest way is to select a tool other than the Pen tool.

 ✔ The third easiest way is to choose Edit⇨Select None or press ⌘+Shift+A.

 ✔ Another way is to hold down the ⌘ key to temporarily turn the Pen tool into the Selection tool and then click someplace other than the path.

Curves Ahead!

The Pen tool's *raison d'être* is to draw curves. Finally, a chance to show off our high school French! It was, in fact, a Frenchman (Pierre Bézier) who came up with the idea of manipulating four control points — two points at the base curve and two at the ends of the direction lines extending from the curve. Thanks to Bézier, Illustrator aficionados can draw perfect curves without clicking and dragging in a perfectly steady arc. Okay, so he didn't come up with the idea just for Macs. But Illustrator still uses Bézier curves, so we're indebted to him just the same.

Creating Bézier curves

Now the fun begins — drawing curves with the Pen tool.

Many new users find it difficult to get used to drawing curves with the Pen tool because curves are created by connecting mouse clicks and dragging, rather than clicking and dragging in an arc-like motion. Once you get the hang of it, you'll see that it really isn't too difficult to create curves with the Pen tool, and you'll appreciate the control it provides when you need to create precise and elegant curves.

The basics of drawing curves with the Pen tool are to click and drag, release the mouse button, move the mouse, and then click and drag. Once you get the hang of drawing continuous curves, you can create more sophisticated shapes. A series of continuous smooth curves is shown in Figure 7-3.

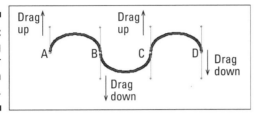

Figure 7-3:
Creating
Bézier
curves with
the Pen tool.

To create these Bézier curves, you need to click and drag at four separate points on-screen. Before you begin, take a look at points A, B, C, and D in Figure 7-3. These are the points on-screen where you will be clicking and dragging the mouse.

Before you start creating curves, you may want to use guides as a grid. The guides can help you make each curve the same width and height. Create three horizontal guides with the top and bottom guides the same distance from the middle guide (we created them about half an inch away). Then create a few vertical guides spaced out the same amount (we created them about an inch apart). For more information about creating guides, see Chapter 4.

Follow the next set of steps to draw a series of continuous smooth curves as shown in Figure 7-3. If you follow these steps, your first curve will point up. If you want your first curve to point down, simply change "up" to "down" and "down" to "up" in all the steps.

1. **Click the Pen tool in the Toolbox to activate it.**

2. **To better see the paths you are creating, set the Fill in the Paint Style palette to None and set the Stroke to black with the stroke weight set to 5 points.**

   This means that your path will be drawn with a black line, with no color inside the curves.

   To open the Paint Style palette, choose Window⇨Show Paint Style. To set the Fill to None, click the Fill icon and then click the swatch with the diagonal in it. This is the one in the upper-left corner of the group of colored swatches in the Paint Style palette.

   You also may want to work in Artwork mode rather than in Preview mode in order to see only the paths that you are creating, without a stroke or a fill. See Chapter 2 for more information about using Artwork and Preview modes.

3. **Now move the mouse to the left side of your document window and click to establish point A. Don't release the mouse. Instead, drag up about an inch and then release the mouse.**

By dragging up, you tell Illustrator that the first part of the curve bump will point up.

The line you see on-screen is a nonprinting line called a *direction line*. The angle at which you create the direction line determines the angle of the curve segment. If you click and drag to create a long direction line, the curve will be higher. The little dot at the end of the direction line is called a *direction point*. Later we cover how to edit curves by clicking and dragging the direction point.

4. **Move the mouse to the right about an inch to point B. Click and drag down about an inch and then release the mouse.**

As you drag down, you create a curve pointing up and a new direction line sprouts from point B.

5. **To continue drawing curves, move the mouse pointer to the right about an inch, from point B to point C. Click to establish an anchor point at point C, and drag up about an inch to create a curve pointing down.**

6. **Move the mouse to point D (about an inch to the right from point C). Then click and drag down about an inch to create a curve pointing up.**

If you want to create more curves, repeat the see-sawing mouse moves of Steps 5 and 6 a few times (replace points B, C, and D with the points you are working with). To make sure the Pen does not reconnect to your last point, click the Pen tool again in the Toolbox.

Creating a snake

Once you know how to create Bézier curves, you can draw wavy objects, like the snake shown in Figure 7-4. The snake on the right was created from the curves on the left.

We drew the snake by creating the curve in Figure 7-4 with the Pen tool. In the Paint Style palette, we set the Fill set to None and the Stroke to 20 points. Then, we used guides to help create the curves. To create the curves for the snake, we started the first curve by clicking and dragging left on point A. We clicked and dragged at three other points (B, C, and D), using similar techniques for drawing curves as described in the previous section. We also used the Pen tool to create the snake's head, the diamond shapes on its back, the grass, and palm tree.

Figure 7-4:
A snake
created with
the Pen tool.

Editing curves

The power of Bézier curves becomes truly evident once you begin to edit a
curve. When you edit a curve, you manipulate the curve's anchor points and
direction lines.

✔ You can change the size of a curve by selecting and moving an anchor
point (use the Direct Selection tool).

✔ While creating a curve using the Pen tool, you can switch to the Direct
Selection tool edit by pressing ⌘+Shift. With ⌘+Shift pressed, drag the
anchor points as you work.

✔ You can change the shape of a curve by clicking and dragging a direction line's endpoint. If you drag a direction line's endpoint to make the direction line longer, you make the curve bigger. If you click and drag to change the angle of the direction line, you change the angle of the curve.

✔ You can change the height of any curve by using the Direct Selection tool to click and drag the bump (curve segment) of a curve. Figure 7-5 shows the curve segment being dragged up. Notice that the direction lines grow when the height of the curve increases.

Direction line

Figure 7-5:
Editing a
curve
segment.

Direction line

✔ The continuous curves that make up the snake in the preceding section are connected by an anchor point known as a *smooth point*. A smooth point is an anchor point bisected by one direction line. Clicking and dragging the direction line that bisects the smooth point edits the curves on either side of the anchor point. (In Figure 7-4, points B and C are smooth points.)

Some curve tips

Here are a few tips and reminders:

✔ Remember to create the first direction line in the direction in which you want the bump of the curve to point. In other words, if the want the curve to bump up, click and drag up to start the curve. If you want the curve to bump down, click and drag down.

✔ When drawing shapes, try to create as few anchor points as possible to ensure that the curves are as smooth as possible. If you need to add anchor points, add them when you edit the curves. Editing anchor points comes up later in this chapter.

✔ To select a curve segment of an unselected path, click the segment with the Direct Selection tool. Once a curve segment is selected, you can delete it by pressing the Delete key.

✔ To create consistent-sized curves, try to make the direction line about a third of the total length of the curve.

Changing directions to draw scalloped curves

Your next stop is drawing scalloped curves — curves whose bumps point in the same direction. Figure 7-6 shows how scalloped curves were used to add frosting to a cake. (The background photograph of the bow and gift wrapping is an edited image from MetaTools' *Power Photos II* CD-ROM.) When you create a scalloped curve, you need to tell Illustrator that you are creating a *corner* rather than a smooth point between curve segments. The corner point allows you to create one curve bump in the same direction as the previous curve bump. When creating scalloped curves, you create a corner point by pressing the Option key and clicking and dragging before you begin to create subsequent curves.

Figure 7-6:
The frosting on the cake was created using scalloped curves.

Figure 7-7 shows a set of scalloped curves. To create the curves, you click at points A, B, C, and D. At points B and C, you press the Option key to create a corner point.

Before you start creating scalloped curves, you may want to use guides as a grid. Create a horizontal guide and a guide above and below that guide the same distance apart (we created them about half an inch away). Then create a few vertical guides spaced out the same amount (we created them about an inch and a half apart).

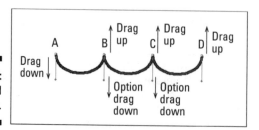

Figure 7-7:
Scalloped
curves.

To create scalloped curves so that your first curve points downward and the subsequent curves follow that lead, follow these steps. If you want your first curve to point upward, simply change "up" to "down" and vice versa in all the steps.

1. **Click the Pen tool in the Toolbox if it is not already selected.**

2. **To better see the paths you are creating, set the Fill in the Paint Style palette to None and set the Stroke to black with the stroke weight set to 5 points.**

   For more information about Filling and Stroking and the Paint Style palette, see Chapters 3 and 10. For more information about the Artwork and Preview modes, see Chapter 2.

   You also may want to work in Artwork mode rather than in Preview mode so you concentrate only on the path you are drawing.

3. **Move the mouse to the left side of your document window to point A. Click at point A, and drag down about half an inch.**

4. **Move to point B (about an inch and a half from point A) and drag up about half an inch to complete the first curve.**

5. **Now you need to create a direction line that points downward because you want the next curve to point downward rather than upward. To establish this direction line, you need to create a corner point. To do this, first move the Pen tool over the last anchor point you created. You'll notice that a small caret icon appears next to the Pen tool. Next, press and hold the Option key. Notice that the status bar says Pen: Make Corner. With the Option key pressed, click and drag down over the last anchor point that you created. A new direction line appears. After you've dragged down about half an inch, release the mouse.**

6. **Move to point C (about an inch and a half from point B). Click and drag up about half an inch to finish the curve.**

7. **Move to point D (about an inch and a half from point C). Once again, you must establish a direction line that points down. To do this, start by pressing and holding the Option key. With the Option key pressed, click and drag down about half an inch. After the new direction line appears, release the mouse.**

Frosting on the cake

After you've mastered creating scallops, you can try using your skills to create a cake with some frosting, as shown in Figure 7-6. We created this cake out of a rounded rectangle and the frosting out of scalloped curves. When creating the cake, we filled the rectangle with white and added a 1-point black stroke. Next we created a few scalloped curves at the top portion of the cake, as shown in Figure 7-7.

After we created a few scalloped curves, we needed to close the path. We used the Pen tool to create a curve at one end of the scallops, as shown in Figure 7-8. Next we created a straight line and another curve to close the path.

Once the cake was complete, we used the Pen tool to create some candles, the Oval tool to create a plate, and the Type tool to create the words Happy Birthday. We moved the plate behind the cake with the Arrange⇨Send to Back command. Finally we dragged and dropped the background photograph of the bow and gift wrapping (MetaTools' *Power Photos II* CD-ROM) from Photoshop to Illustrator. After the photograph was dropped into Illustrator, we chose Arrange⇨Send to Back to move it behind the cake.

If some of these terms make your head spin, don't worry. Keep reading this book and you'll find all the answers you need.

Figure 7-8:
Closed path
used to
create cake
frosting.

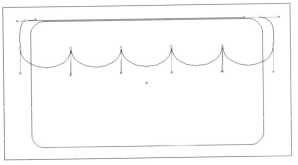

Connecting Lines to Curves and Vice Versa

The world is not created from curves alone. Often objects, such as the vase shown in Figure 7-9, are created from a collection of curves and straight lines. The photo of the flower is from Vivid Details *Flowers Volume 9* CD-ROM. Other simple objects such as paddles and tennis rackets can be created by connecting curves and straight lines.

Once you know how to create Bézier and scalloped curves, connecting straight lines to curves or vice versa is a simple affair. See Figure 7-10 for an example of connecting a line to a curve.

Figure 7-9:
A vase
created by
connecting
straight
lines to
curves.

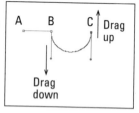

Figure 7-10:
Connecting
a line to a
curve.

Follow these steps to create a line and connect it to a curve. If you want your first curve to point up instead of down, just change "up" to "down" and "down" to "up" in these steps.

1. **Select the Pen tool.**

2. **Click point A to create an anchor point.**

3. **Move to point B. Press and click to create a line.**

   Notice that a tiny caret icon appears next to the Pen pointer. This icon indicates that you will create a corner point by clicking at the anchor point.

4. **Click and drag down to establish a direction line.**

   Dragging down tells Illustrator that you want to create your curve with the bump pointing down.

5. **Move the mouse to point C. Click and drag up to finish the curve.**

Connecting a curve to a line, as shown in Figure 7-11, isn't too different from connecting a line to a curve.

Figure 7-11:
Connecting
a curve to
a line.

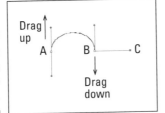

Here are the steps for connecting a curve to a line. If you want your curve to point down, just change "up" to "down" and "down" to "up" in these steps.

1. **Select the Pen tool.**

2. **Click point A, and drag up to establish an upward direction line.**

3. **Move the mouse to point B, click, and drag down to complete the curve.**

4. **Position the mouse pointer over point B. A tiny caret appears next to the pen pointer, indicating that a corner point will be created. Click the mouse on point B.**

5. **To create the line segment, move to point C and click again.**

I've Grown Accustomed to Your Vase

Using the techniques you've learned in this chapter, you can now draw the vase shown back in Figure 7-9. As you create the vase, use Figure 7-12 as a reference. We started by creating guides, as shown in Figure 7-12. In the Paint Style palette, we choose a stroke of 1 point and set the Fill to None. With the Pen tool selected, we clicked points A and B. To create a straight line, we held the Shift key down and moved the Pen tool to point C and clicked. With the Pen tool selected, we clicked point C and dragged to the right to create a direction line.

Then we moved the Pen to point D and clicked and dragged to the left. We clicked point D to convert it to a corner point. Then we clicked point E to create a straight line. With the Pen tool, we clicked point E and dragged to the left to create a direction line. Our next step was to move the Pen tool to point F and click and drag to the right. We then clicked point F again, to convert it to a corner point. Then we pressed and held the Shift key while we clicked point A to create a straight line to close the path. Since the vase is a closed path, it could be filled with a color, a gradient, or a pattern. We filled the vase with a pattern. Chapter 11 covers filling with a gradient. Chapter 12 covers filling with a pattern.

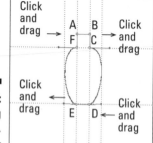

Figure 7-12:
Creating
the vase.

Anchors Away! Adding and Deleting Anchor Points

We can't all be perfect the first time. After you create an object, you may need to add or delete an anchor point to edit or change an object's shape.

When you need to add an anchor point, you click a path segment with the Add Anchor Point tool. To delete an anchor point, you click an anchor point with the Delete Anchor Point tool. Figure 7-13 shows how you can easily change a rectangle into the shape of a house or, if you're a baseball fan, home plate. By deleting two anchor points from this shape, you can convert the home plate to a triangle.

Here are the steps for adding and deleting anchor points to convert a rectangle into different shapes:

1. Use the Rectangle tool to create a rectangle.

2. Activate the Add Anchor Point tool.

To select the Add Anchor Point tool, click the Scissors in the Toolbox. With the mouse button still pressed, drag over to the Add Anchor Point tool; then release the mouse

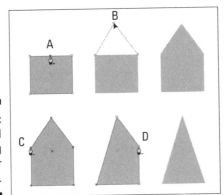

Figure 7-13:
Adding and
deleting
anchor
points.

3. **To create a new anchor point, position the mouse pointer in the center of the top segment of the rectangle (to point A in Figure 7-13); then click the mouse on the top segment of the rectangle.**

   You can also add anchor points by choosing the Filter⇨Objects⇨Add Anchor Points command. Chapter 16 has more about filters.

4. **To create the house shape, activate the Direct Selection tool, click the new anchor point and drag it up (point B in Figure 7-13).**

At this point, you have a new shape created by adding an anchor point. Now use the Delete Anchor Point tool to change the shape into a triangle.

1. **Select the Delete Anchor Point tool.**

   To select the Delete Anchor Point tool, click the Scissors tool in the Toolbox and keep the mouse button pressed. If you see the Add Anchor Point or Convert Direction point tool in the Toolbox instead of the Scissors, click on the tool and keep the mouse button pressed. With the mouse button pressed, drag over to the Delete Anchor Point tool; then release the mouse.

2. **With the Delete Anchor Point tool selected, click once at point C in Figure 7-13 on the house object.**

   The object immediately is redrawn without the anchor point.

3. **Click point D in Figure 7-13.**

   The object is redrawn without the second anchor point and turns into a triangle, as shown in Figure 7-13.

Converting Direction Points

One of Illustrator's handiest editing tools is its Convert Direction Point tool. If you click a corner point with the Convert Direction Point tool, it converts to a smooth point. If you click a smooth point, it converts to a corner point.

Using this tool, you can completely transform objects into different shapes. It's especially helpful to those who don't like drawing curves. For example, you can create a sharp object such as the wedge shown in Figure 7-14 (on the left) by simply clicking the mouse a few times with the Pen tool activated. Then, using the Convert Direction Point tool, you easily transform the corner points to smooth points to create the heart shown on the right of Figure 7-14.

When using the Convert Direction tool to convert a corner point to a smooth point, click and keep the mouse pressed. With the mouse button pressed, click and drag to create a curve.

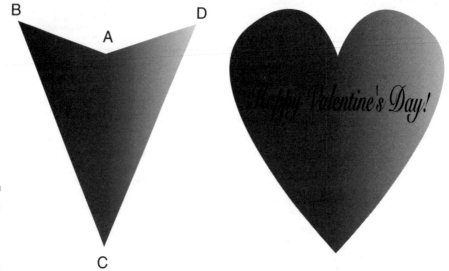

Figure 7-14:
A wedge
converted
into a heart.

Here are the steps for creating the wedge and then converting it into a heart:

1. **With the Pen tool selected, click at points A, B, C, and D to create the wedge.**

2. **Activate the Convert Direction Point tool.**

3. **Convert point D to a smooth point, and drag to create a curve, as shown in Figure 7-15 on the left — that is, position the mouse pointer over point D, and click and drag diagonally up to the left.**

4. **Create the second curve of the heart by clicking point B with the Convert Direction Point tool and dragging diagonally down to the left, as shown in Figure 7-15 on the right.**

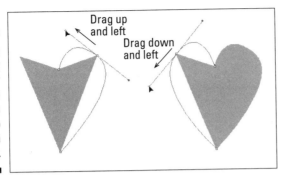

Figure 7-15:
Converting
corner
points to
smooth
points to
create a
heart.

Creating a Wine Glass

Using a combination of the Add Anchor Point tool and the Convert Direction Point tool, you can create artistic magic. Using both tools, you can easily create a wine glass shape by starting with a simple rectangle, as shown in Figure 7-16. We started by using the Rectangle tool to create a rectangle. We created a horizontal guide to help create points A and B on the same horizontal axis. Next, we used the Add Anchor Point tool to add anchor points to the rectangle, as shown at points A and B in Figure 7-16 on the left. With the Convert Direction Point tool selected, we positioned the mouse pointer at point A. Then we clicked and dragged diagonally to the right, as shown in Figure 7-16 on the right. (This step created a curve on the left side of the rectangle.) We positioned the mouse pointer at point B and clicked and dragged diagonally to the left, as shown in Figure 7-16 on the far right. (This step created a curve on the right side of the rectangle.) We also used the Direct Selection tool to click and drag the direction lines to fine-tune the shapes.

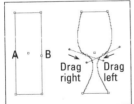

Figure 7-16:
Creating a
wine glass
from a
rectangle.

A Little Path Surgery

Occasionally, as you work with paths, you'll want to cut a path to edit it or to create a more sophisticated shape. For example, in order to create the Saturn image in Figure 7-17 (background image courtesy of Digital Stock™'s *Space & Space Flight* CD-ROM), part of the ring was cut and sent behind the sphere.

Illustrator's path scalpel is its Scissors tool. To use the Scissors tool, you click it in the Toolbox and then click a path segment, which snips the segment. Then you can click and drag the segment away to move it, if necessary.

Figure 7-17: Saturn's ring, created by splitting a path.

Using the Scissors tool, you can snip an open path to create two separate paths, and you can snip a closed path to turn it into an open path. When using the Scissors tool, you can split the anchor points of a closed path, but you cannot split a path at the end-point of an open path — which is fine because there's no reason why you would want to do that anyway.

You can also use the Object⇨Apply Knife command and the Knife tool in the Plug-in Tools palette to slice up a path. For more information about using the Apply Knife command and the Knife tool, see Chapter 6.

You cannot split a path that has text within or along the path. Entering text in a path and along a path comes up in Chapter 15.

 Here's how we used the Scissors tool to cut a path and create the Saturn image in Figure 7-17. First we created a circle using the Oval tool and filled it with a color. Next, we created a horizontal oval for Saturn's ring. In the Paint Style palette, we set the Fill to None and the Stroke to 20 points. With the Scissors tool selected, we clicked at the edge of the oval path at points A and B in Figure 7-18. When we clicked, Illustrator snipped the path into two paths. With the Selection tool selected, we clicked the top segment. This segment was used for the back part of the ring. Next, we sent this segment behind the sphere by choosing Arrange⇨Send To Back. Immediately, the back part of the ring was sent behind the planet. The two paths that make up the ring actually look like one path.

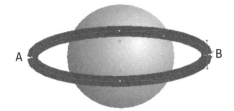

Figure 7-18:
Cutting
the rim at
two points.

Often, after snipping a path with the Scissors tool, you'll need to pull the new path segment away from the old path with the Direct Selection tool.

Joining Points

Sometimes, when trying to create a closed path, you just can't quite get it to close. There's a gap between end-points. The gap is obvious when you stroke an object. If you try to close the gap by just drawing a segment between two points, you end up with two paths instead of one on-screen. The easiest way to close a gap in a path or to simply join two open paths together is to use Illustrator's Object⇨Join command.

The Join command not only joins anchor points that are apart but also anchor points that are on top of each other. When one anchor point is on top of another, the Join command essentially nails them down into one anchor point.

Anchor points that are on top of each other are often referred to as *coincident* points. Why? So you can say they are coincident, rather than having to say they are on top of each other.

Here's how to join two anchor points together that are not on top of each other:

1. **Select the two anchor points that you want to join.**

   You can also select them by clicking and dragging the Selection tool over each point. Or select one with the Direct Selection tool and then press Shift and click the other.

2. **Choose Object⇨Join.**

   The anchor points are joined together by a new segment between the two points.

If you are joining coincident anchor points (described earlier), first select the two by clicking and dragging over them with the Selection tool. After you execute Object⇨Join, the Join dialog box shown in Figure 7-19 appears. In the Join dialog box, choose whether you want the joined point to be a Corner or Smooth point; then click OK.

Figure 7-19:
The Join
dialog box.

Averaging Points

Illustrator's Object➪Average command is sort of like an automatic "make nice" command. After you create an object, Illustrator's Average command can automatically move your anchor points around so that they line up along a vertical or horizontal axis. When the Average command is executed, the selected points move to the average point on an axis among the points. The command is often used to align anchor points that are a little out of whack and make them more symmetrical. The Average command also allows you to completely transform an object. Figure 7-20 shows before and after views of a circle that was averaged both horizontally and vertically. This type of effect can be created by choosing the Both option in the Average dialog box, also shown in Figure 7-20.

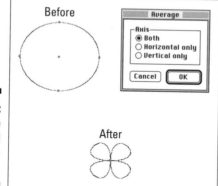

Figure 7-20:
Circle
averaged
to create
new shape.

Here's how to use the Average command:

1. **Create a shape, and then select all the anchor points that you want to average.**

   We selected all the anchor points in a circle path for Figure 7-20.

   To select, click and drag over the anchor points with the Direct Selection tool or Shift-click with the Direct Selection tool.

2. **To line up the objects on a vertical and/or horizontal axis, choose Object➪Average. In the Average dialog box, choose Both, Horizontal, or Vertical.**

You can average and join two paths at the same time by first selecting the two points that you want to join and then pressing ⌘+Option+J. The end-points of the two paths are then joined at a common point between the original two paths.

Chapter 8

Illustrator's Amazing Transformations

Do you still have a few artist friends who refuse to use a Mac? Most of these stubborn sorts will tell you that they can create anything by hand that you can create in Illustrator. Show them a few Illustrator transformations, and they'll soon be singing a different tune. Using Illustrator's transformation tools, you start with a simple shape, slant it, rotate it, and copy it again and again to give it new life as a completely different object. After you create an object, you can also use the transformation tools to enlarge it, shrink it, or create a mirror image from it.

Tools for Transformations

The Scale, Rotate, Reflect, and Shear tools are Illustrator's amazing transformation quartet. Although each member of the transformation quartet creates a different effect, they all work in a similar way.

> ✔ You can use the transformation tools to alter a selected closed or open path or to alter only part of a closed or open path. For more information about open and closed paths, see Chapter 3.

> ✔ You can use the tools manually. That means that you can select the tool and then click and drag on-screen to create a transformation effect. This feature helps when you want to control every step of the transformation

process and stop the process when you're satisfied with the effect. For example, if you manually rotate an image, you can click and drag to begin the rotation effect and stop the rotation exactly where you want by releasing the mouse button.

✔ You can type a value in the transformation tool's dialog box. After you click OK, Illustrator uses the center of the selected object as the origin of the change.

✔ If you don't want to use the center of the selected object as the origin of the transformation, Option+click on-screen where you want to set the point of origin for the transformation. This action opens the transformation tool's dialog box, where you can specify options to control the transformation effect.

When you see the words *Option+click,* it means to press the Option key and, while holding down Option, click the mouse.

✔ Each transformation tool's dialog box enables you to transform a copy of the object. Using this option, you can leave the original object in its place and see the transformed object on-screen. After you copy an object, you can use the Arrange➪Repeat Transform command to create multiple transformed versions of the original object. That process is described later in this chapter.

✔ All of the transformation dialog boxes include Pattern and Object options. By selecting or deselecting the Pattern and Object check boxes, you can choose to transform only the pattern within an object, transform the object without the pattern, or transform the pattern and the object together. To transform just an object, select the Object check box and deselect the Pattern check box. Using the Pattern Check box is covered in more detail in Chapter 12.

Going Upscale

In Illustrator, you can enlarge and reduce an object as many times as you like without adversely affecting image quality. To enlarge or reduce an object, you use the Scale tool. You scale an object by percent values, either uniformly or nonuniformly. When you scale an object *uniformly,* you scale it horizontally and vertically at the same percentage value. Entering values greater than 100 percent makes the object larger; entering values less than 100 percent makes the object smaller. For example, assume that you create a drawing of a movie camera. If you scale the object horizontally and vertically 200 percent, both the width and height of the movie camera grow twice the size of the original.

When you scale an object *nonuniformly,* you scale it horizontally and vertically with different percentage values. For example, assume that you scale your movie camera 200 percent horizontally and 50 percent vertically: The movie camera is now half as tall but twice as wide.

When scaling an object by using the Scale dialog box, you can specify whether you want to scale the line weights with the object. An object's line weight is the stroke width specified in the Paint Style palette. When you scale the line weights, the stroke of the object grows or shrinks according to the scaling percentage. You can also create a copy of the object you are scaling so that the original object is not affected.

Scaling manually

Here's how to scale an object manually by using the mouse:

1. **Select the object you want to scale.**

   To select an object, click it with the Selection tool.

2. **Select the Scale tool.**

   At this point you have the following two choices:

   - To scale from the object's center point, simply click and drag on-screen.

   - Although you can click and drag anyplace on-screen, you may find it easier to control the scaling by clicking and dragging an anchor point.

   As you drag, the object grows or shrinks.

Figure 8-1 shows a movie camera being scaled manually from its center point.

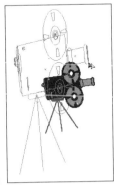

Figure 8-1:
Movie
camera
being
scaled
manually.

Scaling by using the Scale dialog box

Here's how to scale by using the Scale dialog box:

1. **Select the object you want to scale.**

2. **If you want to scale from a point other than the object's center point, Option+click that point to open the Scale dialog box.**

   To use the center point of the selected object as the point of origin, double-click the Scale tool in the Toolbox.

3. **In the Scale dialog box, as shown in Figure 8-2, click the Uniform option to scale horizontally and vertically with the same percentage, or click the Non-uniform option to scale horizontally and vertically with different percentages.**

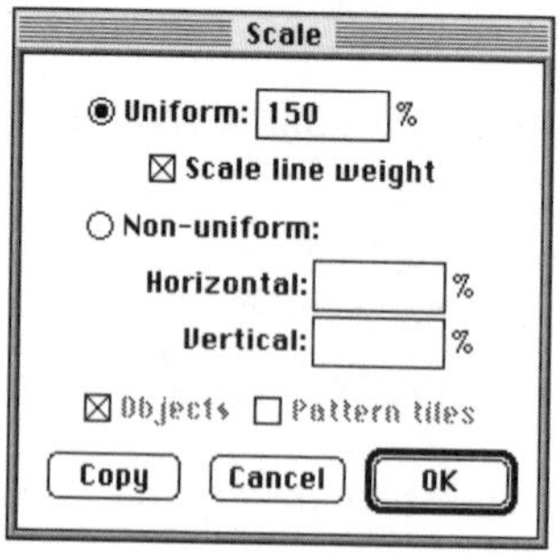

Figure 8-2:
The Scale
dialog box.

Scale
⊙ Uniform: [150] %
⊠ Scale line weight
○ Non-uniform:
Horizontal: [ ] %
Vertical: [ ] %
⊠ Objects □ Pattern tiles
[Copy] [Cancel] [OK]

4. **To enlarge an object, enter a percentage larger than 100 in the percentage field; to reduce an object, enter a percentage smaller than 100 in the percentage field.**

5. **If you scale an object uniformly, you can also choose to scale the object's line weight by clicking the Scale line weight check box to select it.**

6. **To scale the object, click OK; to create a copy of the original object and scale, choose Copy. (The latter choice gives you two images: the unscaled original and a scaled version.)**

Getting the Spin on the Rotate Tool

You can use the Rotate tool to rotate an object by clicking and dragging the mouse or by specifying an angle for the rotation transformation.

Rotating manually

Here's how to rotate an object manually:

1. **Select the object you want to scale.**

2. **Select the Rotate tool.**

3. **Decide whether to rotate the object from its center point or from a specific point on-screen.**

    • To rotate an object from its center, click anywhere on-screen and drag in a circular direction on-screen.

    • To rotate from a specific point on-screen, click the mouse button once at the point you want to rotate from and then click and drag in a circular direction.

Here are a couple of rotating tips:

✔ To rotate at 45-degree increments, press the Shift key when you rotate.

✔ To copy when you rotate, press the Option key as you drag to rotate.

Rotating by using the Rotate dialog box

Here's how to rotate using the dialog box:

1. **Select the object you want to rotate.**

2. **Double-click the Rotate tool in the Toolbox to rotate from the object's center point.**

    To rotate the object from another point on-screen, move the mouse over the area that you want to set as the center point of the rotation. With the Option key pressed, click the point you want to rotate from.

    This action opens the Rotate dialog box.

3. **In the Rotate dialog box, as shown in Figure 8-3, enter a value for the rotation angle.**

    A positive number causes a counterclockwise rotation. If you enter a negative number, the object rotates clockwise.

Figure 8-3:
The Rotate
dialog box.

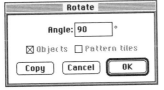

4. **To rotate your object, click OK; to rotate a copy of your object click Copy; to keep rotating more copies, choose Arrange⇨Repeat Transform.**

Creating a sunflower by using the Rotate tool

You can use the Rotate tool to rotate and copy an object at a center point to create all sorts of different objects, from logos to pinwheels to sunflowers. For Figure 8-4, we rotated and copied an oval several times to create a sunflower. To create the sunflower, we started by using the Oval tool to create an elongated oval. Then we Option+clicked at the base of the oval to set the point of origin, as shown on the left. After the Rotate dialog box appeared, we typed in an angle value (in this case, 10) and chose Copy. To create more copies at the same angle, we chose Arrange⇨Repeat Transform. We executed this command several times by using the keyboard shortcut ⌘+D until we created a circle of flower petals on-screen, as shown in the middle. Next, we created a circle over the center of the ovals and filled it. We also created small circles inside the circle to create a sunflower as shown on the right.

Point of origin   Circle of flower petals   Sunflower

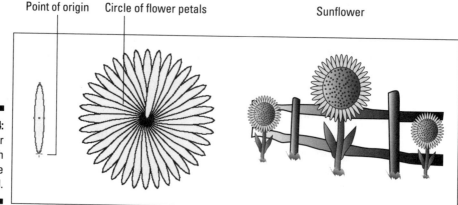

Figure 8-4:
A sunflower
created with
the Rotate
tool.

A Few Moments of Reflection

The Reflect tool enables you to create mirror images of an object. Reflecting can be extremely helpful when you are creating symmetrical objects. For example, assume that you need to create a wine glass. You can create half the wine glass and then copy and reflect it to create the other side of the glass. For Figure 8-5, we created the left antenna and wings of a butterfly, selected them, and used the Reflect tool to reflect and copy the selected items vertically 90 degrees. The photo is from *Vivid Details Flowers Volume 9* CD-ROM.

After reflecting

Before reflecting

Figure 8-5:
Creating a
butterfly by
using the
Reflect tool.

The Reflect tool enables you to create reflections across an imaginary axis. By default, this axis is an imaginary vertical or horizontal line that runs through the center of your object. Essentially, that means that the Reflect tool can flip your object vertically or horizontally. However, if you want, you can change the imaginary axis — which is kind of like taking a mirror and pointing it in different directions to create different reflection effects.

Using different reflection angles takes a little getting used to, so the next couple of sections detail the art of reflection. Each provides you with the option of reflecting vertically or horizontally through an object's center point or reflecting from another point on-screen.

Reflecting manually

To start out, try reflecting a simple shape such as a half-moon or flag or triangle created by connecting segments with the Pen tool. For more information on how to connect segments with the Pen tool, see Chapter 7. Here's how to reflect an object manually:

1. **Select the object that you want to reflect.**

2. **Select the Reflect tool.**

3. **Imagine an invisible axis along which the desired reflection is to occur and then pick a point on this axis and click the mouse.**

    This point is the point of origin of the reflection.

4. **To create the final reflection effect, you can**

    • Click the mouse on another point on the invisible axis to reflect the object along the axis.

    • Click the invisible axis, and drag the mouse to adjust the axis.

    As you drag, the object rotates along the axis. Release the mouse when the object is in the desired position.

You can copy the original selected object while reflecting manually by pressing Option while you click the mouse.

Reflecting by using the Reflect dialog box

If you need to reflect an object, you may find using the Reflect dialog box a bit more comforting than reflecting manually. When the dialog box opens, you can choose to reflect horizontally, vertically, or at an angle.

Here's how to reflect using the dialog box:

1. **Select the object or objects you want to reflect.**

2. **To use the center point of the selected object as the point of origin, double-click the Reflect tool.**

    Alternatively, you can Option+click at a point along an imaginary axis that you want to reflect across.

3. **In the Reflect dialog box, as shown in Figure 8-6, choose whether you want to reflect an object on the horizontal or vertical axis or along a specified angle.**

    If you pick the angle option, enter an angle into the Angle field.

    If you enter a positive number for the angle, Illustrator reflects the object counterclockwise across the axis; enter a negative number, and Illustrator reflects the object clockwise across the axis.

Figure 8-6:
The Reflect
dialog box.

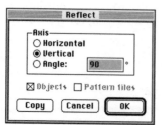

4. **To reflect the object, click OK; to create a copy of the original selected object and reflect, choose Copy.**

Shear Fun

 If you need to create the effect of a splat of goop on the wall, the Shear tool is undoubtedly your best bet. The Shear tool enables you to slant an object horizontally, vertically, or along an axis at a specific angle. Using the Shear tool, you can also create interesting shadow effects or three-dimensional objects.

Shearing manually

Here's how to shear an object manually:

1. **Select the object or objects you want to shear.**

2. **Select the Shear tool by clicking it in the Toolbox.**

3. **If you want to shear the object by using its center point as the origin of the shear effect, simply click and drag on-screen to shear it.**

   This method often creates a slanted version of the original object.

   or

   If you want to shear the object by using another point as the origin of the shear effect, click that spot on-screen; then click and drag to shear.

 Here are a couple of shearing tips:

✔ To copy the original as you shear, keep the mouse button pressed and then press Option while dragging.

✔ To shear at a 45-degree angle or in multiples of a 45-degree angle, press Shift as you click and drag.

Shearing by using the Shear dialog box

Here's how to shear by using the Shear dialog box:

1. **Select the object you want to shear.**

2. **To use the center point of the selected object as the point of origin, double-click the Shear tool.**

To use another point of origin, Option+click the point that you want to set as the origin.

3. In the Shear dialog box, as shown in Figure 8-7, enter the angle at which you want the object sheared.

The shear angle is the angle that the object is slanted at, in relation to the axis chosen at the bottom of the dialog box. Entering a positive number produces a shear angle in a clockwise direction; entering a negative number produces a shear angle in a counterclockwise direction.

4. In the Axis section of the dialog box, choose whether you want to shear the object along a horizontal or a vertical axis or along an axis at a specified Angle.

If you click the Angle option and enter a value into the Angled axis field, the object uses that angle as the shearing axis.

Figure 8-7:
The Shear
dialog box.

Shear

Angle: 45 °

Axis
⦿ Horizontal
○ Vertical
○ Angle: 0 °

☒ Objects ☐ Pattern tiles

[Copy] [Cancel] [OK]

5. To shear the object, click OK; to create a copy and shear the copy, choose Copy; to exit the Shear dialog box and not shear the selected object, choose Cancel.

Creating a three-dimensional object

The Shear tool can help you create three-dimensional shapes, such as cubes, dice, product packages, or a filing cabinet. We created the 3-D shape in Figure 8-8 by using the Rectangle tool to create a square. We filled it with white with a 3-point black stroke. Next, we duplicated the square twice. With the Selection tool and the square selected, we pressed and held the Option key while we dragged to create a copy. When we saw the copy, we released the mouse. We repeated the previous step to create another square. Next, we dragged one square on top and one to the right, as shown on the left of the figure.

Next, we used the Scale tool to scale the top square nonuniformly: 100 percent horizontally and 50 percent vertically. We used the Shear tool to shear the top square 45 degrees on a horizontal axis. We used the Scale tool to scale the bottom square on the right nonuniformly: 50 percent horizontally and 100 percent vertically.

We used the Shear tool to shear the bottom square on the right –45 degrees on a vertical axis. Then, we moved the squares closer together, by selecting them with the Selection tool and dragging each one. To enhance the perspective, we selected the top-left anchor with the Direct Selection tool and used the right-arrow key on the keyboard to move it to the right.

To create the dots on the die, we created an oval, filled it with gray, and moved it into position, as shown on the right of Figure 8-8. we duplicated the dot by selecting it and pressing Option. With the Option key pressed, we clicked and dragged, and a copy of the dot appeared on screen. To create the correct perspective, we used the Shear command to elongate the dots.

Before   After

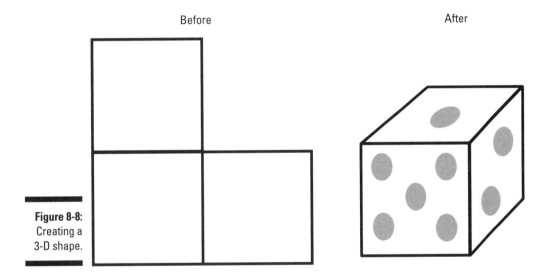

Figure 8-8:
Creating a
3-D shape.

Creating Shadowed Type

You can also use all the transformation tools to create shadowed type, as shown in Figure 8-9. We created the shadowed type by using the Type tool to type a few words. Next we double-clicked the Reflect tool. In the Reflect dialog box, we set the Reflect Axis option to Horizontal and then clicked Copy. We then filled the reflected text with a light color. Then we used the Shear dialog box to shear the reflected text across a 60-degree horizontal axis. We used the Scale tool to scale the reflected and sheared text nonuniformly: 70 percent vertically and 100 percent horizontally. Then we rotated both the text and shadow 5 degrees by using the Rotate dialog box. Finally, we placed an image of a globe behind the text.

SAVE THE EARTH!

SAVE THE EARTH!
————— Shadow type:
Reflected horizontally

SAVE THE EARTH!
————— Shadow type:
Reflected and sheared

SAVE THE EARTH!
————— Shadow type:
Reflected, sheared, and scaled

SAVE THE EARTH!
————— Text and shadow type rotated

Figure 8-9:
Shadowed
type created
with the
transfor-
mation tools.

Great Transformations

Illustrator's Transform tools are great if you want to create one transformation
effect. But what if you want to scale, move, or rotate a group of objects in one
fell swoop? Use the Arrange⇨Tranform Each command. When you execute this
command, Illustrator enables you to scale, move, and rotate all selected objects
using one dialog box.

One of the chief advantages of using the Transform Each command (as opposed
to using the Transformation tools) is that you can scale, move, and rotate from
each object's centerpoint. If you select a group of objects and transform them
by using the transformation tools, each object is transformed from one common point of origin. By using Transform Each instead of the transformation
tools, you can ensure that the symmetry of selected objects remains intact
when you transform them.

1. **Select the objects that you want to transform.**

   To select more than one object, you can click and drag over them with the
   Selection tool or hold Shift down while you click each object with the
   Selection tool.

2. **Select Object⇨Transform Each to open the Transform Each dialog box,
   as shown in Figure 8-10.**

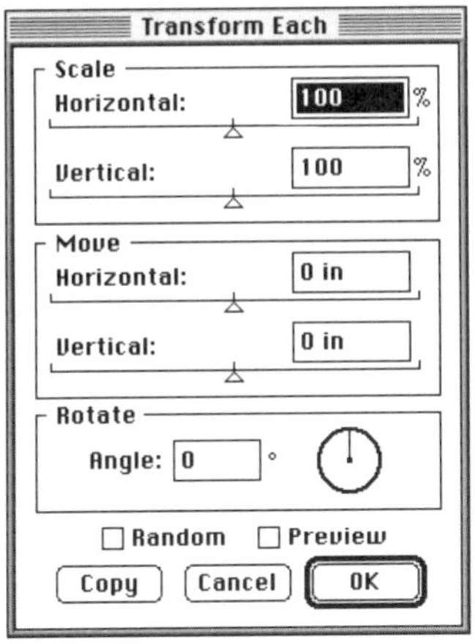

Figure 8-10:
The
Transform
Each dialog
box enables
you to
Scale,
Move, and
Rotate
objects.

3. **To see a preview of the transformation effects while you adjust the dialog box options, click the Preview check box.**

4. **If you want to scale the selected objects, click and drag on the Horizontal and Vertical sliders to enter a Horizontal and Vertical percentage for scaling.**

   You can also enter values from –4000 to 4000 percent in the Horizontal and Vertical fields.

5. **If you want to move the selected objects horizontally or vertically, click and drag the Horizontal or Vertical slider.**

   Dragging right on the Horizontal slider moves the objects right; dragging left moves them to the left. Dragging right on the Vertical slider moves the objects upright; dragging left moves the objects down. You can also enter values from –4000 to 4000 points in the Horizontal and Vertical Text boxes. Negative numbers move objects left or down; positive numbers move objects right or up.

6. **If you want to rotate the objects, click and drag in the circle icon to set the rotation angle.**

   You can also enter values from 0 to 360 degrees into the Angle field.

7. **If you want the transformations to take place randomly, click the Random button.**

   If you click this option, the random transformations are not greater than the values specified in the dialog box.

8. **If you want to copy the original objects and transform them as well, click Copy; otherwise, click OK.**

The 5th Wave — By Rich Tennant

"WELL, MR. BOND, I GUESS THIS IS FAREWELL. LOWER...THE...LASER...PRINTER!"

Chapter 9

Working with Layers and Templates

*W*ouldn't it be nice if you could divide your life up into different compartments? In one compartment would be all job-related things; in another, all the fun stuff in life; and in another, all your bills. This way, you could keep everything organized, and it would keep you from dealing with annoying things — like bills — when you want to concentrate on other things — like fun. Keeping everything divided up like this may be impossible in life, but at least you can do it with your artwork — using layers.

How Things Stack Up

When you begin to work with lots of objects on-screen, several Illustrator features become very important: stacking, grouping, and layering. But, before you begin to deal with the complexities of layers, you should know how to deal with stacks and groups of objects.

When you place an object on top of another object in Illustrator, you're stacking them. The last object you placed on the stack is on top of all of the other objects — just like stacking plates. But manipulating objects in the stack is much easier in Illustrator than in the kitchen.

Here are several things you can do to change the stacking order:

- ✔ **Send To Back:** Choose Arrange⇨Send To Back to send a selected object to the back of all objects that are in front of it. See Chapter 3 for more information about the Send to Back command.

- ✔ **Send To Front:** Choose Arrange⇨Send To Front to send a selected object to the front of all objects it is behind.

- ✔ **Paste In Front:** After you select an object, you can cut or copy it. Either action places the object in the Mac's Clipboard. When you choose Edit⇨Paste In Front, Illustrator pastes the object from the Clipboard in front of objects. If an object is selected, Illustrator pastes the object from the Clipboard in front of the selected object.

- ✔ **Paste In Back:** When you choose Edit⇨Paste In Back, Illustrator pastes the object from the Clipboard behind objects. If an object is selected, Illustrator pastes the object from the Clipboard behind the selected object.

Join my group

Think of trying to carry ten or so dishes, glasses, cups, and saucers stacked on top of each other from the dining room to the kitchen. Wouldn't it be nice to temporarily glue them together so all the objects wouldn't come crashing to the floor? Illustrator lets you temporarily glue objects together by allowing you to *group* objects. Grouping is simple. Just select the objects that you want in your group and choose Arrange⇨Group. After you create the group, you can slide the objects around the screen as one entity. To ungroup objects from the group, select the group and choose Arrange⇨Ungroup.

Here are a few notes to remember about groups:

- ✔ To include a path in a group, you only need to select part of it. After you choose Arrange⇨Group, the entire path is included in the group.

- ✔ If necessary, you can combine groups into other groups by selecting all of the groups (explained in the following section) and choosing Arrange⇨Group.

- ✔ Groups must be in the same layer (more on using layers is coming up in this chapter).

Selecting groups

Once you've placed objects into a group, you may need to select the group so you can fill it, cut it, paste it, or move it as a unit. To select an entire group, click it with the Selection tool.

If you want to fully take advantage of groups, you need to use the Group Selection tool which shares its toolbox location with the Direct Selection tool. Here's how to select the Group Selection tool: If the Group Selection tool isn't visible in the top-right corner of the Toolbox, click the Direct Selection tool and keep the mouse button pressed. When the Group Selection tool (the arrow icon with the plus next to it) appears, select it; then release the mouse.

Once you've selected the Group Selection tool, you can select one path in a group and groups within groups.

If you want to select one path in a group, click the path with the Group Selection tool. If you click again at the same place on the object, the object and its group are selected, as shown in Figure 9-1. If the group that you just selected is within other groups, click again at the same spot to add the next group to the selection. If you keep clicking at the same place with the Group Selection tool, all groups within a group are eventually selected.

If grouping seems a little confusing, assume that you're creating a tea time illustration featuring several cups and saucers, a glass, and a tray. To make it easier to select the multiple objects, you can put them into groups. You could create two groups for the cups, another group for the saucers. You could put the glasses in another group and the tray alone in another group.

By clicking in one spot you can select one of these groups at a time and combine it with previous groups to make up the largest "tea time" group. When you're done, you have one group — within it is the tray group, two cup groups, the saucer group, and the glass group.

Click once   Click twice

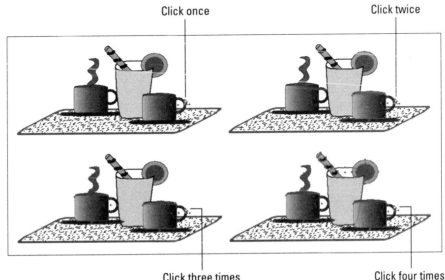

Figure 9-1:
Groups
selected
within
groups,
using the
Group
Selection
tool.

Click three times   Click four times

Now, say you want to select and move the cups, saucers, and glasses without moving the tray (where's David Copperfield when we need him?).

If you activate the Group Selection tool and click the cup handle, you select the cup handle, as shown on the top left of Figure 9-1. If you then click the cup handle again, the cup group is selected, as shown on the top right. If you click the cup handle one more time, the other cup group is selected, as shown on the bottom left. Click the cup handle once more, and the glass group is added to the selected items, as shown on the bottom right. Now you can move the cups, saucers, and glass without moving the tray. If you do want to select the cups, saucers, glass, *and* tray, one more click on the cup handle adds the tray group to the selection.

When working with groups and stacks of objects, you may find it helpful to lock objects on-screen or hide them. If you lock an object, you can't move it on-screen. When you hide an object, you can't see it on-screen. To lock an object, select it and choose Arrange⇨Lock. To hide an object, select it and choose Arrange⇨Hide. To unlock an object, select it and choose Arrange⇨Unlock. To show all hidden objects, choose Arrange⇨Show All.

Laying It On with Layers

Layers add another level of control when you're dealing with multiple objects on-screen. To many Illustrator artists, working in layers is like creating objects on separate sheets of plastic. An object that you create in one layer can be edited and moved independently of objects in other layers. When you work with layers, you can make all layers visible or selectively choose which layers you want to view or hide.

Although it may be easy to conceptualize creating art on sheets of plastic that overlap each other, it's important to understand that Illustrator's layers are a bit more complicated. In Illustrator, unlike programs like Adobe Photoshop, the empty background area is not part of the layer that you are working with. Illustrator layers are somewhat like having your artwork floating at different depths in an aquarium. Not only can you create and edit objects that are floating around at the same depth, but if necessary, you can quickly dart into a new depth by merely selecting an object. In Illustrator, when you click an object in a different layer, you are automatically working in that layer.

As you may imagine, layers can be a lifesaver for working efficiently and keeping your work organized. Creating objects in different layers allows you to concentrate on specific objects without disturbing other objects. For example, you might need to create a complex illustration of a house. You create the basement in one layer, the walls in another, the windows in another, the doors in another, and the roof in yet another layer. Placing objects in more than one layer allows for more design choices and control.

If our introduction to layers doesn't convince you that you need to use them, here are a few more reasons:

✔ You can move one layer in front of another layer, which can be a very quick and efficient way of changing the stacking order of objects.

✔ Layers can be very helpful when you have various items stacked on top of each other and you need to select an item in the stack. Just put the items in different layers, and you can easily select the item after activating the layer it is in.

✔ You can place a scanned image in one layer, dim the image (as if it were covered with a piece of tissue paper), lock it into position, and create another layer in which to trace over the image.

✔ You can experiment with design concepts by placing objects in layers and then hiding and revealing different layers.

✔ Layers can be very helpful when you have a file with a lot of elements filled with gradations, blends, or patterns, which take a long time to redraw on the screen. By putting different items in layers, you can choose to view and work on only a few items. That way, the screen-redraw rate is a lot faster.

Meet the Layers palette

Every time you create a new document, Illustrator creates a layer for you to work in. If you want to create more layers, you need to open the Layers palette. To open the Layers palette, choose Window➪Show Layers.

When you create a new document, the Layers palette contains one layer called — you guessed it — Layer 1, which is the background layer you work in. By default, Layer 1 is the active layer. The *active layer* is the current layer that can be viewed and edited.

Before you start a new layer, you should familiarize yourself with some key features of the Layers palette. The Layers palette is discussed in more detail a bit later in this chapter.

✔ A bar covering the layer's name in the Layers palette means that that layer is the active layer (the layer that you are working on).

✔ A solid dot under the eye icon (in the eye column), as shown in Figure 9-2, means that the layer is visible and is in Preview mode.

✔ You can turn the viewing of a layer off and on by clicking the dot under the eye icon. When the layer is hidden, the dot under the eye icon disappears.

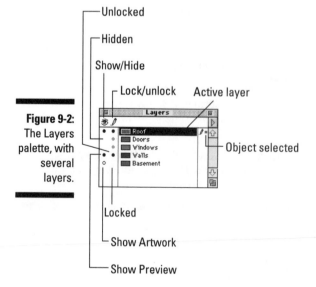

Figure 9-2:
The Layers
palette, with
several
layers.

Unlocked

Hidden

Show/Hide

Lock/unlock Active layer

Object selected

Locked

Show Artwork

Show Preview

✔ A hollow dot under the eye icon, as shown in Figure 9-2, means that the layer is visible and is in Artwork mode.

✔ A solid dot under the pencil icon (in the pencil column) shown in Figure 9-2 means the layer is not locked and can be edited. You can turn the editing of a layer off and on (that is, you can lock and unlock a layer) by clicking the dot under the pencil icon. When no dot appears under the pencil icon, the layer is locked.

✔ When the active layer is not locked, a pencil icon appears to the right of the layer's name. If the active layer is locked, a red bar appears over the pencil icon to the right of the layer's name.

✔ A small colored square to the right of the layer's name (and to the right of the pencil icon) means that an object is selected in the layer.

The Layers palette also allows you to access a group of Layers palette commands. To get to these commands, you must open the palette's pop-up menu, as shown in Figure 9-3. To open the menu, click the arrow in the upper-right corner of the palette.

Figure 9-3:
The Layers
palette
commands.

Creating new layers

In order to work efficiently with layers, you need to know how to create new layers. Here are the steps for creating a new layer:

(Before you create a new layer, create an object in Layer 1. Doing so makes it easier for you to distinguish which layer you are working in.)

1. **Open the pop-up menu by clicking the arrow at the top-right corner of the Layers palette.**

2. **To create a new layer, choose New Layer from the Layers palette pop-up menu, as shown in Figure 9-3.**

3. **In the New Layer dialog box, shown in Figure 9-4, type a name for your layer in the Name field.**

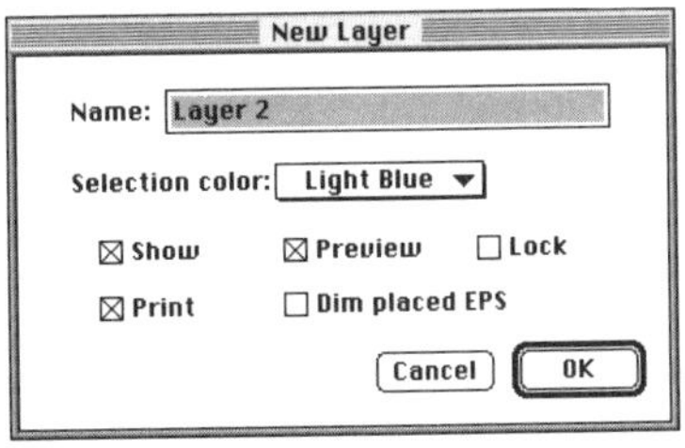

Figure 9-4:
The New
Layer dialog
box.

> **New Layer**
>
> Name: Layer 2
>
> Selection color: Light Blue ▼
>
> ☒ Show   ☒ Preview   ☐ Lock
>
> ☒ Print   ☐ Dim placed EPS
>
> Cancel   OK

4. **Click the Selection color pop-up menu and choose a selection color for your new layer.**

   This step changes the highlight color from the highlight color used in other layers. It's almost as if each object in a layer has its own team uniform to help you figure out what items are in what layer.

   Once you choose a selection color, the colored box to the left of the name of the layer in the Layers palette changes to that color.

   It's important to understand that even though you are in one layer, you can still select and change objects in other layers, unless you lock the other layers. When you select an item on-screen in *another* layer, *that* layer becomes the active layer.

5. **By default, the Show, Preview, and Print options are selected, and the Lock and Dim placed EPS options are not selected, as shown in Figure 9-4. Click OK to create a new layer.**

   You probably won't want to change the settings for these options quite yet — we discuss them later in this chapter. Instantly, a new layer is created, and it appears in the Layers palette.

Deleting a layer

If you decide to delete a layer, select the layer in the Layers palette and choose Delete Layer from the Layers pop-up menu. (To access the Layers pop-up menu, click on the arrow in the upper-right corner of the palette.) If there are objects in your layer, a prompt appears alerting you that artwork on the selected layer will be deleted. If you choose Delete, the layer and the artwork are deleted.

Organizing your layers

Layers help you keep yourself organized when you're creating complex works of art. But if you're not careful, you may actually confuse yourself. For instance, you may not remember exactly what you put in which layer because the layer doesn't have a descriptive name. To help you keep your layers organized, Illustrator provides numerous options in the Layers palette. These options allow you to rename, activate, hide, lock, and reorder layers.

Before you start using the options in the Layers palette, create an object on-screen in the new layer that you created. That helps show you when one layer is hidden and another is in view.

Renaming layers

Before you start examining the different options in the Layers palette, you may want to rename Layer 1 with a more descriptive name. To rename Layer 1 (or any other layer), double-click its name in the Layers palette or choose Layer Options from the palette's pop-up menu. This command opens the Layer Options dialog box. In the dialog box, enter a new name for the layer in the Name field.

Activating a layer

Once you've created several layers, you can pick which layer you want to work in by simply clicking the layer name in the Layers palette. When you work in one layer, you can still access and change objects in other layers as long as you don't lock those layers. You can recognize which item is in what layer because selected objects are outlined in their layer's color.

You can switch active layers by selecting an object in an inactive layer, which makes that layer the new active one.

Hiding a layer

At times, you may want to work in one layer without seeing the objects in other layers, particularly when objects in one layer overlap those in another layer. You can do this by hiding a layer. To hide a layer, click the dot in the column under the eye icon, next to the layer name. To view a hidden layer, click in the eye column to the left of the layer name in the Layers palette. This makes the dot in the eye column reappear. You can also hide a layer by double-clicking the layer name and then deselecting the Show check box in the Layer Options palette.

Here's how to hide more than one layer at a time:

1. **Select the layers that you want to hide by pressing Shift and clicking on the layer names in the Layers palette that you want to hide.**

2. **Choose Layer Options from the Layers palette pop-up menu.**

3. **In the Layer Options dialog box, de-select the Show button check box and click OK.**

To hide all layers except the active layer, choose Hide Others from the Layers palette pop-up menu.

Locking and unlocking a layer

As a safety precaution, you may want to lock a layer. When a layer is locked, changes cannot be made to any objects in the layer. To lock a layer, click the dot in the Pencil column that is next to the layer you want to lock. After you click, the dot disappears and a red slash appears through the pencil icon in the palette — indicating that the palette is locked. To unlock a locked layer, click the pencil column again. After you click, Illustrator removes the red slash in the pencil icon.

If you like doing things the long way, you can also lock a layer by double-clicking the layer name and then selecting the Lock check box in the Layers Options dialog box. The slow way of unlocking a layer is to double-click the layer name and then click the Lock check box to deselect it.

When a layer is locked, the mouse pointer changes to a pencil with a bar through it.

To lock all layers except the selected layer or layers, choose Lock Others from the Layers palette pop-up menu. To select more than one layer, hold down Shift while you click the Layer names in the Layers palette that you want to select.

Reordering layers

You can change the stacking order of layers in the Layers palette, which changes the stacking order of the objects in your document. Thus, if you create a layer called *RR tracks,* it can be below a layer called *street.* You can move the railroad tracks above the street by moving the railroad track layer above the street layer. To reposition a layer, select it in the Layers palette and drag it above or below another layer, as shown in Figure 9-5.

Figure 9-5: Reordering layers.

Changing layer viewing modes

When you create a new layer in Preview mode, the new layer is automatically set to Preview mode. You can turn off Preview mode (which turns on Artwork mode) by deselecting the Preview check box in the Layers Options dialog box. To access this dialog box, double-click a layer name. You can also change any layer to Artwork mode by first pressing Option. With the Option key pressed, click the dot in the Eye column for the layer that you want to switch to Artwork mode. To return to Preview mode, Option+click the Eye column again. For more information about Artwork and Preview modes, see Chapter 2.

If all layers are in Preview mode, you can change them to Artwork mode by choosing Artwork Others in the Layers palette pop-up menu. If at least one layer is in Artwork mode, the Artwork Others pop-up menu command switches to Preview All. You can use the Preview All menu command to switch all layers into Preview mode.

Moving items from one layer to another

You can also move an item from one layer to another by clicking and dragging in the Layers palette. Here's how to do it:

1. **Select the object in one layer.**

   A colored square appears to the right of the active layer name in the Layers palette.

2. **Click and drag the colored square to the layer that you want the object to appear in, as shown on the left side of Figure 9-6. As you drag, notice that the mouse pointer changes to a pointing hand icon.**

   After you drag the colored dot, the object switches layers.

   If you press and hold the Option key as you drag the colored dot, you create a copy of the object as you move it to another layer. When you use this technique, a plus appears in the Layers palette, as shown on the right side of Figure 9-6.

You can also move an object from one layer to another with the Copy and Paste commands. In order to do this, though, the Paste Remembers Layers option in the Layers pop-up menu or General Preferences dialog box must be deselected. If this option is selected, all objects end up in the layer that you originally copied from.

Figure 9-6:
Moving an object from one layer to another (left), and copying an object from one layer to another (right).

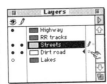 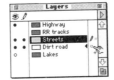

Here's how to copy or paste an object from one layer into another layer using the Copy and Paste commands:

1. **Open the Layers palette pop-up menu to check that the Paste Remember Layers check box is deselected. If it isn't deselected, click it in the pop-up menu.**

2. **Select the object or objects you want to copy.**

3. **Choose Edit⇨Copy.**

4. **Select any object in the layer that you want to paste into.**

5. **Choose Edit⇨Paste.**

Printing layers

As you work on a project, you may want to print several layers without printing other layers. By default, each layer is set to print. To turn off printing for a layer, double-click the layer's name in the Layers palette and then deselect the Print check box in the Layers Options palette.

Placing EPS Art in a Layer

Layers can be very helpful when you want to trace over artwork or logos. When you're finished tracing, you have a sparkling new piece of artwork rather than a jagged scanned logo.

Here are the steps for placing an EPS file in Illustrator and using it in a layer:

1. **Scan a sketch or logo that you want to digitize.**

2. **In your scanning or image editing program (such as Adobe Photoshop or Fractal Design Painter), save the scanned image in EPS file format.**

You can also take a picture with a digital camera and then load it into Photoshop and save it in EPS format.

When saving an EPS file in Adobe Photoshop and other programs, you often are provided with an option of making all white areas in the image transparent. Selecting this option can be very helpful when dealing with placed images in Illustrator because you will be able to see through all the white areas of the placed image.

3. **Create a new document in Adobe Illustrator and open the Layers palette on-screen if it's not already on-screen.**

To access the Layers palette, choose Window⇨Show Layers.

4. **Next, choose File⇨Place. When a dialog box appears, locate the image and choose Place.**

5. **When the image appears, move it into position.**

If you want, you can use the transformation tools to scale, rotate, transform, or reflect the image.

6. **Now double-click Layer 1 in the Layers palette. In the Layers Options dialog box, click the Lock and Dim placed EPS check boxes and name the layer** Scanned image.

After you close the dialog box, your layer will be dimmed, locked, and renamed.

7. **Create a new layer, and name it** Digital Art.

8. **Before you use the Pen tool to digitize the scanned image, set the Fill to None in the Paint Style palette so that you can see through to the scanned image in the layer underneath. Set the Stroke to black or any other color you desire. Use the Pen tool to create the elements and then fill the elements.**

If you're placing colored EPS files from Adobe Photoshop into an Illustrator document and outputting them with the File⇨Separation Setup command, the Photoshop files should be converted to CMYK color images before being placed into Illustrator. For more information about using the File⇨Separation Setup command, see Chapter 21.

If you need to reopen an EPS file created with Adobe Photoshop, press Option and double-click the EPS image in Illustrator.

If you are in Artwork mode, a placed EPS file appears in the document as an empty frame.

You can use Illustrator's Scale tool to shrink the EPS image if needed. However, for best print production of scanned images saved in EPS format, you should do all of your scaling in an image editing program such as Photoshop, where you can set the proper image resolution for the image.

Saving Files with EPS Images for Other Programs

If you are saving Illustrator files with EPS images that need to be imported into other programs, choose File⇨Save As. In the Save As dialog box, choose EPS from the Format pop-up menu, and be sure to select the Include placed images check box in the EPS Format dialog box that appears.

The Template Layer

Illustrator automatically creates a protected layer if you load a PICT image on-screen. The PICT image is called a *template*. After the template appears on screen, you can trace over it with the Pen tool to recreate the image in Illustrator. At this point, you may be wondering what the difference is between using PICT and EPS images for tracing. The main difference is that the PICT file is loaded as a grayed-out image. It doesn't print, and it can be used with Illustrator's Auto Trace tool. When you load an EPS image on-screen, you can use it as a color, gray scale, or black and white image to be integrated into your artwork, and you cannot use the Auto Trace tool with it.

EPS and PICT files

EPS stands for *Encapsulated PostScript*, which doesn't really help explain what an EPS file is. Basically, EPS is a file format. Whenever you save a file, the program that saves it saves it in a special way so that it can reopen the file later. EPS is a generic graphics format that can be used in many scanning software packages and many graphics programs. For example, Adobe Photoshop and Fractal Design Painter can both save a file in EPS format. Adobe PageMaker and QuarkXPress can both load images saved in EPS format.

Another common Macintosh file format is the PICT file format. The PICT file format is the Mac's graphic file format that the Mac uses when it stores objects in the Clipboard. Many graphics programs allow images to be saved in PICT file format. If you need to convert a scanned image to PICT format, you can load it into a program such as Photoshop or Fractal Design Painter and resave it in PICT format. File conversion programs such as Equilibrium DeBabelizer and Equilibrium DeBabelizer Lite will also do the job.

To open a PICT image to use as a template, simply choose File⇨Open. In the standard Open dialog box, open up the PICT file. You see a PICT Image dialog box, as shown in Figure 9-7. In this dialog box, choose the Template option.

If you press and hold the Option key as you choose File⇨New, you can load a PICT file into Illustrator as a new document.

Figure 9-7:
The Open
dialog box
for a PICT
file.

Using the Auto Trace Tool

Years ago, when early Illustrator users learned that Adobe was adding an Auto Trace tool to Illustrator, artists around the country threw up their mouse pads in exaltation. Most thought that autotracing would mean that with a click of the mouse, scanned logos and all sorts of other scanned artwork would be instantly and accurately autotraced. Unfortunately, the Auto Trace tool trips over itself when it tries to figure exactly how to precisely reproduce all of the bumps, gaps, and contours in an image. Consequently, the Auto Trace tool is really only recommended for tracing over simple scanned images. The most accurate way of tracing over an image is to pick up the Pen tool and trace over it manually.

For an example of auto-traced art, see Figure 9-8, which shows an image of William the Silent (Father of the Dutch Republic) created by Knight-Ridder Tribune Grapics artist Ron Coddington. A photograph of William was loaded into Adobe Photoshop where the image's contrast was increased using the Brightness & Contrast command. The image was then saved in PICT format and loaded into Illustrator where Ron used the Auto Trace tool to create the effect in Figure 9-8. To give the final effect a rough look, Ron applied the Illustrator's Tweak filter to the image. (See Chapter 16 for more information on filters.)

You may want to invest in Adobe Streamline, an autotracing program that allows for more precise tracing features than Illustrator's Auto Trace tool. Streamline is discussed in more detail in Chapter 20.

Figure 9-8:
An image
created
using the
AutoTrace
tool by
Knight-
Ridder
Tribune
Graphics.

Here's how to use the Auto Trace tool to trace over a PICT template:

1. **Load the template by choosing File⇨Open.**

2. **Turn off the Fill and Stroke options in the Paint Style palette.**

3. **Select the Auto Trace tool from the Toolbox.**

   If the Auto Trace tool is not visible in the Toolbox, click the Freehand tool in the Toolbox and hold the mouse button down until the Auto Trace tool appears. Drag the pointer to the Auto Trace tool and release the mouse.

   Once the Auto Trace tool is selected, the mouse pointer changes to a crosshair.

4. **Click the edge areas of the template to be traced. (Position the crosshair pointer within 6 pixels of the edge of the template.)**

   Illustrator automatically begins tracing the object.

Depending upon the object you are tracing, you may need to run the Auto Trace around the outer edge *and* the inner edge of the object.

Template gaps and Freehand tolerance

Often, templates have gaps that you want to trace over. You can instruct Illustrator's Auto Trace tool to ignore these gaps, based on a specified distance that you type into the Auto Trace gap field in the General Preferences dialog box. To Open the General preferences dialog box, choose File⇨Preferences⇨General. In the Auto Trace gap field, enter a value in pixels. The value you enter is the largest distance Illustrator uses to ignore gaps. For example, if you enter a value of 2 (the maximum value allowed), Illustrator ignores all gaps of 2 pixels or less.

You can also use the Freehand tolerance option to change the effects of autotracing. The larger the value entered into the Freehand tolerance field (you can enter values from 0 to 10), the smoother the paths created by the Auto Trace tool. Unfortunately, a high value can result in less accurate autotracing. If you enter a low value, you'll get a bumpier path but probably a more accurate one.

Autotracing Part of a Template

You do not need to autotrace an entire template. If you want to trace just part of a template, click and drag with the Auto Trace tool from the beginning of the area that you want to trace to the end of the area that you want trace.

When you autotrace only part of a template, you must drag within two pixels of the edge of the object.

Using Layers to Create an Image

We used layers to create the television image shown in Figure 9-9. We started by double-clicking Layer 1 in the Layers palette and then we named it Rectangle. We used the Rectangle tool to create the outer area of the TV set, filled it with gray, and stroked it with a thick, black stroke. Next we created a new layer and named it Rounded-Rectangle. In this layer, we used the Rounded Rectangle tool to create the TV's picture screen. We gave the screen no fill and a thick, black stroke.

Next, we created a new layer and named it Knobs. We created three ovals for knobs in this layer. We then created a new layer and named it Antenna. In this layer, we added a triangle and two diagonal lines for an antenna.

Then, we created a new layer called Stand. In this layer, we created the stand for the TV out of a rectangle and a triangle. (To create the second leg of the stand we duplicated the triangle.)

Finally, we created a new layer and named it Picture. We used the File↪Place command to load an EPS image into this layer and then we moved it over the TV. We moved this layer between the Rounded and Rectangle layers so that the stroke of the picture tube covered the EPS image.

That's all there is to it. By creating a few shapes in separate layers we've effectively duplicated a television set worthy of any college dorm room.

Figure 9-9:
A TV set
created
using layers.

Chapter 10

Color Me Happy

*I*magine a world without color — pretty dull. Not only would art be a lot more boring, but just think how hard it would be to find your car in a parking lot. When you want to spice things up with color, the place to turn is the Paint Style palette.

Using the Paint Style Palette

Illustrator's Paint Style palette is your ticket to the world of color. As discussed in Chapter 3, the Paint Style palette can be used to fill and stroke objects with different colors. The palette can also be used to create tints or shades of colors; to choose colors by combining percentages of cyan, magenta, yellow, and black (more about these four colors later); and to apply patterns and gradients. The Paint Style palette, shown in Figure 10-1, can be accessed via the Window menu or the Object menu. To open the Paint Style palette from the Window menu, choose Window⇨Paint Style. From the Object menu, choose Object⇨Paint Style.

The best way to approach using the Paint Style palette is to imagine that it's a cabinet containing three compartments filled with artistic tools. The different compartments are called panels. The left panel contains the Fill and Stroke boxes and paint swatches, the right panel contains the palette's color selection choices, and the bottom panel contains line attribute options covered in Chapter 6.

When working with color, you'll undoubtedly want to see both the left and right panels open on-screen. If these panels are not visible you can view them by clicking either the first or second choice in the Paint Style's Panel pop-up menu. To access the Panel pop-up menu, click the tiny arrow in the upper-right corner of the palette.

You can also switch panels in the Paint Style palette by clicking on the panel icons next to the Panel pop-up menu.

You can quickly expand or collapse the Paint Style palette to see more panels or fewer panels by clicking the palette's Zoom box in the palette's upper right-hand corner.

You can control exactly what types of colors the Paint Style fills or strokes with by clicking the Illustrator's color selection options, the tiny boxes at the top of the right panel of the palette. When you click any of these boxes a black bar appears below it and the name of the color selection option is shown at the top of the panel. For instance, if you click the process color selection option (the box with cyan, magenta, yellow, and black triangles in it), the word Process appears above the left box in the panel (see Figure 10-1). After you make your choice, the object or objects are filled or stroked.

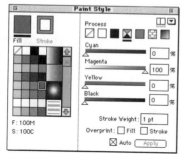

Figure 10-1:
The Paint Style palette and color selection options.

Here's how to use the color selection options at the top of the right panel in the Paint Style palette.

✔ Click the box with the diagonal in it if you do not want to fill or stroke with a color. Filling with this option chosen creates a transparent object.

✔ Click the White box to fill or stroke with white or create shades of gray. When creating a shade of gray, you click and drag the Tint slider in the Paint Style palette to pick a percentage of white. (The Tint slider appears after you click the white box.)

✔ Click the Black box to fill or stroke with white or create shades of gray. When creating a shade of gray, click and drag on the Tint slider to pick a percentage of black. (The Tint slider appears after you click the black box.)

✔ Click the Process color box (the icon with cyan, magenta, yellow, and black triangles in it) to fill or stroke using percentages of cyan, magenta, yellow, and black.

✔ Click the Custom box icon (the green icon) to fill or stroke colors that you choose by name. This icon allows you to choose colors using color-matching systems such as PANTONE and TRUMATCH (described later in this chapter). You can also pick custom colors that you create and name in the Custom Color dialog box (also described later in this chapter).

✔ The Pattern box (the one filled with a scale pattern) allows you to fill objects with patterns. Patterns are covered in Chapter 12.

✔ The Gradient box allows you to fill objects with gradients. Gradients are covered in Chapter 11.

Using the CMYK color sliders

The CMYK sliders in the Paint Style palette are quite easy to use. First, make sure that you click the Process color option in the Paint Style palette. Next, simply click and drag any of the slider controls in the palette. As you drag with the mouse, the color in the Fill or Stroke swatch changes. Also, a percentage readout shows exactly what percentage of each color component you are using to create the process color.

Using process colors

Nature provides us with an infinite variety of colors. But Illustrator's Paint Style palette includes only about 80 swatches of colors. If you want to use other colors, you can click the Process color icon. When you do, four sliders appear in the Paint Style palette, as shown in Figure 10-1. The four sliders allow you to choose colors using the percentages of cyan, magenta, yellow, and black. These four colors are known as *process* colors because they're used in the four-color printing process that commercial printers use for print jobs that require many different colors.

Looking at the Paint Style palette, you may wonder why cyan, magenta, yellow, and black were chosen as the colors used to create other colors. The reason is that commercial printers can combine cyan, magenta, yellow, and black ink on four printing plates to create millions of different colors. By adding and subtracting percentages of the CMYK colors (K stands for black), countless colors can be created. In color theory, the combination of CMY colors should create black. But because printing inks aren't really pure, they create a muddy brown instead. Thus, printers add black ink to create pure black and grays to help add shadows.

How do you figure out exactly what percentage makes what color? One simple way is to purchase a process guide book. Companies such as Agfa and PANTONE publish swatch books that show the CMYK percentages making up a variety of colors. All you do is hunt in the book for the color you want to create and then enter the percentages on-screen by dragging the sliders or by entering values in the percentage fields. If you use this technique, it helps provide you with an excellent indication of how the on-screen colors will look when printed. (Unfortunately, because of differences in monitors and printers, screen colors do not always match the colors you get when printing.)

A color often comes out darker on the printed page than it looks on your monitor. That's because on your screen, colors are created by the light emitted from your monitor. Colors on the printed page are created from light that is absorbed into and reflects off the ink combinations on the page.

Using a color wheel

Another helpful way of choosing colors is to use a color wheel, as shown in Figure 10-2.

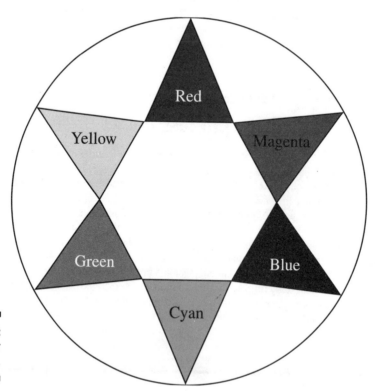

Figure 10-2:
A color wheel.

The color wheel may look familiar to you. At some point, most art classes delve into the physics of color theory. The color wheel includes the primary colors: red, green, and blue. Between the primary colors are other colors: cyan, magenta, and yellow. The positions on the color wheel can help you recreate colors on-screen because each color is positioned between the two colors that create it.

According to the color wheel, here's how you create the primary colors using the sliders in the Paint Style palette:

- ✔ To create red, click and drag the Magenta and Yellow sliders to 100%. Drag the Cyan and Black sliders to 0%.

- ✔ To create green, click and drag the Cyan and Yellow sliders to 100%. Set the Magenta and Black sliders to 0%.

- ✔ To create blue, click and drag Cyan and Magenta to 100% and click and drag Yellow and Black to 0%.

You can use Filter➪Colors➪Adjust Colors to increase or decrease the Cyan, Magenta, Yellow, and Black percentages of a color. Other commands in the Filter➪Colors submenu also allow you to adjust colors. More about these filters comes up in Chapter 16.

To move all of the CMYK sliders at the same time, press Shift and click and drag one of the sliders.

Those dynamic sliders

Right before your eyes is another very helpful aid in choosing process colors. Take a close look at each of the four sliders in the Paint Style palette. Notice how the color in a slider gradually blends to another color.

The sliders are actually showing you what colors you create if you drag the slider to that color point on the slider. Try it out. Start with a green color. If your sliders aren't set to green, click and drag the Cyan and Yellow sliders to 100% and the Magenta and Black sliders to 0%. Now assume that you want to create a yellow-green color. Notice the yellow color in the Green slider. All you need to do is drag the slider to the color you see on the slider, and that will be the color you create. The slider is telling you that if you drag all the way back to 0%, you create yellow. The sliders also tell you that you can create a darker green by increasing the Black slider or by adding more magenta. So, as you work with the CMYK sliders, always pay attention to the colors in the sliders.

If you click any process color in the color swatch group, the CMYK sliders change to show the percentage of each color component in that color.

Adding and deleting colors in the Paint Style palette

To keep the colors that you choose with the CMYK sliders close at hand, you'll probably want to add them to the color swatches in the Paint Style palette. After you choose your color with the CMYK sliders, simply click and drag the color that's in the Fill or Stroke box to the swatch area. After you release the mouse, the color is added to the swatch group.

Here are a few color swatch tips that can help you when you use the Paint Style palette:

✔ You can change the current Fill color to the Stoke color by dragging the Fill color icon over the Stroke color icon in the Paint Style palette. You can reverse the process by dragging the Stroke color icon over the Fill color icon.

✔ To delete a color from the swatch group, move the mouse pointer over the color that you want to delete. Press and hold ⌘. The mouse pointer changes to a scissors icon. With the scissors icon on the color that you want to delete, click the mouse.

✔ To set all colors in the Paint Style palette back to the original default colors, ⌘+Shift+click the swatch area.

Using custom colors

As you work with color in Illustrator, you'll probably want to start creating your own colors using the CMYK sliders and save them so you can use them again. Illustrator allows you to create colors from CMYK color components and name them as custom colors.

Here's how to create a new color using the Custom Color dialog box:

1. **Choose Object⇨Custom Color to open the Custom Color dialog box, shown in Figure 10-3.**

   You can also open the Custom Color dialog box by clicking the Custom color box in the Paint Style palette and then double-clicking any custom color in the Custom color list.

2. **Click the New button.**

3. **Enter a name for your color in the Name field.**

4. **To create a custom color from CMYK percentages, click the CMYK color box and then adjust the Cyan, Magenta, Yellow, and Black sliders to create your custom color. To create a custom color that is a shade of**

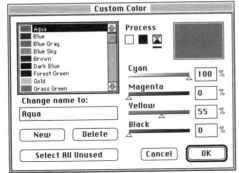

Figure 10-3:
The Custom
Color dialog
box.

**black or white, click the Black or White color option box and then click
and drag the Tint slider in the Paint Style palette to create the shade of
gray.**

For more information about tints, see the next section.

After you create your color, the color appears in the Custom color list. The
color is then available for filling and stroking in the Paint Style palette
when you click the Custom color icon.

When Illustrator creates a custom color, it considers it a *spot color* — not a
process color, even though you created it with process sliders. Don't worry
about such complicated issues now. These issues are discussed in Chapter 21.

Tantalizing tints

Often, when you are filling or stroking an object with color, you don't want to
color it something pure red, pure black, or pure green. You want to create a *shade*
of a color. To produce a shade of a color in Illustrator, you create a *tint* of the
color. Tints can be created after clicking the Black, White, or Custom color
selection option at the top of the Paint Style palette. After you click one of
these color selection options, a Tint slider and tint % field appear in the Paint
Style palette.

Tints are created by changing a color's percentage to less than 100 percent. If
you don't want to create a solid color, you simply select a custom color and
then change the percentage in the Paint Style palette by clicking and dragging
the Tint slider or by entering a number in the Tint percentage field. The higher
the percentage, the darker the color. Figure 10-4 shows the Paint Style palette
with the Custom color selection option selected. The figure shows the custom
color with a 50 percent tint.

Once you've created a tint, using it is a simple matter: Simply select the
object that you want to fill, and click Fill in the upper-left corner of the Paint
Style palette.

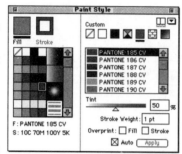

Figure 10-4:
The Paint
Style palette
with the
Custom
color icon
selected.

Once you click and drag the Tint slider to change a custom color's percentage, the Tint slider stays at that percentage when you click another custom color.

Working with spot colors

The Custom Color dialog box and the Paint Style palette allow you to access preset colors from color-matching systems such as those created by PANTONE and TRUMATCH. Such colors are often used to output *spot colors*. Spot colors are usually used when you want to place a color or two in an image. For example, assume that you want to print a logo in one color. Instead of wasting money printing the color using percentages of cyan, magenta, yellow, and black, you can pick the color from a swatch book of spot colors that can be purchased from PANTONE. Typically, you pick a color by number, such as PANTONE 711. After you pick the color in the swatch book, you search for the color in the PANTONE library of colors that can be loaded into Adobe Illustrator from Illustrator's Color Systems folder.

In order to use PANTONE colors or color from other color-matching systems, you must load them by choosing File⇨Import Styles. Next, open up Illustrator's Utilities folder to access the Color Systems folder. Here you'll find PANTONE, TRUMATCH, FOCOLTONE, and Toyo color systems. To load the colors from the color system, select a color system filename and then click open.

You can then access the custom colors by clicking the Custom color icon in the Paint Style palette or by choosing Object⇨Custom Color.

You can click any of the colors and use it as your fill or stroke color. You can also alter the colors to create your own custom version and add these to the Paint Style palette. To create your own custom color version, double-click the custom color that you want to edit. In the Custom Color dialog box that appears, use the familiar CMYK color sliders to adjust the colors. After you've adjusted the sliders, enter a name in the Change name to field and then click OK.

Creating a Custom Paint Style

You might have noticed that every time you create a new document, the Paint Style palette is filled with the same colors. If you created any custom colors, they're only saved in the documents you created them in, not in all new documents. Fortunately, you can make Illustrator load specific palettes by creating a custom startup file that contains a Paint Style with your most commonly used colors, gradients, and patterns. You can even create various custom startup files for different jobs.

Before you create a custom color startup file, duplicate Adobe Illustrator's Startup file, by selecting it (the file is in the Plug-ins folder within the Adobe Illustrator 6 folder) and choosing File⇨Duplicate from the Finder menu (or ⌘+D). Move the original startup file outside the Plug-in folder. This way you can always drag this file back into the Plug-ins folder and reuse the original startup file. Now delete the word "copy" from the duplicated startup file in the Plug-ins folder so the filename is "Adobe Illustrator Startup."

Next, double-click the duplicated startup file to load it into Illustrator. Once the file opens, delete or add any colors, gradients or patterns from both the Paint Style palette and Artboard area. Save the file, and quit Illustrator. From now on, anytime you work in Illustrator, any new file you create will contain the items you placed in the Paint Style palette. You can create additional startup files, but you can only have one in the Plug-in folder at a time. You might even want to make a separate folder with startup file backups in it.

For more information, patterns are covered in Chapter 12 and Gradients are covered in Chapter 11.

Eyedropping Colors

Once you start creating your own custom colors, you'll find that you occasionally need to reuse a color that you already used in an on-screen illustration. Often the easiest way to replicate the color is to click it with the Eyedropper tool. After you click, the fill and/or stroke color in the Paint Style palette matches the color you clicked.

For example, assume that you need to recreate a color that you used in an image. You created the colors with your own CMYK percentages and didn't store the color in the Paint Style palette; how do you copy the color? Very simple: by activating the Eyedropper tool and then clicking the color that you want to copy. As soon as you click, the current color in the Paint Style palette automatically switches to the color you clicked. The fill and stroke colors in the palette match the fill and stroke colors of the object you clicked. The CMYK sliders jump to show you the precise CMYK percentages of the color you clicked. Once the fill and stroke colors appear in the palette, click the Apply button to apply the colors to any selected object.

Or, if you'd like, you can use the following shortcut to change the fill and stroke of an object with the Eyedropper's help:

1. **Select the object whose color and stroke and other attributes you want to change.**

2. **Select the Eyedropper tool in the Toolbox.**

3. **Position the Eyedropper tool over the object that has the color attributes that you want to copy, and double-click it.**

   Immediately, the color attributes of the selected object change to those of the image you double-clicked.

Controlling the Eyedropper tool

When you select the Eyedropper tool, it automatically samples the fill, stroke, caps, and all sorts of other attributes of the object that you click. You can change how the Eyedropper tool works by double-clicking the tool. In the Paintbucket/Eyedropper dialog box, shown in the sidebar figure, deselect what you do not want the Eyedropper to sample. For example, if you don't want the Eyedropper to copy the stroke, deselect Stroke in the Eyedropper picks up section and in the Paintbucket applies section. The Paintbucket tool is coming up next.

Paintbucket/Eyedropper

Paintbucket applies:
- ☒ Fill
  - ☒ Color
  - ☒ Overprint
- ☒ Stroke
  - ☒ Color
  - ☒ Overprint
  - ☒ Weight
  - ☒ Cap
  - ☒ Join
  - ☒ Miter limit
  - ☒ Dash pattern

Eyedropper picks up:
- ☒ Fill
  - ☒ Color
  - ☒ Overprint
- ☒ Stroke
  - ☒ Color
  - ☒ Overprint
  - ☒ Weight
  - ☒ Cap
  - ☒ Join
  - ☒ Miter limit
  - ☒ Dash pattern

[Cancel] [OK]

Filling with the Paint Bucket Tool

 The Paint Bucket tool is your portable paint filler. It makes filling colors and applying paint attributes easy. You can easily fill an object by selecting it and then clicking the Fill button in the Paint Style palette. However, a faster way of filling an object with the current settings in the Paint Style palette is to simply click it with the Paint Bucket tool.

Here's how to use the Paint Bucket tool. (It's great for people who don't like to select before filling.)

1. **Set all attributes in the Paint Style palette.**

2. **Activate the Paint Bucket tool.**

3. **Position the mouse pointer over an object whose paint attributes you want to change and click the mouse.**

   When you click, the object fills with color. If the object is a closed path, the entire object is filled. If it isn't a closed path, Illustrator fills from end-point to end-point.

 You can double-click the Paint Bucket tool to set the attributes that it fills with. The attributes choices are the same for both the Paint Bucket tool and the Eyedropper tool.

Now that you know how to use the Paint Bucket tool and the Eyedropper, you can put them to work as a team that samples and applies colors. With the Eyedropper tool, simply click the color that you want to sample. To change another object's color to the sampled color, activate the Paint Bucket tool and then click the object whose color you want to change. Immediately, Illustrator changes the new object's color attributes to match the attributes of the sampled color.

The 5th Wave

By Rich Tennant

CPLATENNANT

"My gosh Barbara, if you don't think it's worth going a couple of weeks without dinner so we can afford a color printer, just say so."

Chapter 11

Graduating from One Color to Another

- -

- -

*Y*ou want to create a beautiful indoor scene. You've sketched out the scene, you've chosen your colors, and now you need to create some nice lighting and 3-D effects. Where do you turn? To Illustrator's great gradients.

What's a Gradient?

A gradient is a smooth blend from one color to another that fills an object. In Illustrator, a gradient can be as simple as a smooth transition from black to white or white to black, a transition from one color to another, or several transitions among colors.

Gradients are often used to create background effects. For example, you can easily create a background that simulates the sky by creating a gradient that starts with a deep, rich blue and gradually turns to light blue. Gradients can also help you create lighting and three-dimensional effects. Figure 11-1 shows gradients used to add depth to an illustration of a stoplight, created by artist John Ryan.

Figure 11-1:
A stoplight
created with
gradients
(art by
John Ryan).

Using Illustrator's Predefined Gradients

The easiest way to get started in the world of gradients is to use Illustrator's predefined gradients, which are accessed from the Paint Style palette. The steps to using the predefined gradients are simple: You create an object. With the object selected, click the Gradient color selection option icon in the top of the right panel in the Paint Style palette. A list of gradients appears. Choose a gradient from the scrolling list by clicking a name.

Figure 11-2 shows the list of gradients in the Paint Style palette. Most of the gradients are *linear,* meaning that the colors start and change as if in a straight line — of any angle. A *radial* gradient means the color starts in the center and then spreads out in circles of colors. Figure 11-3 shows a ball, created with a radial gradient, and its shadow, created with a linear gradient. The background image is from Fotoset's *Photographic Originals* CD-ROM.

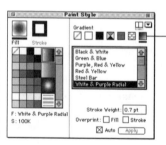

Gradient color selection option icon

Figure 11-2:
The list of
gradients in
the Paint
Style
palette.

Figure 11-3:
A ball and
shadow
created with
radial and
linear
gradients.

Although the Paint Style palette does not provide the means for customizing a gradient, you can change the angle used to create the gradient by typing a value in the Angle field. (The Angle field only appears in the palette when you click on the Gradient color selection option in the palette.) Changing the gradient angle can make your gradient look more interesting, but if you really want to add variation to your gradients, you need to use the Gradient Vector tool.

Using the Gradient Vector Tool

The Gradient Vector tool allows you to manually edit gradients by clicking and dragging the mouse. Using this tool, you can not only change the angle of gradient fills by clicking and dragging the mouse, but you can also apply the same gradient over several objects at once. Artists frequently use this technique of applying a gradient to several objects at once to fill the letters of a word with colors that gradually blend from one to another.

By clicking and dragging the mouse, you control exactly how much of the starting color of the gradient appears in the object and how much of the ending color appears in the object. For example, assume that you want to create a gradient from black to white. You want one inch of black at the beginning of the gradient and one inch of white at the end of the gradient. Your first step is to select an object and then fill it with the Black & White gradient in the Paint Style palette. To fill the object with a gradient, first select the Fill box at the top of the left panel in the Paint Style palette. Next, click the gradient color selection option in the right panel of the palette, and then click the Black & White gradient in the gradient list. To edit the gradient, select the Gradient Vector tool, and then click one inch into the object, drag, and release the mouse one inch before you get to the end of the object.

You can also use the Gradient Vector tool to switch the direction of a gradient. The image on the left of Figure 11-4 shows a gradient created in a lightning bolt. The gradient was originally created using a gradient fill chosen in the Paint Style palette. The image on the right was edited by dragging the Gradient Vector tool from the bottom of the lightning bolt up towards its top. The background image is from Image Club's *Photogear Volume Six: Skyscapes* CD-ROM.

Figure 11-4:
Original gradient (left) and edited gradient using the Gradient Vector tool (right).

Used with express permission. Adobe® and Image Club Graphics Inc.™ are trademarks of Adobe Systems Incorporated.

Here's how to use the Gradient Vector tool to edit a gradient:

1. **Select an object and fill it with a gradient using one of the gradients in the Paint Style palette.**

   To access the gradients, first click the gradient color selection option in the right panel of the Paint Style palette. (The gradient color selection option is the last small box at the top of the right panel.)

2. **Select the Gradient Vector tool in the Toolbox.**

3. **Move the mouse pointer over the selected object, positioning it where you want the color of the gradient fill to start changing colors. Click and drag the mouse at the angle that you want your gradient changed to. Release the mouse where you want the gradient to stop changing colors.**

The gradient fills the entire object, even if you don't click and drag from the very start of the object to the very end. The first color of the gradient appears solid up to the point where you click the mouse in the object. The last color appears solid from the point you release the mouse to the end of the object.

To constrain the gradient in increments of 45 degrees, press Shift as you click and drag.

One of the handiest features of the Gradient Vector tool is that it allows you to create a blend that runs across several objects. Here's how to create this effect:

1. **Select the objects that you want to fill with a gradient.**

   If you want to fill text with a gradient, you must first convert the text to a path. To do this, create some text using the Type tool. Select the text with the Selection tool, and then choose Create Outlines from the Type menu. Instantly, the text is converted into paths.

   See Chapters 13, 14, and 15 for more on working with text.

2. **With the objects selected, choose a gradient fill from the Paint Style palette.**

   Instantly, the objects are filled with a gradient.

3. **To edit the gradation that spans several selected objects, activate the Gradient Vector tool and then click and drag over the selected objects, as shown in Figure 11-5, in the direction in which you want the gradation to start and end.**

Figure 11-5:
Using the
Gradient
Vector tool
to edit a
gradation
over several
selected
objects.

Creating Custom Gradients with the Gradient Palette

In many drawing programs, a gradient is a simple blend from one color to another. Illustrator provides custom gradient options that can allow you to create multiple color blends in one gradient. This power is provided by Illustrator's Gradient palette.

Using the Gradient palette, you can choose multiple starting and ending color points within one gradient, which allows you to create a variety of multicolor effects. Here are the steps for creating a custom gradient:

1. **Start by opening the Gradient palette. Choose either Object⇨Gradient or Window⇨Show Gradient.**

   The Gradient palette appears.

   If the entire palette does not appear, click the tiny flag icon in the upper-right area of the palette to open it all up.

   You can open the Gradient palette by double-clicking a custom gradient in the Paint Style palette.

2. **To create a new gradient, click the New button.**

   By default, Illustrator names your first new gradient New Gradient 1. You can edit the name by clicking and dragging over the default name and then typing a new name for your gradient.

   If you want to create a gradient based upon an existing gradient, click the gradient name that you want to duplicate and then click the Duplicate button instead of the New Button. Rename the gradient, if you like.

3. **By default, Illustrator creates a gradient from white to black. Now you must choose the starting color of your gradient.**

   To change the starting color, first make sure that the left triangle situated below the gradient bar is selected. If it isn't, click it.

   To choose a starting color, you can click the White, Black, Process, or Custom icon in the Gradient palette shown in Figure 11-6. If you click the Black or White icon, you can click and drag the Tint slider to choose a percentage of black.

   If you want to create a process color as your starting color, click the Process color icon and then set the colors using the CMYK sliders in the palette. For more information about using the CMYK sliders, see Chapter 10.

If you want to use a custom color as your starting color, click the Custom color icon and pick a color. If you'd like, you can also choose a tint for your Custom color. To make a tint, click and drag the Tint slider or enter a percentage into the Tint field.

White   Process

Black   Custom   Gradient bar

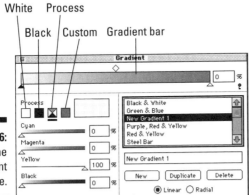

Figure 11-6:
The
Gradient
palette.

4. **To choose the ending color of your gradient, click the right triangle of the gradient bar and then choose a color as described in Step 3.**

    Illustrator also allows you to create intermediate gradients (multiple start and end points). This subject is covered later in the chapter.

5. **If desired, click and drag the bottom triangles to adjust the specific points at which you want your gradient to start and end.**

    As you drag the mouse, you see the changes reflected in the gradient bar. The colors in the gradient bar preview how the gradient will look when you apply the gradient. Applying gradients created in the Gradient palette is covered in the next section.

6. **Set the type of fill desired by clicking the Linear or the Radial option at the bottom of the Gradient palette.**

7. **At this point, your gradient starts at one color and gradually changes to another, with the midpoint of the blend directly between your starting and ending colors. If you want to change the position of the midpoint, click and drag the diamond at the top to the left or the right.**

    Dragging left shifts the midpoint to the left. Dragging to the right shifts it to the right.

If you want to delete a gradient, simply select the gradient in the Gradient palette and click the Delete button. Any object using the gradient fill that you delete is then filled with black.

Applying Custom Gradients

Once you've created your gradient, Illustrator automatically adds it to the list of gradients in the Paint Style palette. To apply your custom gradient, select an object. Then select the gradient color selection option at the top of the right panel in the Paint Style palette (see Chapter 10 for more information about using the Paint Style palette). If the Auto check box is selected, the gradient is automatically applied to the object. If the check box isn't selected, click the Apply button. Alternatively, you can use the Paint Bucket tool to apply the gradient to objects just by clicking them with the tool (see Chapter 10 for more on how to use the Paint Bucket tool). If you want, you can now edit the gradient in the Gradient palette, and the effects are automatically updated.

Editing Gradient Fills

At any time, you can return to the Gradient palette, select a gradient by name, and edit the fill. To edit the start or end or intermediate point, simply click the appropriate triangle and change colors. To change the midpoint, click and drag any of the top midpoint diamonds on the bar. To delete an intermediate fill, click and drag an intermediate diamond down to below the gradient bar and then release the mouse. After you edit your fill, all objects utilizing that fill are updated accordingly.

Adding intermediate colors to a gradation

You can make Illustrator's gradations quite sophisticated by adding intermediate colors to a gradient. You can use this technique to create interesting color transitions and effects. For example, you can create a gradation that starts at white and blends to black, with multiple intermediate blends between white and black, as shown in Figure 11-7. This feature essentially allows you to string one gradient to another. Figure 11-8 shows a simple object filled with the gradation in Figure 11-7. This fill produces a metallic effect.

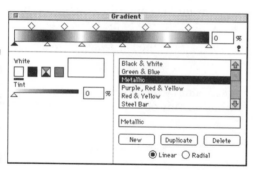

Figure 11-7: The Gradient palette with intermediate colors.

Figure 11-8:
An image filled with the gradation specified in Figure 11-7.

Adding intermediate blends is quite easy: Simply position the mouse pointer over the point on the Gradient bar where you want to start an intermediate blend, and then click the mouse. As soon as you click, another triangle is created, which defines another point on the blend. After you click, adjust the colors using the same techniques described earlier. You can continue creating triangles and adjusting colors as desired. Also, as you create intermediate colors, you may find that you want to change the end color. To do this, simply click the last triangle and adjust the colors.

Switching starting and ending gradient colors

After creating your gradient, you may decide that you want to reverse the starting and ending colors of the gradient. If so, you can easily transpose the colors by simply clicking the starting triangle on the left side of the gradient and dragging it over the end marker at the right-side triangle. Alternatively, you can drag the right triangle over the starting triangle on the left.

Moving Gradients from Document to Document

Once you start building a library of gradients, you're probably going to want to use gradients created in one document in other documents.

To import all gradients from one file into another, choose File↪Import Styles. In the dialog box, choose the file that contains the gradients that you want to load and then click Open. This loads all of the gradients and colors from one document into another.

If you create a new document and want to use a gradient from a different file, you can also simply load on-screen the file that has the desired gradient in it. After you load the document, activate the file that you want to move the gradient to. When that file is on-screen, click the Gradient icon at the top of the right panel in the Paint Style palette. The gradients from all open documents appear. You can then use the Paint Style palette to fill an object with a gradient from another document. This method is handy if you just want to use one or two gradients (or colors) from other documents, rather than all of the gradients and colors from other documents.

If you want every new document that you create to have the same custom patterns, you need to change Illustrator's Startup file. To find out how to do this, see Chapter 10.

If you are going to be using gradients for print jobs, you should be aware that gradients can cause problems when printing. A gradient should appear to be a smooth transition from one color to another. Unfortunately, sometimes printed gradients look like individual discrete blocks of colors placed side by side.

Here are some tips for printing gradients:

- ✔ Make sure that the screen frequency and output resolution you are using can produce 256 levels of gray. If you are unsure, ask your pre-press house or service bureau. For more information about printing, see Chapters 5 and 21.

- ✔ For best results, at least one of the process color components should change by 50 percent or more.

- ✔ It's generally a good idea to keep blends under 7.5 inches long.

- ✔ Light colors usually produce better blends. If you are going to use dark colors in blends, try to keep the blended area as short as possible.

Chapter 12

Working with Patterns

*T*he easiest way to understand the importance of patterns is to simply look around you at the clothes people are wearing. Patterns, patterns everywhere. Without patterns, most of your fabrics, packaging, and home furnishings would look downright dull. So, obviously, adding a pattern to your artwork can liven it up. Fortunately, Illustrator provides some powerful pattern creation features. Using Illustrator's patterns, you can create fabric and paper designs and unusual background images. Not only can patterns help you jazz up your artwork, but Illustrator makes this potentially tedious task a quick and simple one. For example, assume that someone asks you to create a poster for a local zoo. You create the shapes for the zebras, leopards, and giraffes. Then it comes time to fill in the spots for all the wild beasts. If you had to manually draw and fill in all the spots for each of the animals, you'd be seeing spots before your eyes for days. The easiest solution is to create and name custom patterns and then fill the animals with the spot patterns. All you need to do is figure out how to create and use Illustrator patterns.

Trying Out a Few Test Patterns

Adobe's pattern-making capabilities allow you to create your own designs for patterns and then fill objects on-screen with your custom patterns. If you don't want to create your own patterns, you can use those that are included in Illustrator's Paint Style palette. Figure 12-1 shows a sundress filled with Illustrator's Scales pattern. The pattern was scaled 200 percent. Using predesigned patterns like Scales is quite easy. (The figure's background is from ColorBytes' *Sampler One* CD-ROM, photography by Carlye Calvin.)

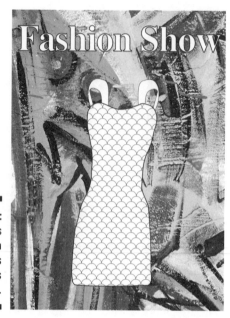

Figure 12-1:
A dress
filled with
Illustrator's
Scales
pattern.

Here are the steps for filling a path with a pre-set pattern from the Paint Style palette:

1. **Start by creating a closed path for your pattern. Keep the path selected.**

2. **If the Paint Style palette is not open on-screen, open it by choosing Window⇨Show Paint Style or Object⇨Paint Style.**

3. **With the path still selected, select the Fill box at the top of the left panel of the Paint Style palette. Next, click the Pattern color selection icon at the top of the right panel in the Paint Style palette.**

   The Pattern color selection icon is the box with the scale pattern in it (the second box from the right).

   When you click the Pattern icon, a list of patterns appears in a scrolling list, as shown in Figure 12-2.

4. **Click a pattern name to see a preview of it in the Fill box. If the Auto check box is selected, the path is then automatically filled with the pattern. If the Auto check box is not selected, click the Apply button and apply the pattern to your object.**

Selected pattern

Fill box with pattern | Pattern icon

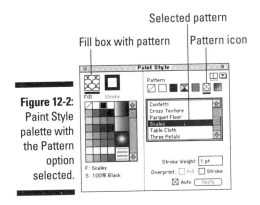

Figure 12-2:
Paint Style
palette with
the Pattern
option
selected.

Pattern Transformations

If you'd like to add a little spice to a pattern's life, you can create all sorts of unusual effects by applying Illustrator's transformation tools. Here's how to use a transformation tool with a pattern:

1. **Select the object that is filled with a pattern.**

2. **Double-click the transformation tool that you want to use.**

   See Chapter 8 for more on the transformation tools.

   At the bottom of the transformation tool's dialog box, the options Objects and Pattern tiles appear.

   - If you want to alter the pattern within the object and not affect the object, select the Pattern tiles option and make sure that the Objects option is not selected, as shown in Figure 12-3.

   - If you want to alter the object and not the pattern, you must select the Objects option and not the Pattern tiles option.

   - If you want to alter both the Objects and the Pattern tiles, both options must be selected.

3. **Specify the transformation options that you'd like to apply to your pattern. Click OK, and the pattern is transformed.**

Figure 12-3:
Rotate
dialog box
with only the
Pattern tiles
option
selected.

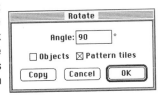

The image on the left of Figure 12-4 shows Illustrator's Yellow Stripe pattern applied to a gift package. The image in the center shows the pattern after scaling and rotating. The image on the right shows the pattern after rotating, reflecting, and shearing.

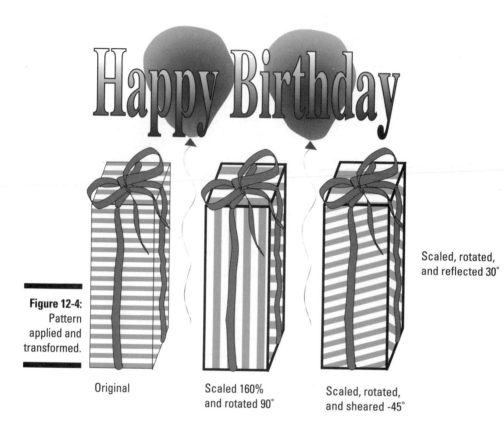

Scaled, rotated, and reflected 30°

Figure 12-4: Pattern applied and transformed.

Original

Scaled 160% and rotated 90°

Scaled, rotated, and sheared -45°

Here are a few tips and reminders:

✔ In order to transform pattern tiles, the Transform Pattern tiles option must be selected in the General Preferences dialog box. By default, this option is turned on. To access the General Preferences dialog box, choose General from the File⇨General Preferences submenu.

✔ You can also move a pattern that is within a selected object by choosing Object⇨Move.

✔ You can quickly apply a transformation to a pattern by first selecting the object with the pattern and then selecting the transformation tool. Next, press P as you click and drag the mouse to manually produce the transformation. You can also move a pattern within an object by selecting the object and pressing P while you drag inside the object.

✔ In order for patterns to print, the Preview and print patterns check box must be selected in the Document Setup dialog box. This setting is on when you first install Illustrator. If you need to access the Document Setup Dialog box, choose File⇨Document Setup.

Creating and Applying a Custom Pattern

After you see how you can enhance images with Illustrator's predefined patterns, you're undoubtedly going to want to try your hand at creating patterns from your own artwork. When you create a pattern, you are essentially creating a type of rectangular tile with your design in it. When you apply the pattern, the object is filled with repeated versions of your tile.

Figure 12-5 shows a custom pattern we created using the Pen and transformation tools. Figure 12-6 shows the custom pattern applied to a shirt. We also used the Brush tool to add some detail to the neck and cuff areas of the shirt.

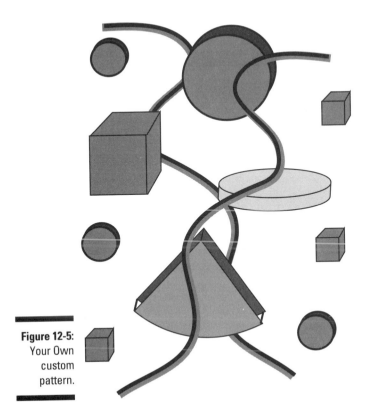

Figure 12-5:
Your Own
custom
pattern.

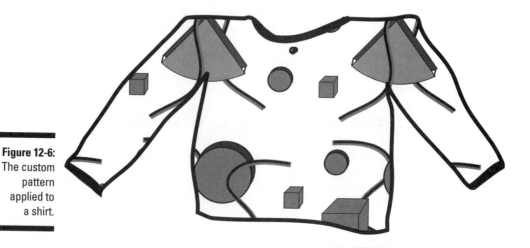

Figure 12-6:
The custom
pattern
applied to
a shirt.

Here are the steps for creating a custom pattern:

1. **Create a design for the pattern using any tool, and fill the design with colors, if desired.**

   You can't use a gradient in a pattern or another pattern within a pattern. However you may be able to work around this limitation by selecting a gradient or pattern on-screen and executing the Object⇨Expand command. This command turns gradients and patterns into objects that are masked. (Masks cannot be used in patterns, either. To learn more about Masks, see Chapter 18.) You can then release the mask by choosing Object⇨Masks⇨Release. After executing these commands, you can then create a new pattern using the unmasked objects (which used to be a gradient or pattern).

2. **After you create the design that you want to repeat in your pattern, you may decide to create a *bounding rectangle* around the pattern. The bounding rectangle allows you to set how much background or blank space appears in each rectangular tile when the pattern is applied. If you don't create a bounding rectangle, Illustrator creates a rectangular tile that borders your pattern design as closely as possible.**

   To create a bounding rectangle, use the Rectangle tool to create a rectangle that borders your design, as shown in Figure 12-7.

Pattern design

Bounding rectangle

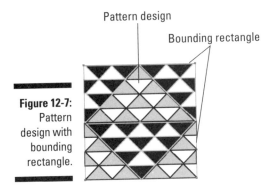

Figure 12-7:
Pattern
design with
bounding
rectangle.

3. **After you create a rectangle over your pattern, you must place the rectangle at the very back of all of the objects in your pattern. To do this, select the rectangle and then choose Arrange⇨Send To Back.**

4. **If you'd like, you can apply a fill or stroke to the bounding rectangle or set both the fill and the stroke to None.**

   If you fill with a color, the color appears throughout the pattern. If the fill and stroke are set to None in the Paint Style palette, the background and fill of the pattern are transparent, which means that you can place a colored item behind the pattern and see the colored item through the transparent background. If you don't create a bounding rectangle, any blank areas in the tile surrounding your pattern are transparent also.

5. **Now use the Selection tool to select both the pattern and the bounding rectangle. If you didn't create a bounding rectangle, just select the pattern.**

   The easiest way is to click and drag with the Selection tool over the bounding rectangle and pattern to create a marquee. For more information about using the Selection tool, see Chapter 3.

6. **With both the pattern tile and the bounding rectangle selected, choose Object⇨Pattern from the Object menu.**

7. **In the Pattern dialog box, choose New. Illustrator helpfully shows a preview of your tile, as shown in Figure 12-8. Name your pattern in the Change name to field, and click OK to define your pattern.**

   After you close the dialog box, Illustrator adds your pattern's name to the pattern list in the Pattern dialog box.

   When you save your document, the pattern is saved with it. It does not automatically appear in other documents. (Copying your pattern into other documents is covered later in this chapter.)

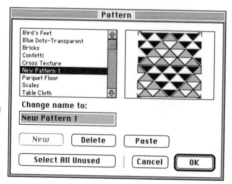

Figure 12-8:
The Pattern
dialog box.

8. **Before applying your pattern, select an object or several objects. To apply your pattern to the selected objects, first click the Fill box in the Paint Style palette. Then click the Pattern color selection icon in the right panel of the palette, and select your custom pattern's name from the list in the dialog box.**

Now that you're on the road to creating your own patterns, here are a few handy suggestions to make using patterns more efficient:

✔ You can add a swatch for your pattern to the swatches in the Paint Style palette by clicking the swatch when it appears in the Fill icon and then dragging it to the swatch area in the palette.

✔ When creating your bounding rectangle, you may want to use horizontal and vertical guides to help you place the box exactly where you want it to be.

✔ For faster viewing and printing, your best bet is to create a bounding rectangle about 1-inch square. If your pattern is very intricate, the size of the bounding rectangle should be smaller than an inch.

✔ You can make the printing process more efficient if you use the Group command to group pattern areas that are similar in color.

✔ You can rename a pattern by selecting it in the Pattern dialog box, typing a new name into the Change name to field, and clicking OK.

Editing Custom Patterns

What happens when you've filled lots of intricate objects with a pattern and then decide that you want to change the pattern? Fortunately, you can edit a pattern and leave it to Illustrator to take care of everything else by updating all the patterns on-screen to the newly edited pattern.

Here are the steps for editing a pattern if your original pattern is on-screen and that pattern has been applied to an object:

1. **With your pattern and bounding rectangle still on-screen, simply edit the pattern in the bounding rectangle using any of Illustrator's tools or commands (remember you can't put a gradient, pattern, or mask in a pattern).**

2. **Select the bounding rectangle and its contents, and choose Object⇨ Pattern.**

3. **In the Pattern dialog box, click the pattern name and then click OK to edit the pattern and have Illustrator automatically apply the changes to the pattern in your object on-screen.**

If you don't want the original pattern to change, click New in the Pattern dialog box to create a new version of the pattern. Type in a new name for the pattern, and click OK to define the new pattern. If you create a new version of your pattern, objects on-screen with the old pattern are not updated, so you'll need to apply the new pattern to an object if you want it to appear on-screen.

If you deleted the pattern that you created in the document on-screen, you can paste it back into your document and then edit the pattern. Here's how:

1. **Make sure that nothing on-screen is selected. Choose Edit⇨Select None to deselect.**

2. **Open the Pattern dialog box by choosing Object⇨Pattern.**

3. **Select the name of the pattern that you want to edit.**

4. **Click the Paste button and then the OK button.**

   Your pattern is now pasted on-screen.

The Paste button pastes a pattern in the middle of the screen. If you don't want the pattern pasted in the middle of your artwork, scroll left or right so that Illustrator pastes beyond your document's border.

5. **Edit the artwork by using any of Illustrator's tools or commands.**

6. **Select the pattern tile and bounding rectangle. Then choose Object⇨ Pattern. If you want all the patterns on-screen updated, do not click the New button in the Pattern dialog box. Instead, click the name of the pattern you're editing and then click OK.**

Deleting a Pattern

If you've had enough of a pattern, you can delete it by first choosing Object➪Pattern. Then, in the Pattern dialog box, select the pattern. Click the Delete button and click OK to delete the pattern. Any object on-screen that was filled with the deleted pattern turns black.

Copying Patterns from Documents

Once you start building a library of patterns, you're probably going to want to use patterns created in one document in other documents. If you want to load all the patterns from one document into the document that is currently open, Choose File➪Import Styles. In the dialog box that appears, select the file that contains the patterns that you want to use. Then click Open.

If you create a new document and want to use a pattern from another file, you can access the other file's patterns by opening that document on-screen also. After you load the document with the pattern or patterns, activate the file that you want to move the pattern to. When that file is on-screen, either choose Object➪Pattern or click the Pattern color selection option in the right panel of the Paint Style palette. Notice that all the patterns from all open documents appear. You can then use the Paint Style palette to fill an object with a pattern from another document, or you can paste the pattern into the document on-screen by clicking the Paste button in the Pattern dialog box. If you do use the Paste button in the Pattern dialog box, you then need to define the pattern in the new document using the steps described in the "Creating and Applying a Custom Pattern" section of this chapter.

If you want every new document that you create to have the same custom patterns, you'll need to change Illustrator's Startup file. To find out how to do this, see Chapter 10.

Patterns on a Path

By now you probably agree that patterns are great for filling in objects to make them more interesting. But patterns can also be used to easily create intricate and decorative border effects by placing them along paths. By placing patterns on paths, you can even create complete illustrations, as shown in Figure 12-9 (artwork created by artist Eve Elberg). The patterns used to create Figure 12-9 are shown on the left; the final illustration (the pattern on a rectangular path) is shown on the right. Using the Path Pattern command, you can place a pattern on the side of an object and another on the corners of the object. For instance, when Eve created the breakfast scene, she used the Path Pattern command to

Figure 12-9: Image created by artist Eve Elberg, using the Path Pattern command.

position the cup pattern on the corners of her image and to place the breakfast pattern on the sides. As you can see, the result is breakfast for six rather than breakfast for one.

Here's how to use the Path Pattern command. Before you follow the steps, create the object or objects that you want to place (as patterns) on a path. Use the steps described in the Creating and Applying Custom Patterns section to turn the object or objects into custom patterns.

1. **Create the path that you want to place the patterns on.**

2. **Choose Filter⇨Stylize⇨Path Pattern.**

3. **In the Path Pattern dialog box shown in Figure 12-10, select the pattern name in the scrolling list of patterns.**

4. **In the dialog box, click the Sides, Outer Corner, or Inner Corner box to specify which part of the selected path that you want to apply the pattern to. Figure 12-11 shows the differences between sides, outer corners and inner corners.**

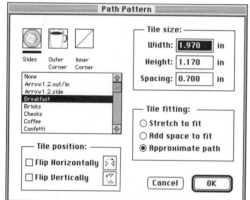

Figure 12-10:
The Path
Pattern
dialog box.

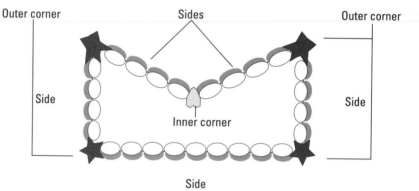

Figure 12-11:
Path
Pattern's
sides, outer
corners, and
inner
corners.

After you select, a sample of the pattern appears in the selected box.

If you don't want to apply a pattern to a specific portion of the path, select Sides, Outer Corner, and/or Inner Corner and select None from the scrolling list of pattern names.

5. **Repeat steps 3 and 4 with different patterns if you want to apply different patterns to different parts of the path.**

6. **Choose an option in the Tile fitting section to control how the pattern tile fits onto the path.**

   • To stretch or shrink the tile to fit the path, choose Stretch to fit.

   • To add a blank space between each tile, choose Add space to fit. If you want to control the amount of spacing between each tile, enter an amount into the Spacing field in the Tile size section of the dialog box. If you don't enter an amount, Illustrator automatically decides the spacing amount.

- To place the tile on the inside or outside of a rectangular path, choose Approximate path. If you don't choose this option, the pattern is centered onto the path.

- If you want to make the pattern larger or smaller, enter a value in the Width or Height field in the Tile size section of the dialog box. If you enter a value in one field, the other field changes proportionally.

- To create a wreath effect when applying a pattern to a circular path, enter a width that is smaller than the circle's circumference. If you enter a width that is the same size as the circle's circumference, Illustrator scales the pattern to fill the circle.

7. **If desired, you can flip the pattern horizontally or vertically by clicking the icons in the Tile position section of the dialog box.**

Part III
All About Working with Text

The 5th Wave — By Rich Tennant

"NOT ONLY DID WE GET YOU AN APPLE WITH A MOUSE, LIKE YOU ASKED, WE ALSO GOT YOU A BANANA WITH A LIZARD."

In this part . . .

Sometimes you need more than an illustration to get your point across. Sometimes you need to get in a few words as well. The chapters in this part show you all the amazing things that you can do with text in Illustrator. You see how to put text on curves, inside shapes, and around objects. After reading this part, you may find that many projects you're doing in a page layout program can actually be done in Illustrator.

Chapter 13
Putting It in Writing

They say that a picture is worth a thousand words, but sometimes a picture isn't worth anything without a word or two to help explain it.

Words can help your art make a statement, add humor, sell a product, or grab attention. Perhaps two of the most tempting words in the human language are shown in Figure 13-1. The words *sale* and *50%* are almost always guaranteed to trigger a response. Words like these can be almost as eye-catching as the best computer graphics.

Figure 13-1:
Text and graphics create a sales tag.

Illustrator provides numerous possibilities to be creative with type. You can add type to a document using the Type, Area Type, and Path Type tools. You can even import type into Illustrator from other programs. As we explain in later chapters, you can flow type around graphics, bend it around curves, stretch it, or shrink it. But before you start making type jump through flaming hoops, you need to know how to create type on-screen.

Typing Away with the Type tool

The easiest way to get a few words on-screen is to use the Type tool. To activate the Type tool, you simply select it in the Toolbox. Because the Type tool shares its Toolbox location with the Area Type and Path Type tools, you may need to click either one of these tools and wait until the Type tool appears before you can choose it.

When the Type tool is selected, the mouse pointer changes to an I-beam when you move it into the document window.

Before you start adding your words of wisdom to the screen, move the I-beam pointer to the area where you want to start writing. Next, click the mouse. After you click, a blinking cursor appears. At this point, you can start typing. By default, Illustrator starts you off in its default typeface, Helvetica, and its default type size, 12 points. If the type is too small to see, simply zoom in using the Zoom tool. Now try your hand at creating some prose, and start typing some words on the keyboard. As you type away, the text appears on-screen. If you make a mistake, simply press the Delete key to delete the last character you typed and then type in the correct character.

Don't know what typeface and type size you're using? Look at the Info palette, which displays the current typeface and type size when the Type tool is activated. You can also use the Character palette. To open the Info palette on screen, choose Window⇨Show Info. To open the Character palette, choose Show⇨Character or Type⇨Character.

Proper typography requires that you use *smart quotes*. These are the curly quotes that look like " ". If you're worried about those unprofessional-looking vertical quotes cropping up in your text, Illustrator has a solution. It can automatically replace all vertical quotes with smart quotes. All you need to do is choose Type⇨Smart Punctuation. In the Smart Punctuation dialog box, select the Smart Quotes check box. This command is like having a professional typesetter at your disposal. It will not only ensure that smart quotes appear in all your type, but the dialog box also has settings that can replace two keyboard dashes (--) with the typographically correct em dash (—). It also replaces three dashes with an ellipsis and allows you to change all the text in a document or only selected text.

If you want to use standard Mac keyboard commands to create smart quotes, here's a list:

Smart Quote	Keyboard Shortcut
"	Option+[
"	Option+Shift+[
'	Option+]
'	Option+Shift+]

Did your Caps Lock key get stuck, and did you accidentally type all of your text in uppercase? Illustrator has a solution. Just select the text and choose Font➪Change Case. Options in the Change Case dialog box allow you to change all selected text to lowercase, a mixture of uppercase and lowercase, or uppercase.

Creating New Lines and Blocks of Text

Once you start working with Illustrator's Type tool, you're probably going to be typing more than a word or two — probably a few lines. There are lots of tricks to get Illustrator to type text so that it wraps from one line to the next. They're covered in the next chapter. For the time being, the easiest way to move from one line to the next is to press the Return key. To create a few lines of text, type what you want on the first line, press Return, type the next line of text, press Return, and so on.

As you type, you're probably thinking that working with type in Illustrator is not too different from working with a word processor. To some degree, you are correct. However, there are some major differences between using Illustrator and using a word processor. One of the major differences to understand is that when you click to establish a new block of text, that text has no relation to any previous text. Each block of text is a separate entity that you can select and move separately from all other blocks of text. To create a new block of text, however, you can't just click someplace else on-screen to establish another insertion point. In fact, if you are working in one block of text and then click someplace else and try to begin writing there, Illustrator ignores you. It doesn't allow you to type someplace else. In order to end one block of text and begin writing someplace else, click the Type tool in the Toolbox again, move to where you want to type, click, and start typing.

In order for PostScript typefaces to look smooth on-screen, you should have Adobe Type Manager (ATM) installed in your system. ATM probably isn't installed if the type on your screen looks jagged. If ATM is installed, you should be able to see an ATM icon in your Control Panel folder. To see if ATM has been installed, click the Apple menu, then choose Control Panels in the list of choices in the Apple menu. When the Control Panel folder opens, you should see the ATM icon in the folder. You can also double-click the ATM icon to see if ATM has been turned on or off. If you need to install ATM, find the ATM installation disk that comes with your Adobe Illustrator installation disks and follow the installation instructions.

If ATM is installed and your fonts still look bad, the printer font of your Postscript typeface probably has not been installed. If this is the case, read the installation guide that comes with your fonts.

Selecting Type

After you get accustomed to typing in Illustrator, your next goal is to be able to edit text, change the type size and typeface, delete, and change the text color. Before you can make these changes to type, you need to know how to select text. Once the text is selected, virtually all of Illustrator's editing commands affect only the selected text.

Here's a list of text-selecting options available when you have any of the type tools selected. Using the type tools, you can select any letter or group of letters in a text block.

✔ To select one letter or several letters, click and drag with the I-beam pointer over the letter that you want to select.

Once you select the text, it becomes highlighted. Figure 13-2 shows the word *people* selected and highlighted. If you want to select several lines of text, you can click and drag with the mouse over the lines to select the words.

Figure 13-2:
Text
selected
with the
I-beam
pointer.

- ✔ To select a word, double-click the word.
- ✔ You can select a paragraph of text by triple-clicking the mouse in the text.
- ✔ A paragraph is established every time you press Return while typing.
- ✔ You can select all type in a text block by clicking in the type with the I-beam pointer and then choosing Edit⇨Select All or pressing ⌘+A.

You can also select type using Illustrator's Selection tool. Once you select text with the Selection tool, the entire text block is selected. If you change typefaces or colors, the entire text is changed. As you see later in this chapter, before moving a block of text, you must select it with a Selection tool. Here's how to select text with the Selection tool:

1. **Activate the Selection tool.**

2. **Move the Selection tool to the baseline of the text that you want to select and click.**

   The *baseline* of the text is like an invisible horizontal line that all text sits on.

3. **After you click, Illustrator underlines the selected text, as shown in Figure 13-3.**

With any tool selected, you can temporarily activate the Selection tool by pressing ⌘.

Figure 13-3:
Text
selected
with the
Selection
tool.

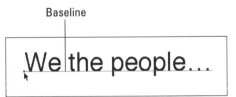

Baseline

We the people…

To quickly duplicate a block of text, select it with the Selection tool. Next press and hold Option while you click and drag the text with the Selection tool. As you drag, a duplicate of the text block appears on-screen, making your prose purple.

Once you know how to select text, you can start to create a few simple effects using the Paint Style palette. If you want to fill text or stroke it with color, all you need to do is select the text and then choose the color and fill in the Paint Style palette. Illustrator also allows you to fill and stroke text with different colors, as shown in Figure 13-4. In this figure, the text was duplicated, sent to the back, and filled with black to create a shadow effect. Using the Paint Style palette, you can also create reversed type, as shown in Figure 13-5, which is commonly used to draw attention. For more information about filling and stroking, see Chapters 3 and 10. The Send to Back command is covered in Chapter 3. For more information about duplicating, see previous tip and Chapter 3.

Figure 13-4:
Text stroked
and filled
with
different
colors.

Here's how to create reversed type:

1. **Create a rectangle, using the Rectangle tool.**

   For more information about using the Rectangle tool, see Chapter 3.

2. **Open the Paint Style palette by choosing Window⇨Paint Style. Click the Fill box at the top of the left panel of the palette, and then click a black swatch to fill the rectangle with black.**

3. **In the Paint Style palette, set the Fill to white.**

4. **Activate the Type tool, and type the text.**

Figure 13-5:
White text
on a black
background.

Made in USA

Type on the Move

Once you create type, you may need to reposition it on-screen or create special type effects, such as having the phrase "Up, Up, and Away" gradually climb up the screen. In order to create these effects, you need to know how to move the type. To move type, select it with the Selection tool and then click and drag it into the desired position. You can also select type and then move it by choosing Arrange➪Move. Once type is selected, you can also move it using the Arrange➪ Average command, which is discussed in Chapter 7. You can also evenly distribute the type by clicking the different distribute options in the Align palette.

Once you select type, you can also scale, rotate, shear, and reflect it. Figure 13-6 shows pinwheels created simply by rotating and copying the letters *A* and *V.*

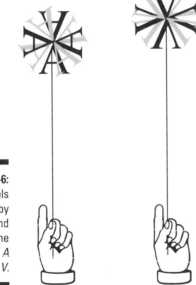

Figure 13-6:
Pinwheels
created by
copying and
rotating the
letters *A*
and *V.*

Text with Character

Part of the fun of working with type is changing its size, face, and other attributes. Illustrator provides several roads to type effects: the Font menu, the Type menu, and the Character palette. Use the Font menu if you want to change the typeface. The Type menu is handy if you want to change just one type attribute. For example, to change the size of some text, select the text, choose Type➪Size, and pick a size from the pop-up menu. If, however, you'll be making numerous type changes, you'll want to open the Character palette, shown in

Figure 13-7. Every character attribute option available in Illustrator's menus is available in this one palette. To open the Character palette, choose Window⊅Show Character or Type⊅Character. You can also open the Character palette by pressing ⌘+T. To see the entire expanded palette, click the little flag on the right side of the palette.

Figure 13-7:
The
Character
palette.

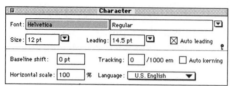

Changing fonts and font size

The easiest way to get accustomed to working with the Character palette is to try changing the typeface and the type size of some text. Start by using the Type tool to create some text. Next, select the type by clicking and dragging over it. To change the typeface, click the down arrow in the upper-right corner of the Character palette, which activates a Font pop-up menu. In the pop-up menu, position the mouse over the typeface that you want and press and hold down the mouse button. When the mouse button is pressed, another pop-up menu appears, allowing you to choose whether you want the type to have attributes such as Normal, Bold, Italics, Bold Oblique, or Bold Italics, as shown in Figure 13-8. Select the style you desire. As soon as you release the mouse, the text is updated accordingly. To change type size, you can simply enter a number into the Size field in the Character palette. Alternatively, you can choose a size from the pop-up menu (the down arrow next to the Size field). After you choose a size, the text on-screen is updated. After you change typeface and type styles, you can integrate the text with graphic objects that you create on-screen. Figure 13-9 shows the word *congratulations* in the Zapf Chancery font. We used the Pen tool to create the banner.

You can change typefaces by typing a letter into the Font field in the Character palette. After you type a letter, Illustrator changes the typeface to one that begins with the letter you typed.

You can search for a specific font and replace it with a different font using the Type⊅Find Font command.

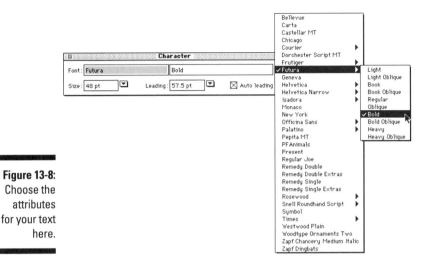

Figure 13-8:
Choose the attributes for your text here.

Figure 13-9:
Zapf Chancery font in a banner created with the Pen tool.

Congratulations

Finding characters with Key Caps

The character sets of most typefaces include copyright symbols, trademark symbols, bullets, and a cast of other unusual characters. How do you know what keys to press to place these characters in your document? Choose Key Caps from your Apple menu. Key Caps provides an on-screen keyboard that shows you what characters will appear when you press Option, ⌘, and Option+Shift on your keyboard. Notice that when you press Option+G, the copyright symbol appears. Press Option+2 for the Trademark symbol, and Option+8 for a bullet.

As the type kerns

To create just the right effect with type, you may want to squeeze letters closer together so that the letters almost step on the toes of those nearby. If you want to tighten the spacing between letters or send type farther apart, you can *kern* or change the *tracking*. When you kern type in Illustrator, you adjust the spacing between two letters. When you change the tracking, you adjust the spacing between more than two letters. Kerning and tracking are not always necessary. But if you start working with larger type sizes, the gaps between certain letters give the type an uneven look.

The Character palette allows you to kern or change tracking depending upon what you have selected. If you click with the I-beam pointer between two characters, you see the word *Kern* in the Character palette (you'll also see the word *Kern* in the Type menu). If you click and drag over a letter or several letters, you see the word *Tracking*, and the word *Kern* changes to *Tracking* in the Type menu.

When you kern or track, Illustrator makes you enter values in something called an *em space*. An em space is essentially the size of the type measured horizontally rather than vertically for a specific type size, which means that an em space at 12 point is 12 points, and an em space for a 48-point type is 48 points. When you enter values in the Kerning field, you are entering them in $^1/_{1000}$ of an em space — an extremely small increment. The bottom example in Figure 13-10 shows you how small the increment $^1/_{1000}$ of an em really is. The spacing between the letters *V* and *A* is $^{115}/_{1000}$ of an em.

Figure 13-10:
The *VA* in
VALENTINO
(at the
bottom)
kerned at
$^{115}/_{1000}$ em.

Here are the steps for kerning or tracking:

1. **Activate the Type tool.**

2. **To kern, put the I-beam pointer between two letters and click. To change tracking, select all the letters that you want to track.**

3. **If the Character palette isn't open, choose Type⇨Tracking or Type⇨ Kern. This opens the Character palette and moves the cursor to the Tracking/Kern field.**

4. **To increase the distance between characters, enter a positive value in the Tracking/Kerning field. To decrease the distance between characters, enter a negative value in the Tracking/Kerning field.**

Many typefaces have kerning values built in between specific pairs of letters. For example, between the letters *VA* or *WA*, font designers often create specific kerning values. To use preset pair kerning values, leave the Auto kern check box selected.

5. **Press Tab or Return.**

The kerning or tracking is applied to the text.

Here are a few kerning tips:

✔ To change tracking or kerning using the keyboard, first select the type or click the I-beam pointer between two letters. To squeeze the type closer together, press Option+left-arrow key. To move letters apart, press Option+right-arrow key.

✔ If you want to see the kerning value between two letters, open the Info palette and click to place the insertion point between two letters, as shown in Figure 13-11.

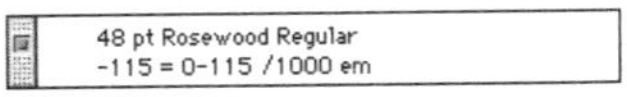

Figure 13-11:
The Info palette displaying the font size, font, and kerning value.

48 pt Rosewood Regular
-115 = 0-115 /1000 em

Superscripts, subscripts: My baseline has shifted!

E=MC^2, H$_2$O, Deluxe Designs©. You often need to send a character up or down in the middle of the line of text, as in these examples. Fortunately, you don't need to create a new block of text and manually move the letter up or down. All you need to do is use the Baseline Shift option in the Character palette.

Using Illustrator's Baseline Shift option, you can move type 1,000 points above the baseline or 1,000 points below it. To use the Baseline Shift option, first select the character or characters that you want to shift. To move a letter up, enter a positive number in the Baseline Shift field. To move a letter down, enter a negative number. If you've got both hands on the keyboard, you can press Option+Shift+up-arrow key to move characters up and Option+Shift+down-arrow key to move characters down. The increments moved is based upon the settings in the Baseline Shift field set in the General Preferences dialog box. To access the General Preferences dialog box, choose File⇨Preferences⇨General. By default, the Baseline Shift is set to 2 points.

Stretching it to the limits: expanded and compressed type

Illustrator allows you to treat type as if it were rubber. You can expand or compress type to create different effects or to add emphasis. Expansion and compression are handled by changing the percentage values in the Horizontal scale field in the Character palette. Figure 13-12 shows type unaltered and then with a horizontal scale of 200 and a horizontal scale of 50.

Illustrator considers the normal horizontal scaling of a character to be 100 percent. To compress the type, enter a value less than 100 percent into the Horizontal scale field; to expand the type, enter a value greater than 100 percent. After you enter a number, press Tab or Return to see the text adjustment.

Changing the horizontal scale does not change the height of the type.

Getting the lead out

When you want to change the spacing between lines of text in Illustrator, you can't change the spacing by choosing single, double, or triple spacing from a pop-up menu. Instead, you enter a *leading* (pronounced like: ledding, rhymes with wedding) value. The term *leading* is used because the earliest printers placed lead between lines of type to space the lines apart. Changing leading in Illustrator is quite a bit easier, and quite a bit safer.

Figure 13-12:
Horizontal
scale
applied at
100 percent,
200 percent,
and 50
percent.

Illustrator's leading option allows you complete control over how far the baseline of one line of text is from the next line of text. By default, all leading of type is set to Auto leading. The Auto leading value is set to 120 percent of the type size, which means that if your type size is 10 points, the leading is 12 points. If the type size is 50, the leading is 60 points.

To change leading, start by selecting the lines of text that you want to adjust. Next, enter a leading value in points in the Leading field in the Character palette. Then press Tab or Return to have Illustrator adjust the text. If the Character palette is not on-screen, you can also change leading by choosing Type⇨Leading and then choosing a value from the submenu that appears. If you are unsure of exactly what leading value to enter, think of leading in terms of the type size that you are using. For example, to create a double-spaced line of text, type a value in the Leading field that is twice the size of the selected type. For example, if your type size is 12, a leading value of 24 would double-space the text.

Creating a Pop Can

The Type tool can be used to create the pop can shown in Figure 13-13. To make the image, we first created a rounded rectangle for the basic shape of the can and then created an oval at the top and an oval at the bottom of the can. Next, we used the Oval, Rectangle, and Rotate tools to create the label area inside the can. The Type tool was used to add the text to the labels. We created the Letters *P, o,* and *P* and the exclamation mark in separate text blocks — we did this so that we could move each letter independently of the others. For the text, we used different fonts and font sizes. We selected some of the text and several of the letters and then used the Rotate tool to rotate letters or words. We pressed Option+8 to create the bullets and Option+2 to create the trademark symbol.

Figure 13-13:
Text added
to pop can.

Chapter 14

Goin' with the Flow of Text

In This Chapter

▶ Creating text rectangles

▶ Linking text

▶ Importing text

▶ Fitting headlines

▶ Wrapping text around graphics

▶ Using the Paragraph palette

▶ Creating tabs

▶ Creating rows and columns

*W*hen most people need to slap a few paragraphs of text on-screen, they usually turn to their word processor. When they want the text to take a detour and run around graphics, they usually turn to their page layout program. If you've got Illustrator, you don't need to turn anyplace else.

Boxing Your Text

When you need to place several lines of text on-screen, it's often helpful to have the text automatically wrap to the next line. In Illustrator, you can make text automatically wrap to the next line by creating a *text rectangle*. When you create a text rectangle, you can confine the text to a specific area where it wraps according to the size of the rectangle you've created, as shown in Figure 14-1. Thus, the rectangular text box basically defines a rectangular border for the type. The text rectangle appears on-screen as a rectangle, but the rectangle doesn't print. When you are in Artwork mode, the rectangle always appears on-screen. When you are in Preview mode, the rectangle appears when you create it and when you select it with a selection tool or when you select the text that is inside of it. To learn more about Artwork and Preview modes, see Chapter 2.

Figure 14-1:
A typical
text
rectangle.

You create a text box rectangle by clicking and dragging the Type tool. Once the rectangle has been created, you can move it, resize it, and flow text from one rectangle to another rectangle. Here's how to create a text rectangle:

1. **Select the Type tool in the Toolbox.**

2. **With the Type tool activated, click and drag diagonally to create a rectangle.**

3. **As soon as you create the rectangle, a blinking cursor appears in it. At this point, you can start typing away.**

   As you type, the words wrap to the next line as they do in a word processor. If you want to force a line break, simply press the Return key to create a new paragraph.

To duplicate a text rectangle, press Option and then click and drag the edge of the rectangle with the Selection tool. After the duplicate rectangle appears, release the mouse and then release the Option key.

Resizing a text rectangle

If you type lots of text into the rectangle, the rectangle does not automatically enlarge to accommodate the text you type. Instead, Illustrator warns you that the text doesn't fit by placing a tiny plus sign at the bottom of the rectangle, as shown in Figure 14-2. In order to see all of the text, you need to resize the text rectangle.

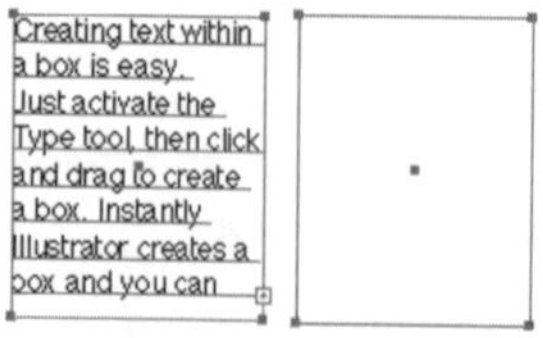

Figure 14-2:
Text with
overflow
icon.

Creating text within
a box is easy.
Just activate the
Type tool, then click
and drag to create
a box. Instantly
Illustrator creates a
box and you can

Here's how to resize the text rectangle:

1. **Select the Direct Selection tool in the toolbox. (The Direct Selection tool is the hollow arrow.)**

2. **In order to resize the rectangle, the text in it must not be selected. If the text is selected, simply click outside the text rectangle to deselect it.**

3. **To resize the rectangle, click and drag any of the rectangle's edges.**

   If you click and drag a corner point, you can reshape the rectangle, as shown in Figure 14-3. If you click and drag a segment, the entire side of the rectangle stretches.

Figure 14-3:
Resizing
a text
rectangle
with the
Direct
Selection
tool.

When resizing a rectangle, you can press Shift to constrain while you click and drag. This constraint helps you click and drag in a straight line.

No matter how great you can spell, everyone makes typos. Your best defense against typos is to spell-check your text. To run Illustrator's Spell checker, choose Type⇨Check Spelling.

Linking text

To create different type effects, you may want to *link* text rectangles so that you can flow text from one rectangle to another. Using this technique, you can create columns of text where text snakes from the bottom of one column to the top of the next column. Here's how to link two text rectangles together:

1. **In order to link more than one text box together, first create the text boxes and then select them, as shown earlier in Figure 14-2.**

   To select a group of text rectangles, activate the Selection tool and then click and drag over each box. Alternatively, you can select one box and then Shift+click to select other text boxes.

2. **Choose Type⇨Link Blocks.**

   Any text that doesn't fit into the first text flows into the other text boxes.

Here are a few linking notes that can help you while you work:

 ✔ Text flows according to the stacking order of text rectangles; in other words, according to which rectangle is on top of another. The bottom object in the stack of rectangles is where text flows first; it then flows into the next highest object. You can change the stacking order by using the Arrange⇨Send To Back and Arrange⇨Bring To Front commands. For more information about Send to Back and Bring to Front, see Chapter 3.

 ✔ If you want to unlink text, select the text rectangles and then choose Type⇨Unlink Blocks.

 ✔ To delete a line segment of a text rectangle without deleting the text in it, click the edge of the rectangle with the Direct Selection tool and then press Delete.

Importing Text

Although you can easily type paragraphs of text into Illustrator, you may be working on a project with clients or colleagues who prefer to do all their work in a word processing program so that you do the designing and they do the typing — which is probably fine by you. If they are working in a standard Mac word processor such as MacWrite, WordPerfect, or Word, you should be able to import their text into an Illustrator text rectangle.

You can import text into a path that is not a rectangle by using the Area Type tool. Using the Area Type tool is covered in Chapter 15.

Illustrator's Import Text command uses file translators created by Claris Corporation. In order to import files from word processors, you must install the Claris Translators and the Claris XTND files — both of which are installed in your System folder.

When you import text, you can have Illustrator import it into a graphic object or you can import the text into a text rectangle.

Here are the steps for importing text into Illustrator:

1. **Activate the Type tool.**

2. **With the Type tool activated, click and drag to create a text rectangle.**

3. **To import the text from a disk file, choose File⇨Import Text. In the Open dialog box, double-click the file that you want to open or select the file that you want to Import and then click Open.**

Once the file is loaded, it flows directly into the text box. Figure 14-2, shown earlier, shows some text that was imported into a rectangle.

You can export your Illustrator text to other programs by selecting the text with the Type tool and choosing Type⇨Export. A dialog box appears allowing you to save the text in different file formats for other programs.

If the Headline Fits

Once you've got a line of text in a rectangle, you may want to turn it into a headline that stretches from one end of the text box to the other. In other programs, this situation often means endlessly changing the type size to try to make the text fit as snugly as possible.

Illustrator makes fitting headlines easy. For example, in Figure 14-4, the Hong Kong headline was automatically stretched to fit in the text box after we executed Illustrator's Fit Headline command. When we executed Fit Headline, the spacing between the words was stretched so the text fit in the text box. Then, we increased the type size using the Type⇨Size command.

Here's how to fit a headline into a text rectangle:

1. **Create a text rectangle and type your heading in it.**

   Creating text in a rectangle is covered in the Boxing Your Text section of this chapter.

2. **Select the Type tool in the toolbox.**

Figure 14-4: A Hong Kong headline resized using the Fit Headline option.

3. **Select the text by clicking and dragging over it with the Type tool.**

4. **Choose Type⇨Fit Headline.**

For most typefaces, the tracking of the type changes so that the type stretches across the width of the rectangle when you execute the Fit Headline command. If you're using Adobe multiple master fonts, the width of the type changes. For more information about tracking, see Chapter 13.

Wrapping Up a Graphic with Text

Wrapping text around a graphic is one of the most common techniques for keeping a page full of dull-looking text from putting the reader to sleep. Figure 14-4, in the preceding section, shows an example of some text wrapped around a scanned image of Hong Kong Harbor. Guides were used to set up the placement for the text columns and headline. First, we fit the headline into a text rectangle, and then we created and linked text rectangles for the columns. Next, we created an oval over the two text columns. After we used the Make Wrap command to wrap the text around the oval, we placed the photograph over the image.

Here are the steps for wrapping text around a graphic:

1. **Create text in a text rectangle.**

2. **Place the graphic object or objects in front of the text rectangle by choosing Arrange⇨Bring To Front or Edit⇨Paste In Front.**

3. **Select the text rectangle and the graphic object or objects that you want to wrap the text around.**

   Usually, the easiest way to select all the objects is by clicking and dragging over them with the Selection tool.

4. **To create the wrap text effect, choose Type⇨Make Wrap.**

   The text flows around the selected graphic objects.

To create a border around the graphic object so that the type does not wrap too close to the graphic, create a separate graphic box, oval, or path to surround the object that you want to wrap the text around. Next, select the border object and the text before choosing Type⇨Make Wrap. We used this technique twice in Figure 14-4: to create a shape to wrap the text around between the columns and to create a shape behind the initial cap at the beginning of the text.

Using the Paragraph Palette

Once you've got lots of text on-screen, you may want to format it — center or justify the text, for example — or change the spacing between paragraphs. Your control center for handling paragraphs is the Paragraph palette, shown in Figure 14-5. To open the Paragraph palette, choose Window⇨Show Paragraph or Type⇨Paragraph. The keyboard shortcut is ⌘+Shift+P.

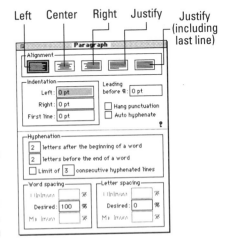

Figure 14-5:
The
Paragraph
palette.

The easiest commands to use in the Paragraph palette are those that control alignment. The icons at the top provide a picture of how each choice changes selected text. The only icons that may be a bit confusing are the last two. If you choose the last icon, the text is *justified,* which means that all the text lines up flush left and flush right, including the last line of the text. If you choose the second to last icon, all the selected text is justified *except* the last line of the text.

Here are some helpful keyboard shortcuts that can speed up your work. Remember to select the text before using any of the keyboard shortcuts.

- ✔ **Align left:** ⌘+Shift+L
- ✔ **Align center:** ⌘+Shift+C
- ✔ **Align right:** ⌘+Shift+R
- ✔ **Justified (last line is *not* justified):** ⌘+Shift+J
- ✔ **Justified (including last line):** ⌘+Shift+B

Changing indents

Like most word processors, Illustrator's Paragraph palette allows you to control the indents of text. The options in the Paragraph palette allow you to indent by entering a value in points in the Left, Right, and First line fields of the Paragraph palette. When you enter a value, it's measured from the left or right side of the text rectangle or the path that the text is in.

- ✔ **Left field:** Indents every line on the left side of the selected paragraph
- ✔ **Right field:** Indents every line on the right side of the paragraph
- ✔ **First line field:** Indents the first line of every paragraph

If you enter a negative number in the First line field, you create a *hanging indent* — which means that the first line of the paragraph extends to the left of the rest of the text in the paragraph.

If you want to create a hanging indent inside the text rectangle, enter a value into the Left field as well the First line field. For example, if you enter **–30** in the First line field and **30** in the Left field, the first line of each selected paragraph will extend to the left 30 points. The first paragraph in Figure 14-6 shows the effect of entering these values in the Paragraph palette. The second paragraph shows the effect of entering **30** in the Left, Right, and **-30** in the First line fields.

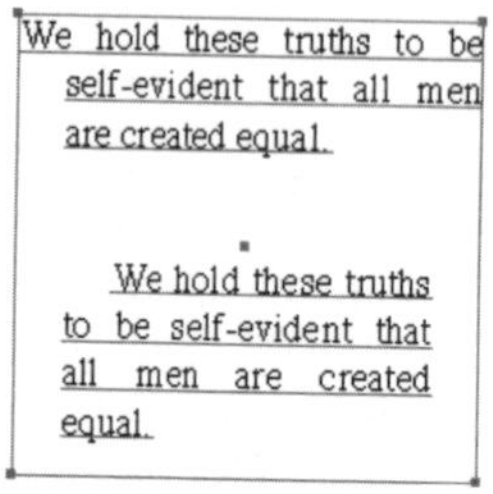

Figure 14-6:
Indents
created
with the
Paragraph
palette.

We hold these truths to be self-evident that all men are created equal.

We hold these truths to be self-evident that all men are created equal.

"I'd like to hang some punctuation right over here"

Sometimes working in a text rectangle gets a little too confining. Occasionally, you may feel the need to pop a hole in the surrounding box and place something outside it. For example, graphic artists often like to place punctuation marks so that they hang to the left of the left margin of text. This effect is shown in Figure 14-7, which includes some words of wisdom uttered by former New York Yankee catcher Yogi Berra.

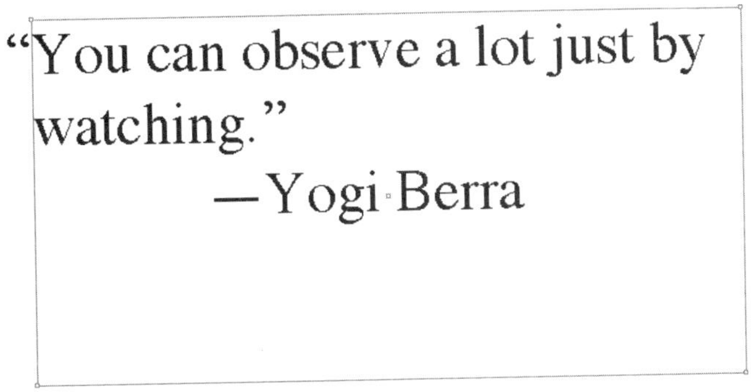

"You can observe a lot just by watching."
—Yogi·Berra

Figure 14-7:
Text with
hanging
punctuation.

To create this effect, simply select the text and then select the Hanging Punctuation option in the Paragraph palette. Press Return or Tab to see the effects.

More leading

No, you're not seeing double. The word *leading* appears in the Paragraph palette and in the Character palette. The leading option in the Character palette — which we cover in Chapter 13 — controls the spacing between each line in a selected block of text. The Leading Before Paragraph option only changes the spacing between different paragraphs. Here's how to add or reduce the leading between paragraphs:

1. **Activate the Type tool.**

2. **Select the text that includes the paragraphs that you want to adjust.**

3. **Enter a value in points in the Leading Before Paragraph field.**

4. **Press Tab or Return to see the change.**

Hyphenation and word spacing

You can use the Paragraph palette to control hyphenation and word spacing. To see these options, you must expand the palette by clicking the palette's flag in its lower-right corner. If you want to adjust when and where Illustrator places hyphens in text, you can enter values in the letters before the beginning and after the ending of a word field. You can also control how many consecutive lines can contain hyphens by selecting the Limit consecutive lines check box and entering a value in the field.

You use the Word and Letter spacing options in the palette primarily to control the spacing of justified text. The best way to learn how to use these options is to experiment with the Desired Text fields. When the Word spacing text field is set to 100 percent, no additional spacing is added to the letters. If you set the Desired Word spacing field to 125 percent, the Minimum to 100, and the Maximum to 200, you're telling Illustrator that you prefer that all spacing be 25 percent more than normal, but it's okay to have no spacing added or as much as double the original spacing (200 percent). If you leave the Desired Letter spacing set to 0, no letter spacing change will occur. If you increase the Desired Letter spacing field to 5 and leave the Maximum Letter spacing field set to 5, you're telling Illustrator that you want an increase in letter spacing of 5 percent, but the spacing cannot go beyond 5 percent.

Put It on My Tab

When you create text, you often need to produce tidy columns of words or numbers. If you had a typewriter, you would accomplish this by setting tab stops. Illustrator's electronic version of tabs far surpasses the tab power of any typewriter and even many word processors. In order to set tabs in Illustrator, you need to open the Tabs palette, shown in Figure 14-8. To open the palette, choose Window⇨Show Tab Ruler or press ⌘+Shift+T.

Figure 14-8:
The Tabs
palette.

Left Center Right Decimal

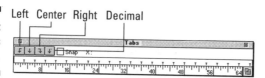

Illustrator's Tabs palette allows you to set left, right, center, and decimal tabs.

- **Left-aligned tab:** Lines up all words in a column on the first letter of each word

- **Right-aligned tab:** Lines up all words in a column on the last letter of each word

- **Decimal tab:** Aligns all numbers in a column on the decimal point

- **Center tab:** Centers each tabbed word in the column

The Tex-Mex menu in Figure 14-9 shows how decimal tabs can be used to line up columns of numbers.

Tex-Mex Food

Sal's Sizzling Soup $3.25

Susan's Sumptuous Salad $3.95

Ted's Terrifying Taco $6.95

Barry's Bursting Burrito $12.95

Edie's Enormous Enchilada $10.95

Charlie's Cha-Cha Chili $11.22

Specials of the Day

Figure 14-9:
Menu
created
using tabs.

By default, Illustrator automatically creates tabs a half-inch apart. These tabs are the tiny "T"s you see along the tab ruler when you first open the Tabs palette. If you want to create your own tabs, you can specify where you want to set the tabs and what type of tab you want by using the tab ruler.

Here's how to set your own tabs:

1. **If the Tabs Ruler palette isn't on-screen, open it by choosing Window⇨Show Tab Ruler.**

2. **If you want to set the tabs for text that is already created, select the text first, using one of the Type tools.**

3. **Choose the type of tab that you want to create by clicking one of the tab icons: left, right, center, or decimal.**

4. **Position the mouse pointer over the point on the tab ruler where you want to set the tab, and then click the mouse.**

Illustrator places a tab marker at that point.

The Snap check box in the Tabs palette forces all tab stops to be set to the closest ruler mark that you click near. If you want to turn off this feature, click the check box to deselect it.

5. **Continue setting tabs as desired by clicking the appropriate points on the ruler. If you want to change tab styles, click the appropriate icon.**

6. **After you have set your tab, move to the tab position by pressing the Tab key on your keyboard.**

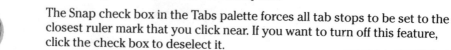

Here are a few tab tips:

- ✔ If you make a mistake and need to change a tab style from right to left, left to right, or center to tab — or whatever — first, select the tab position on the ruler that you want to change. After you click the stop, it's selected. Next, click the tab icon that you want to change it to.

- ✔ If you want to delete a tab, click the tab icon on the ruler and then drag the icon above the tab ruler. You can release the mouse after you see the word Delete in the ruler.

- ✔ You can also create columnar text, using Illustrator's Rows and Columns command, coming up next in this chapter.

Creating Rows & Columns

If you've got text that you want to arrange into rows and columns of text boxes, you'll find Illustrator's Rows & Columns command to be a tremendous time saver. When Illustrator executes the command, it takes a selected rectangle on-screen and slices it up into rows and columns, rows only, or columns only.

Here's how to use the Rows & Columns command:

1. **Create a rectangle or text box.**

   You may need to create a large rectangle or text box because Illustrator creates rows and columns out of the text box or rectangle you create.

2. **If the rectangle or text box isn't selected, select it with the Selection tool.**

3. **Choose Type⇨Rows & Columns.**

4. **In the Rows & Columns dialog box, shown in Figure 14-10, enter the number of rows and columns you want to create in the Rows and Columns fields.**

   You can also click on the left and right arrows to adjust the numbers. As you enter data, Illustrator automatically calculates the column width and the row height.

   If the Preview check box is selected, you'll see the rows and columns appear on-screen as you change options in the dialog box.

5. **If you want to add guides on the rows and columns, select the Add Guides check box.**

6. **You can control the text flow by clicking the Text flow icon.**

   The text snakes from left to right or top to bottom. The arrows show the direction of text flow. If the arrows create a Z shape the text flows from left to right. If the arrows create an N shape, the text flows from top to bottom.

Figure 14-10:
The Rows &
Columns
dialog box.

Rows & Columns			
Columns: 3	⬌	Rows: 2	⬌
Column Width: 2.132 in	⬌	Row Height: 2.063 in	⬌
Gutter: 0.167 in	⬌	Gutter: 0.167 in	⬌
Total Width: 6.729 in	⬌	Total Height: 4.292 in	⬌
Text Flow:	☒ Preview	Cancel	OK
	☐ Add Guides		

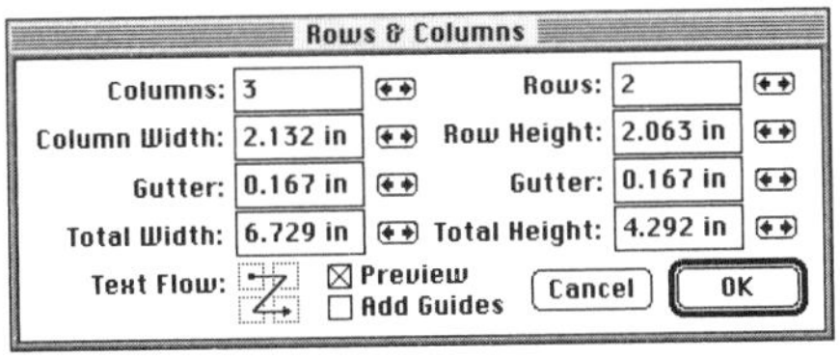

7. **Click OK.**

   Illustrator divides the rectangle or text into a matrix of columns and rows.

8. **You can now use the Type tool to enter or edit text in the rows and columns created.**

Chapter 15

Text Tricks

• •

• •

Sometimes, to get a message across, graphics alone won't do, and text alone just won't do. What you really need is a combination of both — text with a spark of creative artistry. At these times, Illustrator provides several simple-to-use options that can help light up your art with a few typographical tricks. You can add text within an object and along an object, and you can even convert text into an object. Once you convert text into an object, you are able to bend, move, and twist the text to make it dance. The style of the dance is up to you.

Shaping Up Your Text

If you've got a message to deliver, text poured across a page in one monotonous row after another can easily make a reader nod off into slumberland. One surefire way of waking up your audience is to put a little shape into your text by typing the text into an object. Figure 15-1 shows type placed inside the shape of a swimming pool. To create this effect, we created a shape with the Pen tool, copied the shape, and enlarged it using the Scale tool. After filling this larger shape with a pattern, we sent the larger shape behind the smaller shape. In order to make the text wrap within the smaller shape, we created text with the Area Type tool.

Figure 15-1:
Text created
inside a
shape with
the Area
Type tool.

Here's how to use the Area Type tool to create text inside an object:

1. **Create an object using the Oval, Rectangle, Pen, or Freehand tool. See Chapter 1 for an overview of Illustrator's tools.**

   The path can be open or closed. See Chapters 3, 6, and 7 for more information on paths.

2. **If the object you've created is not selected, select it with the Selection tool.**

3. **Activate the Area Type tool.**

Remember, the Area Type tool shares its Toolbox location with the Type and Path Type tools. If you don't see the Area Type tool in the Toolbox, click the Type tool in the Toolbox. Keep the mouse pressed until the Area Type tool appears, and then click the Area Type tool with the mouse. After you select the Area Type tool and move the pointer into your document, the mouse pointer changes to the Area Type pointer.

4. Move the mouse pointer over the object, as shown in Figure 15-2.

Then click the edge of the object. When you click the mouse, a blinking cursor appears.

Figure 15-2:
The Area
Type tool
positioned
over an
object.

5. Start typing.

As you type, the text appears within the shape. In Figure 15-3 the Area Type tool was used to create the text inside the leaf. The background photograph is from MetaTool's *KPT Power Photos I* CD-ROM.

Figure 15-3:
Text created
in an object
using the
Area Type
tool.

Here are a few handy notes to remember when working with objects filled with text:

- ✔ If the text doesn't fit in the object, a plus icon appears at the bottom of the text. To make all of the text appear, enlarge the object or link it to another object using techniques described in Chapter 14.

- ✔ Filled or stroked objects become unfilled or unstroked after you fill them with text using the Area Type tool. After filling an object with text, however, you can select the object with the Direct Selection tool and then fill or stroke it separately from the text. For more information on filling and stroking, see Chapters 3 and 10.

- ✔ You may want to change the type alignment to Justified to better fit the text into the shape. See Chapter 14 for more information on justifying text.

- ✔ If the object is very small or the type is very big, you may want to enlarge the object or reduce the size of the type. See Chapter 8 for more information on enlarging and reducing objects.

Text on a Roller Coaster

If you're looking for the ultimate type thrill, you'll want to send your text reelin' and rockin' along a roller coaster path, as shown in Figure 15-4. To create this effect, you need to use Illustrator's Path Type tool, which allows you to create type along a curved path. After you create type along a curve, you can click and drag it along the path and flip the type.

Figure 15-4:
Text created
along a
curve with
Illustrator's
Path Type
tool.

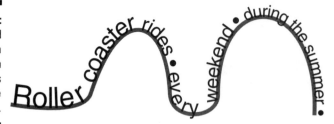

Here's how to create text along a path:

1. **Create a path.**

   If you want the text to appear on a curve, create a curved path using either the Pen tool or Freehand tool. For more information on using the Pen tool, see Chapter 7. For more information on using the Freehand tool, see Chapter 6.

2. **If the path is not selected, select it with the Selection tool.**

 3. **Activate the Path Type tool.**

   After you select the Path Type tool, move the pointer into your document. The mouse pointer changes to the Path Type tool I-beam pointer.

4. **Move the Path Type tool directly over the path as shown in Figure 15-5, and then click the mouse.**

   A blinking cursor appears at the point where you clicked the mouse.

5. **Start typing.**

   As you enter the text, Illustrator places it along the edge of the curve.

Figure 15-5:
Path Type
tool
positioned
over path.

Path Type tool I-beam pointer

When you create text along a path that you already filled or stroked, the path loses the fill or stroke. However, after you create the text along the path, you can select the path with the Direct Selection tool and then fill it or stroke it again.

You can use the Direct Selection tool to adjust the path's shape. When you edit the path, the text adjusts itself according to the shape of the path.

Moving text along a path

After you create the text along a curve, you may want to reposition the text. Fortunately, Illustrator allows you to click and drag the text to its new position. As you click and drag, the text slides along the path as if it were a train gliding along some very smooth railroad tracks. Here's how to put your text in motion:

1. **Click the path with the Selection tool.**

2. **Position the mouse pointer directly over the I-beam that appears in the text.**

3. **Click and drag the mouse.**

   The text moves in the direction that you're dragging.

If you click and drag the text across the path rather than along the path, you'll flip the text upside down. If this happens, double-click the I-beam pointer.

Placing text on the top and bottom of an oval

One of the most common type tricks is to place text around the circumference of an oval. This technique is easily created in Illustrator and is often used to create eye-catching designs and logos, such as the ones in Figure 15-6 and Figure 15-7. To create text along the bottom of the curve (as in Figure 15-7), you can't just start typing text along a circular path. You must first type text along the top of a circular path and then copy and rotate the text and oval 180 degrees to make it appear at the bottom of the curve.

Figure 15-6:
Type
created
along the
top of a
curve.

Figure 15-7:
Type
created
along a
curve, with
the bottom
text copied
and rotated
to appear at
the bottom
of the
image.

To place text at the bottom of an oval, follow these steps:

1. **Use the Oval tool to create an oval.**

   See Chapter 3 for more information on the Oval tool.

2. **If the oval is not selected, select it with the Selection tool.**

3. **Activate the Path Type tool.**

4. **To create the text at the top of the circle, move the Path Type tool to the top of the circle.**

5. **Click the mouse at the top anchor point to create an insertion point.**

   Then choose Type⇨Alignment⇨Center to ensure that your text appears centered at the top of your curve.

6. **Type several words (as on the left of Figure 15-8).**

7. **To create the text at the bottom of the circle, as in the center figure of Figure 15-8, copy the text using the Rotate tool and rotate the text 180 degrees.**

   To do this step, double-click the Rotate tool in the Toolbox. In the Rotate dialog box, set the Rotate angle to 180 degrees and then click Copy. The copied and rotated text now appears at the bottom of the circle; the original text remains at the top.

8. **Select the text by clicking and dragging over the letters with the Path Type tool, and type new text over the duplicated text. As you type the new text, you replace the old text.**

9. **To flip the text, activate the Selection tool; then double-click the I-beam.**

   The text automatically flips inside the circle, as shown on the right of Figure 15-8.

10. **To shift the text below the circle, use the Baseline shift option in the Character palette.**

    To open the Character palette, choose Window⇨Show Character or choose Type⇨Character. Set the Baseline shift to a negative number to make the text appear below the oval. You may have to experiment with different numbers to get the effect you want. If you don't see the Baseline shift field on-screen, click the tiny flag in the lower-right corner of the Character palette.

11. **For the finishing touch, use the Pen tool to create a new graphic or one that you've already prepared in the middle of the circle.**

Figure 15-8:
Type the words at the top of the oval; then copy and rotate the text, and finally double-click the I-beam pointer to flip the text.

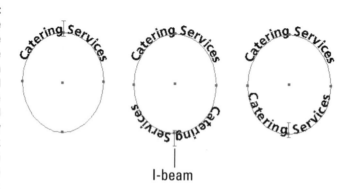

I-beam

Converting Text into Path Outlines

If you want to make your text dance, you can transform type into a team of graphic objects using Illustrator's Create Outlines command. This handy command converts the text into a set of paths that can be edited like any other path. You can click and drag anchor points and direction lines, fill the text with patterns and gradients, and apply more sophisticated effects using blends (see Chapter 17) and masking (see Chapter 18). Figure 15-9 shows a simple example of how you can put a little kick in a few words of text. We converted the word *Can* to a path outline. Because the *n* was converted to a path, its "leg" could be bent up and manipulated. After we manipulated the leg, we used the Brush and Pen tools to create the face and hair. Next, we selected and duplicated the entire image to create the second *Can* in *Can Can*.

Figure 15-9:
Type
changed
into outlines
and then
edited using
the Direct
Selection
tool.

To turn type into a path, all you need to do is select the text using the Selection tool (see Figure 15-10). Then choose Type➪Create Outlines. In a few moments, the type is transformed into a path or series of paths. You can now edit the type by clicking and dragging its anchor points and direction lines with the Direct Selection tool. You also can fill the type with a pattern. Figure 15-11 shows another example of converting type into path outlines. After we converted the type to paths, we filled the type with a pattern. Because the letters were paths, they could also be filled with text using the Area Path tool.

Onward with More Type Effects

Once you convert text to outlines, a whole world of possibilities for type effects opens. You can create multiple-stroked type and gradients in type, and you can even apply various filters to manipulate the type.

Figure 15-10:
Type changed into outlines using the Create Outlines command and then manipulated.

Figure 15-11:
Type changed into outlines and then filled with a pattern. The text inside the letters was created with the Area Path tool.

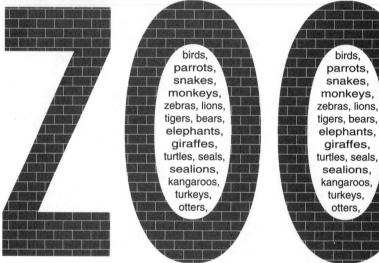

Creating multiple-stroked type

Figure 15-12 shows the word *cruise* created by duplicating the word into different layers and then applying a pattern to the text in one layer and different stroke sizes to the text in other layers. The background image in Figure 5-16 is from Digital Stock™'s *Ocean & Coasts* CD-ROM (image courtesy of Digital Stock™).

Figure 15-12:
Type
converted to
an outline
and then
copied to
different
layers and
stroked.

Here's how to create the effect:

1. **Start by creating some text using the Type tool.**

2. **Select the text with the Selection tool by clicking at the baseline of the text.**

3. **With the text selected, convert the text to outlines by choosing Type⇨Create Outlines.**

4. **Group the text paths by choosing Arrange⇨Group.**

   By converting the text to a group, you can select all the letters with the Group Selection tool and apply a stroke to all the letters.

5. **Copy and paste the grouped text into different layers.**

   For more information about layers, see Chapter 9.

   In each layer, stroke the text with different-size strokes in different colors. The back layer should have the largest stroke, the top layer the thinnest stroke. If desired, you can fill the text in the top layer with either a pattern or a gradient.

Creating 3-D type

Another commonly used, attractive type effect is a gradient in type. Creating a gradient in text can only be accomplished if the text is first converted to outlines. After the text is converted to a path, you can apply a gradient to each text path by selecting each path and choosing a gradient fill from the Paint Style palette (for more information on using the Paint Style palette, see Chapter 10). If you want to edit the gradient, use the Gradient Vector tool (for more information on using the Gradient Vector tool, see Chapter 11). Figure 15-13 shows a gradient created in type with a 3-D effect.

Here's how to create the 3-D text effect. Before you start, convert some text to outlines:

1. **Group the text outlines by selecting each path and then choosing Arrange⇨Group.**

2. **Copy the text paths twice into two different layers, and send the copies behind the original text.**

   You should now have text in three layers. (For more information about layers, see Chapter 9.)

3. **To create the highlight area, slightly offset (drag) one of the duplicated text paths diagonally up to the right and fill it with white.**

4. **To create the shadow area, slightly offset (drag) the other duplicated text paths diagonally down to the left and fill it with black.**

5. **Adjust the text in each layer as desired to control the amount of depth in the 3-D effect.**

Figure 15-13:
Type converted to an outline and then stroked in different layers, with the pattern created in the top layer.

Using Adobe Dimensions to create 3-D type effects

Adobe Dimensions (which is included on the Illustrator 6 CD-ROM) allows you to import any 2-D art created in Illustrator and convert it into 3-D. We created the 2-D text at the left in Figure 15-14 in Illustrator and then imported it into Dimensions, where we extruded it to make it a 3-D wireframe — a wireframe is like a skeleton of a 3-D image, without color or lighting effects. The wireframe was then rendered with a fill, stroke, and lighting. The 3-D rendered text appears on the right of Figure 15-14.

Chapter 20 has more about how to use Illustrator with other programs to create artwork.

Figure 15-14:
2-D type
converted to
outline (left)
and
imported
into
Dimensions
to make it
3-D (right).

Filter fun

Illustrator's plug-in filters allow countless possibilities for creating unusual and fantastic type effects. You can take an in-depth look at filters in the next chapter. To get a taste of what's in that chapter, take a look at the cracked-type effect shown in the bottom image in Figure 15-15.

If you ever need to shatter some text, follow these steps:

1. **Type a word.**
2. **Convert the word to path outlines by selecting it and choosing Type⇨Create Outlines.**
3. **Create a path over the letters using the Freehand tool, as shown in the top image of Figure 15-15.**

4. **To break the text in two, first select the Freehand path and text path outlines; then choose Filter⇨Pathfinder⇨Divide.**

   This step divides the text into two halves.

5. **To split the text, select the bottom half with the Group Selection tool and then drag the selected text away from the other half.**

   You may want to move the text away from the other half using the down-arrow key on your keyboard.

Figure 15-15:
Text effect
created with
the Divide
filter.

a) **EARTHQUAKE**

b) **EARTHQUAKE**

Part IV
More Amazing Illustrator Stuff

The 5th Wave   By Rich Tennant

"This Illustrator color scheme is really going to give our presentation _style_!"

In this part . . .

You'll have lots of fun working in this part. In it, we show you how to use filters to quickly edit and distort objects with the touch of a mouse button. Also, we show you how to create morphing magic with blends and special effects with masks and compound paths. In this part's last chapter, you find out how to transform your artwork into a graph. And you are sure to leave this part with lots of Illustrator tricks up your design sleeve!

Chapter 16

Filter Fun

. . . .

In This Chapter

▶ Using filters

▶ Understanding plug-in filters

▶ Distorting and stylizing objects with filters

▶ Manipulating objects and shapes with filters

▶ Selecting with filters

▶ Adjusting colors with filters

▶ Using third-party filters

. . . .

To most people, a filter is something that they use to make coffee. To the coffee lover, a filter transforms some boring, ground-roasted beans and boiling water into a delicious, savory drink. To the Illustrator user, a *filter* can transform a few boring old paths into attractive and interesting elements in your artwork.

Without filters, the coffee drinker would be out of luck. Without filters, the Illustrator artist couldn't quickly transform paths and create special effects. Fortunately for most Illustrator artists, they can have the best of both worlds: a good cup of coffee and some unique filters that create special effects and save lots of time.

Plugging In to Plug-In Filters

The *plug-in filter* is one of the hottest crazes in the digital-imaging world. It's hot because it can save time and can automatically create unusual special effects. What exactly is a plug-in filter? It's a little program module that sits on your hard disk waiting to be called into action by the main program — in this case, by Illustrator.

Many of the first plug-in filters served to sharpen, add contrast, or change colors in an image. To some degree, they worked in computer programs as camera filters did in photography. But the world of plug-in filters goes far beyond the effects of photographic filters. Illustrator's plug-in filters now allow you to completely change the look of a path. Plug-in filters can distort paths and create new paths from overlapping path areas.

Because filters are separate programs, they must be installed properly for Illustrator to find them. During installation, Illustrator places the plug-in filters in its Plug-ins folder. If you move a filter out of this folder, it doesn't appear in the Filter menu and is not accessible.

Recently, software companies such as MetaTools and Letraset have created their own plug-in filters for use in Illustrator. These filters create neon and 3-D effects. You can purchase the plug-in filters separately and install them on your computer in Illustrator's Plug-ins folder or in another folder that you select. If you install the filters in a folder other than Illustrator's Plug-ins folder, you need to tell Illustrator where to find them. To inform Illustrator of the new location, choose File⇔Preference⇔Plug-ins. In the dialog box that appears, select the folder that contains your plug-in filters.

Using Filters

Although each of Adobe Illustrator's filters creates a different effect, most are consistent and quite simple to use. Before applying a filter, you often select the object or objects that you want the filter to change. Next, you click the Filter menu and choose a filter group. The filter categories are Colors, Create, Distort, Gallery Effects: Classic Art 1, Gallery Effects: Classic Art 2, Gallery Effects: Classic Art 3, Ink Pen, Objects, Pathfinder, Select, and Stylize.

After you select a filter group, a list of individual filters appears on-screen. You can select an individual filter from this list. Often, a dialog box appears providing you with several options for customizing the effect. A few of the filters allow you to see a preview of the filter's effect before it is applied. To see a preview, make sure that the Preview check box in the dialog box is selected.

After you use a filter, its name appears at the top of the Filter menu; this feature lets you reapply the filter easily by choosing its name in this top position. You can also press ⌘+Shift+E to reapply a filter. For instance, after you execute the Pattern on a Path filter by choosing Filter⇔Stylize⇔Path Pattern, you can reapply the filter by simply choosing Filter⇔Path Pattern.

When you run a filter by choosing its name at the top of the Filter menu, the filter's dialog box is bypassed, and the filter effect is immediately applied. If you want to use the filter that appears at the top of the Filter menu but want to open its dialog box first, press Option while choosing the filter name.

If you don't like the effect of a filter, you can reverse the effect by choosing Edit⇨Undo or pressing ⌘+Z. For more information about using the Undo command, see Chapter 3.

Creating Objects with Filters

Some of the easiest filters to use are the Create filters. These filters save you time by automatically creating simple objects. The filters in the Filter⇨Create submenu are Fill & Stroke for Mask, Object Mosaic, and Trim Marks.

The Fill & Stroke for Mask filter creates two objects that can be used as a fill and stroke for a mask. We discuss this filter in Chapter 17.

Creating object mosaics

The Mosaic filter is a filter that allows you to transform PICT images into mosaics. PICT is the standard graphics file format used by the Mac. For more information about PICT images, see Chapters 9 and 20. Figure 16-1 shows an image transformed into a mosaic. The filter works by analyzing the colors in the image and then rearranging similar colors together into tiles so that the image looks like a mosaic.

PICT files can be created in Adobe Photoshop and numerous other painting and illustration programs.

To use the Mosaic filter, choose Filter⇨Create⇨Object Mosaic. A dialog box appears and allows you to choose a PICT file for transformation. After you choose a PICT file, the Object Mosaic dialog box appears, as shown in Figure 16-2. In this dialog box, you can specify the tile size of the mosaic, the spacing between tiles, and the number of tiles. After you click OK, Illustrator creates the Mosaic. Try this feature out for yourself to get an idea of what the options do.

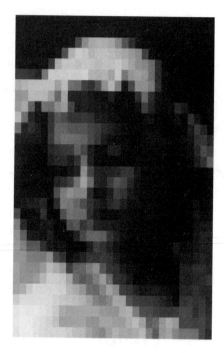

Figure 16-1:
A photograph transformed into a mosaic. Photograph courtesy Boraventures Publishing, *America Remembered* CD-ROM collection.

Figure 16-2:
The Object Mosaic dialog box.

Object Mosaic	
Current Size (pts):	**New Size (pts):**
Width: 242	Width: 0
Height: 382	Height: 0

Use Ratio ● Lock Width ○ Lock Height

Tile Spacing:	**Number of Tiles:**
Width: 100	Width: 30
Height: 100	Height: 30

● Color ○ Gray   ☐ Delete Raster

Cancel   OK

The Trim Marks filter

Starting your own business? One of the first things you need is a set of business cards. Assume that you plan to create business cards on a regular sheet of paper. You want to create *trim marks* around the edges of each card to show where you (or your print shop) should trim the cards. You can create trim marks around several business cards by using the Trim Marks filter.

You may find that the Trim Marks filter is more versatile than Illustrator's Object⇨Cropmarks⇨Make command (as discussed in Chapter 5). The Cropmarks command puts crop marks around the entire page or around one rectangular area. The Trim Marks filter places trim marks around a selected object — and you can create the trim marks around several objects on a page.

To use the Trim Marks command, simply select an object and then choose Filter⇨ Create⇨Trim Marks. Illustrator creates the trim marks at the edges of an imaginary rectangle surrounding the *imageable* or printable area of the object. Figure 16-3 shows a business card with trim marks around it. If you create cards in Illustrator and want to create a set of trim marks around each individual card, select each card and then apply the filter to each individual card.

Figure 16-3: Trim marks around a business card.

Distorting Objects

The Distort filters — Free Distort, Punk, Bloat, Roughen, Scribble, Tweak, Twirl, and Zig Zag — allow you to create unusual shapes out of simple objects and text. You may think that filters called *distort* would be used to create only grotesque objects. If you're looking for the grotesque, you're better off using a program like Elastic Reality. Illustrator generally uses the Distort filters to create unusual and intricate shapes and text effects that would normally be quite time consuming to create by hand. Figure 16-4 shows examples of each of the Distort filters.

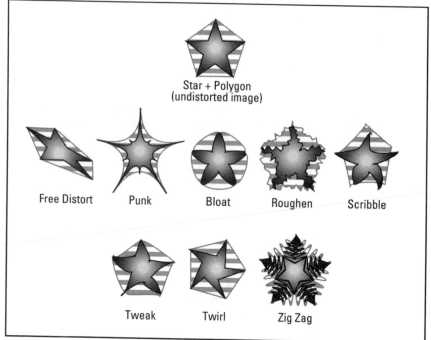

Figure 16-4:
Examples of
the applied
Distort
filters.

Using Free Distort to create perspective

You can use the Free Distort filter to create a variety of special effects. The Free Distort filter can change the size and the shape of an object. You can also use it to create perspective, as shown in Figure 16-5. To use the Free Distort filter, select the object or objects and choose Filter⇨Distort⇨Free Distort. In the Free Distort dialog box (shown in Figure 16-6), a rectangle surrounds your object. Click and drag any of the corner points to create the distortion; then click OK.

Figure 16-5:
Text before
and after
using the
Free Distort
filter.

Figure 16-6:
The Free
Distort
dialog box.

Punking and bloating

You may think that a Punk filter would shave the head of your path, stick earrings on its direction lines, and paint its anchor points purple. In actuality, creating a punk look in Illustrator means shifting anchor points to make them look jagged.

To use the Punk filter, select the object to be punked and choose Filter⇨Distort⇨ Punk and Bloat. In the Punk and Bloat dialog box, drag the slider to the left to create a punk effect. As you drag, negative numbers appear in the percentage field. The further left you drag, the greater the punk (jagged) effect. If you want, you can also enter a value into the percentage field in the dialog box. To create the greatest Punk effect, enter –200.

If you drag the slider in the Punk and Bloat dialog box to the right, you bloat an object. Bloating expands a shape as if it were a balloon that you huffed and puffed into. The further right you drag the slider, the greater the bloat effect and the greater the object is distorted. To create the greatest Bloat effect, enter 200 into the dialog box's percentage field. To see a preview of the effect before applying the filter, make sure that the Preview check box in the filter's dialog box is selected.

Using the Roughen, Scribble, and Tweak filters

The Roughen filter roughs up your art work. The Roughen filter distorts a path by adding anchor points and creating jagged edges in the original path. When you run the filter, a dialog box appears allowing you to set the size and whether the edges are smooth or sharp. To learn how the filter works, experiment with different settings, with the Preview check box selected.

The Scribble and Tweak filters are two filters in one dialog box. The Scribble filter turns text or objects into scribbles by randomly moving anchor points away from the selected object. Now, you are probably saying to yourself, "Why would I want to transform my art into scribbles?" Good question. You probably wouldn't unless you want to create a random look in your illustrations. You have to wonder, "When is Adobe going to come out with a Perfection filter that turns scribbles and rough sketches into perfect artwork?"

The Tweak filter is handy if you want to fine-tune your artwork. It works by incrementally moving anchor points on selected objects. Although you can use the Tweak filter to fine-tune the placement of anchor points, you can also use it to distort and twist paths.

To apply the Scribble or Tweak filter, select an object and then choose Filter⇨Distort⇨Scribble and Tweak. The Scribble and Tweak dialog box allows you to choose whether you want to Scribble or Tweak. After choosing Scribble or Tweak, you can adjust the Horizontal or Vertical sliders to vary the effect. To see a preview of the effect before applying the filter, make sure to select the Preview check box in the filter's dialog box.

Spinning an object with the Twirl filter

If you want to take an object out for a spin, try out the Twirl filter. The Twirl filter is one of your best choices for putting a twist into type, as shown in Figure 16-7.

If you're going to twirl some type, remember to select the type and convert it to paths before applying the filter. To convert type to paths, choose Type⇨Create Outlines.

Figure 16-7:
Type twirled with the Twirl filter.

Twirl

Step 1

| Twirl |
| Angle: 70 ° |
| Cancel | OK |

Step 2

Twirl

Step 3

Here's how to use the Twirl filter:

1. **Select the object to be twirled.**

2. **Choose Filter⇨Distort⇨Twirl.**

3. **In the Twirl dialog box, enter a value in the Twirl Angle field and click OK.**

    The value range for the Twirl Angle field is –4000 to 4000. Negative numbers move the twirl to the left; positive numbers move the twirl to the right.

You can apply the Add Anchor Points filter (see "Adding anchor points" later in this chapter) to an object and then apply the Twirl filter for a more dramatic effect.

Adding a Touch of Style

The Stylize filters can change the style of paths in your illustration. Unfortunately, you find no Stylize filters called *elegant, refined,* or *polished.* Illustrator's styles are a bit more mundane. To Illustrator, stylizing paths can mean adding arrowheads, creating drop shadows, and rounding corners. The Stylize filter options include Add Arrowheads, Calligraphy, Drop Shadow, Path Pattern, and Round Corners. Figure 16-8 shows examples of some of the various Stylize filters.

Figure 16-8:
Examples of applied Stylize filters.

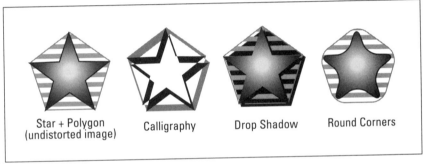

Star + Polygon (undistorted image)   Calligraphy   Drop Shadow   Round Corners

"I shot an arrow into the air . . . "

If you ever need to direct attention to a specific area in your illustration, you may want to create arrows that point to that area. But there's no point in trying to create arrowheads yourself; just let Illustrator's Add Arrowheads do it for you. Figure 16-9 shows some arrowheads that Illustrator can create. Here's how you can add an arrowhead to a line:

1. **Select the open path(s) that you want to add an arrowhead or arrow tail to.**

2. **Choose Filter⊅Stylize⊅Add Arrowheads.**

3. **Choose the type of arrowhead by clicking one of the pointing-hand buttons.**

   Each time you click, a new arrow type appears.

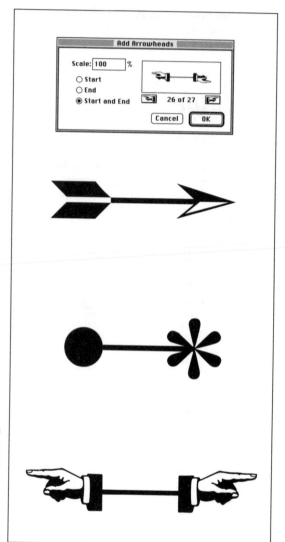

Figure 16-9:
Arrows
created with
the Add
Arrowheads
filter.

4. **Choose whether you want the arrowheads at the start, at the end, or at the start *and* end of the path.**

   If you create a path from left to right, the start of the path is on the right. If you create a path from right to left, the start of the path is on the left.

5. **Make the arrowhead larger or smaller by entering a value in the Scale field.**

   If you leave the Scale value set to 100%, the arrowhead appears as its default size. If you enter 200%, the arrowhead becomes twice the default size.

If you want to create a path with one type of arrowhead at the start of the path and a different arrowhead at the back of the path, you must apply the filter twice. Apply it once to create an arrowhead at one end of the path; apply the filter again to place the different arrowhead at the other end of the path.

Creating calligraphy

The Calligraphy filter can make an object look as if it were created with a calligraphy pen. To use the Calligraphy filter, select a path and then choose Filter➪Stylize➪Calligraphy. You can control the calligraphic effect by entering a value into the Pen Width field of the Calligraphy dialog box. Also, you can change the angle of the calligraphic stroke by changing the value in the Pen Angle field.

Dropping a few shadows

Creating a drop shadow is one of the most frequently used (and possibly most overused) techniques for adding depth and 3-D effects to an image. Illustrator's Drop Shadow filter is undoubtedly the easiest way to accomplish this task. The Drop Shadow filter automatically duplicates an object and allows you to manipulate the duplicate. That is, you can darken the duplicate, and you can offset the duplicate by moving it up, down, left, or right. Figure 16-10 shows the effect of the Drop Shadow filter when you apply it to text.

You must convert the text to paths with the Type➪Create Outlines command before you can apply the Drop Shadow filter to text.

Here's how you can create a drop shadow:

Figure 16-10:
Drop
shadow
created with
the Drop
Shadow
filter.

1. **Select the object that you want to apply the filter to.**

2. **Choose Filter➪Stylize➪Drop Shadow.**

3. **In the Drop Shadow dialog box, type values into the X Offset and Y Offset fields to specify the shadow's distance from the original image.**

When you enter a positive value in the X Offset field, you move the shadow to the right; entering a negative value moves the shadow to the left. When you enter a positive value in the Y Offset field, you move the shadow downward; entering a negative value moves the shadow upward.

4. **Enter a value in the Darker field to control the shadow's level of darkness.**

Entering a higher value makes a darker shadow; entering **100** produces a black shadow, and entering **0** produces a shadow that is the same color of the original object.

5. **Click OK to apply the drop shadow.**

Putting patterns on paths

You can put Illustrator's patterns, or those that you create, along a path by using the Filter⇨Stylize⇨Path Pattern command. For more information on creating patterns and using the Path Pattern command, see Chapter 12.

Rounding up those corners

The Round Corners filter takes an object's corner points and rounds them. You can turn any corner point into a rounded corner, regardless of the tool that you used to create the object.

To use the Round Corners filter, select the object or objects that you want to round and choose Filter⇨Stylize⇨Round Corners. In the Round Corners dialog box, you can enter a Radius value to set how round you want the corner to be. The larger the number, the greater the rounding effect. For information on creating rounded rectangles using the Rounded Rectangle tool, see Chapter 3.

Using the Ink Pen Filter

The Ink Pen filter allows you to fill objects to make them look as though they were created with an ink pen. The Ink Pen filter is especially good at creating old time pen and ink drawing effects where the strokes are created from very thin lines drawn very close together. This drawing technique is often referred to as *hatching* and is frequently used to create variations in light and shading. The Ink Pen filter can even create pen patterns that make images appear as if they were filled with grass or wood.

When the Ink Pen filter is applied, it creates the effect of filling an object with pen strokes by transforming the selected object into a mask and placing the lines behind the mask. For more information about masks, see Chapter 18.

Using the Ink Pen Effects dialog box

Here are the steps for filling a selected object using the Ink Pen filter:

1. **Select the objects or objects that you wish to fill with the Ink Pen filter.**

2. **Choose Filter⇨Ink Pen⇨Effects.**

This opens the Ink Pen Effects dialog box, shown in Figure 16-11. Looking at the dialog box, which may be the largest dialog box in all of Illustrator, you may be somewhat alarmed and think that using the Ink Pen filter requires hours of study and contemplation. Fortunately, you can figure out what most of the options do by simply clicking and dragging the sliders, making choices from the pop-up menus, and then viewing the preview box that appears towards the top of the dialog box (make sure that the Preview check box is selected).

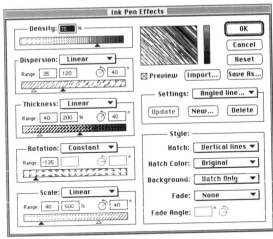

Figure 16-11: The Ink Pen Effects dialog box.

For instance, clicking and dragging the Density slider to the right makes the hatching pattern more dense. You can figure out how dense the slider adjustment is going to be by simply looking at the pattern that appears in the Density slider and watching how the change integrates with the other options in the Preview area of the dialog box. To vary the type of hatching pattern, click in the Settings pop-up menu.

After you've made adjustments in the Ink Pen Effects dialog box, click OK. The selected objects on-screen are filled with the pattern that was previewed in the dialog box.

Creating and editing hatch styles

If you really get excited about using the Ink Pen filter, you may want to create your own hatch style out of objects you create in Illustrator or edit existing hatch styles.

Here's how to create a hatch style:

1. **Create and select an object that you want to use as a hatch style.**

2. **Choose Filter⇨Stylize⇨Ink Pen⇨Edit.**

3. **In the Ink Pen Edit dialog box, choose New. Name the hatching pattern if you want and click OK to close the Hatch Name dialog box.**

4. **If you want to save your hatch style so it can be used in other documents, click Save As to save the hatch file to your hard drive. (You may want to create a Hatch folder in which to save all of your hatch files.)**

5. **Click OK to close the Ink Pen Edit dialog box**

To edit a preexisting hatch style, select a style from the Hatch pop-up menu in the Ink Pen Edit dialog box. Then click Paste to paste the hatching pattern into your document. To close the Ink Pen Edit dialog box, click OK. Now you can edit the hatching pattern and follow the steps above to name and save the edited hatching pattern.

Adjusting Objects Using the Objects Filters

The filters in the Objects submenu allow you to manipulate objects and shapes. These filters are Add Anchor Points, Clean up, Offset Path, and Outline Path.

Adding anchor points

The Add Anchor Points filter places a new anchor point between every two existing anchor points. It is often helpful to use this filter before you apply the Bloat, Punk, and Twirl filters. To use the filter, select your object and choose Filter⇨Objects⇨Add Anchor Points. For information on adding anchor points using the Add Anchor Point tool, see Chapter 7.

Cleaning up

The Clean Up filter allows you to clean up paths on-screen. When you choose the filter, a dialog box appears in which you can delete stray points (extra anchor points that you inadvertently create), delete unpainted objects and/or delete empty text paths. (An empty text path is a path created with the Type, Area Type, and Path Type tools that doesn't have any text on or in it.)

Offsetting a path

The Offset Path filter allows you to copy a path and create the copy at a specific distance from the original path. You can use the Offset Path filter to help you create 3-D effects such as beveled buttons for multimedia presentations.

To use the Offset Path filter, select the object or objects that you want to offset and choose Filter⇨Objects⇨Offset Path. In the resulting dialog box, enter the *offset distance* in points. The offset distance is the distance between the original path and the copy. Use the Line Join pop-up menu to choose a line join and to set the point size for the miter limit. See Chapter 6 for more information about line joins and miter limits.

Outlining a path

The Outline Path filter turns the stroke of a path into a filled, closed path. This filter can be handy if you want to replace a stroke with a pattern or fill. Figure 16-12 shows an example of the effect that you can produce with this filter. To create this effect, convert the type to paths (using Type⇨Create Outlines) and then stroke the paths. Next, apply the Outline Path filter to replace the stroked area with a closed path. To finish the look, fill the closed paths with a pattern. To do this, you need to first deselect the original path, select the new outline (surrounding the original path), and then fill it with a pattern.

Figure 16-12:
Text effect
created with
the Outline
Path filter.

Custom
Wallpaper

Because the Outline Path filter creates a filled path out of a stroke, it also is helpful when you trap artwork. See Chapter 21 for a discussion of *trapping*.

Manipulating Objects Using the Pathfinder Filters

The Pathfinder filters conjure up the romantic notion of western scouts hunting in the great outdoors. In actuality, the Pathfinder filters are more like *path modifiers* than *pathfinders*. Most of these filters follow the edge of a path and then change it depending upon the shape or color of overlapping objects. The filters can save you a lot of time when you need to add to or subtract objects from a path. In many instances, these filters can eliminate the need for cutting up paths using the Scissors and Knife tools.

The filters in the Pathfinder submenu, as shown in Figure 16-13, are Unite, Intersect, Exclude, Minus Front, Minus Back, Divide, Outline, Trim, Merge, Crop, Hard, Soft, and Trap. The icons in the Pathfinder submenu give you a preview of what happens when you apply each filter.

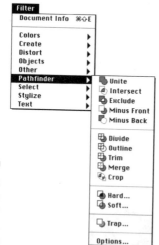

Figure 16-13:
The Pathfinder submenu.

Unite filter

The Unite filter unites all selected objects into one path. To create the united path, the filter makes one path along the outside edge of all selected objects and ignores the inside parts.

You can use the Unite filter to create a new path from overlapping paths. A simple example appears in Figure 16-14 and shows two overlapping paths automatically combined into one. In this example, the filter united an oval and a rectangle.

Figure 16-14:
An object
created
using the
Unite filter.

Intersect filter

The Intersect filter creates a single path from overlapping areas of all selected paths. When the final path is created, non-overlapping areas are deleted.

Exclude filter

The effect of the Exclude filter produces the opposite of the Intersect filter's effect. The Exclude filter creates a path from the area of selected objects that do not overlap. The overlapping areas become transparent. When you make a new path from overlapping paths with the Exclude filter, Illustrator creates a compound path. A *compound path* is a path created from two or more paths, with overlapping areas becoming transparent. For more information on compound paths, see Chapter 18.

Minus Front and Minus Back filters

If you subtract your back from your front, you'll probably end up with a pretty odd shape. If you subtract the back from the front of a path in Illustrator, you can create some pretty nifty designs that would otherwise be quite time consuming to create.

If you apply the Minus Front filter, Illustrator traces over the back-most object in a stack of objects. When it creates the new path, the filter subtracts the shapes of the objects in front of the back object. The areas in front of the back disappear. Any areas of the back object that are covered by the objects in front are deleted. If all of this sounds complicated, think of all of the front objects in a stack of objects combining together to form a magic cookie cutter that slices through all paths. After the cookie-cutter cuts, a hole in the shape of the cookie cutter is seen through all of the objects.

The effect of the Minus Back filter is the opposite of the Minus Front filter's effect. When you apply the Minus Back filter, the front-most object in a stack becomes the basis for the new path. The shapes of all objects in back of the front object are subtracted from the front path. The objects in back disappear, along with any areas of the front object that cover the objects in back.

To create the stamp in Figure 16-15, we used the Minus Front, Exclude, and Free Distort filters. We started by applying the Minus Front filter to the rectangle with overlapping ovals in Step 1 to create the stamp shape in Step 2. In Step 3,

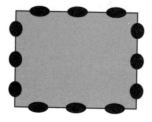

Step 1

Figure 16-15:
Image
created
using the
Minus Front,
Exclude, and
Free Distort
filters.

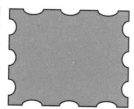

Step 2

Step 3

we selected the words *Art Fair* and the black paint and applied the Exclude filter to create the transparent area. We applied the Free Distort filter to the Union Square text to finish the stamp.

Divide filter

Using the Divide filter, you can divide an object into different segments to create interesting effects. Figure 16-16 gives you an idea of what you can do with the Divide Filter. To create the target shown on the right in Figure 16-16, you need to complete several steps. First, create the lines through the original circle object, as shown on the left. Select the lines and the circle and then apply the Divide filter to use these lines to create the separate paths (the lines themselves disappear when you apply the filter).

Select the separate paths with the Group Selection tool, and alternately fill them with white and black to create the target area. Next, duplicate and scale the original circle. Give the new circles different fills and strokes. Add the arrow by using the Add Arrowheads filter. Apply the text to the curve with the Path Type tool, and you're done.

Figure 16-16:
Image
before and
after
applying the
Divide and
Add
Arrowheads
filters and
text.

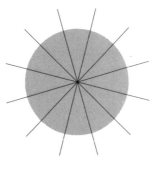

You can also apply the Divide filter to overlapping objects, to separate the overlapping areas and create separate closed paths. Figure 16-17 shows an example of applying the Divide filter to text paths.

Before applying the filter to the word *Type* in Figure 16-17, you must convert it to paths by using the Type⇨Create Outlines command.

Outlining with a filter

The Outline filter allows you to convert *filled* paths to *stroked* paths. It works similarly to the Divide filter. When you select overlapping closed paths, the Outline filter divides the overlapping areas into new open path segments and strokes the paths with the fill color. This effect is shown in Step 2 of Figure 16-18. After applying the filter, you can use the Group Selection tool to select different line segments and stroke them with different colors, as shown in Figure 16-18, Step 3.

Merging and trimming

The Merge and Trim filters remove the hidden (or underlying) portions of overlapping paths. The difference between the two filters is based on the colors of the overlapping or adjoining object. The Merge filter creates one merged path out of overlapping paths when overlapping or adjoining paths are the same color. If you apply the Trim filter instead, the paths are not merged into one path if the overlapping colors are the same. Nevertheless, Trim still removes the hidden portion of overlapping paths.

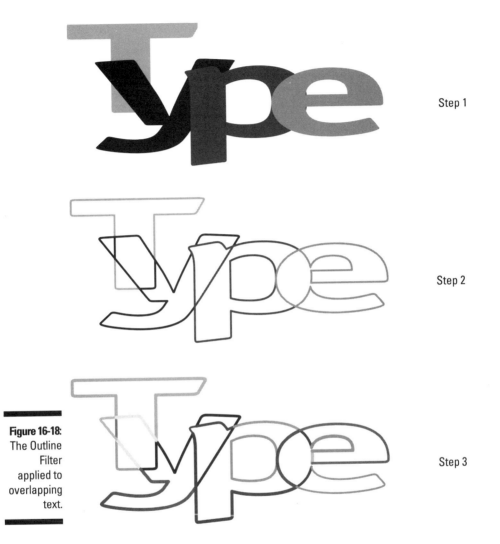

Step 1

Step 2

Figure 16-18:
The Outline
Filter
applied to
overlapping
text.

Step 3

Crop filter

The Crop filter is like a cookie cutter for paths. When you apply the filter, the topmost object cuts out and deletes objects that fall outside its boundaries. To use the Crop filter, create an object to serve as your cookie cutter and position it over another object or objects (the objects that you want to crop). Next, choose Filter⇨Object⇨Crop. The paths underneath are cut out by the top object (which acts just like a cookie cutter). Any areas outside the boundary of the cookie cutter object are deleted.

Hard and Soft filters

The Hard and Soft filters have nothing to do with how hard or soft anything is. The Hard filter produces a color that is often called the *overprint color,* the result of mixing one process color over another process color. When Illustrator mixes the colors, it uses the darker of each CYMK component to create the new color. For more information about CMYK colors, see Chapter 10.

The Soft filter lets you control the transparency of colors that overlap each other. You can specify just how transparent the final color will be by entering a Mixing Rate percentage in the Soft filter's dialog box. Enter a high number for a more transparent effect; enter a low number to create a less transparent effect.

Trap filter

The Trap filter helps you change paths to adjust for *color gaps* that can occur when artwork is printed on a printing press. The color gaps occur because of registration problems on the press. See Chapter 21 for a discussion of the Trap filter and color separations.

Selecting with Filters

The Select filters, Select Inverse and Select Masks, can perform handy selection tricks. The Select Inverse filter selects all objects that are not selected and leaves the selected objects deselected. The Select Masks filter selects the objects that a mask is created from.

Adjusting Colors with Filters

The filters in the Colors submenu — Adjust Colors, Blend Front to Back, Blend Horizontally, Blend Vertically, Invert Colors, Overprint Black, and Saturate — let you quickly change the colors of objects on-screen.

Illustrator applies all but one of these filters automatically when you choose the filter. The exception is the Adjust Colors filter, which lets you specify the color adjustment before you apply the filter. When you choose the Adjust Colors filter, a dialog box appears. To add more of a color, drag any one of the Cyan, Magenta, Yellow, and Black sliders to the right. To subtract a color, drag any of the sliders to the left. Make sure to click the Preview button to see a preview before applying the filter.

Here are some points to be aware of when using the Colors filters:

✔ The Adjust Colors, Invert Colors, Blend Horizontally, and Blend Vertically filters affect only process color fills. Process color fills are created from cyan, magenta, yellow, and black color components. See Chapter 10 for more information about process colors.

✔ To apply the Blend Front to Back, Blend Horizontally, and Blend Vertically filters, you must select at least three paths. All other filters work when you have one path or more selected.

✔ The Blend Front to Back filter is the only one that works when you have a pattern in a path.

✔ The Overprint Black filter allows you to overprint black fills and strokes or remove overprinting from fills or strokes. For more information on over-printing see Chapter 21.

Using the Gallery Effects Filters

The Gallery Effects filters create painterly effects out of your artwork. You can create spatter, fresco, pastel, and Japanese brush stroke effects. Each Gallery Effects filter includes a preview window. This means that you can easily learn how to use each filter by adjusting the filter's dialog box options and clicking the Preview button.

Each of the filters was originally created to work with Adobe Photoshop, not Illustrator. You might be wondering, then, what filters created for Photoshop are doing in a drawing program. They appear in Illustrator because Illustrator 6 allows you to convert your vector images into bitmap images by using the Object⇨Rasterize command (how to use the Rasterize command is discussed in the next section). Once you convert the image, your objects are no longer based on mathematical formulas but upon how many pixels per inch are in the image. (A pixel is the smallest image element in a bitmap image. See Chapter 1 for more information about the difference between Vector and Bitmap — also called *raster* images.)

Once you rasterize an image, you can run a Gallery Effects filter by selecting the object or objects you want to apply the filter to and then choosing a Gallery Effects filter from the Filter⇨Gallery Effects submenu.

You can also apply Gallery Effects filters to images that have been dragged and dropped from Photoshop, and TIFF images that have been loaded into Illustrator using the File⇨Place command. (TIFF is a standard file format used when saving digitized images that have been scanned or digitized using Digital cameras.) For more information about the File⇨Place command, see Chapter 9. For more information about dragging and dropping files from Photoshop, see Chapter 3.

You can copy the filters that come with Photoshop into Illustrator's Plug-in folder and use them in Illustrator with rasterized images, placed Tiff images, or images dragged and dropped from Photoshop. You can also purchase filters created for Photoshop and apply them in Illustrator to rasterized, placed Tiff images or images dragged and dropped from Photoshop. Some of the Photoshop compatible filters you can purchase are Andromeda Software Series 1 and 2, Alien Skin Black Box, Xaos Tools Paint Alchemy and Terrazzo, MicroFrontier Pattern Workshop, Virtus' Alien Skin Textureshop, MetaTools Kai's Power Tools, MetaTools Convolver, Knoll Software CyberMesh, and Human Software Squizz. To be able to access these filters in Illustrator, you must copy them into Illustrator's Plug-in folder.

Rasterizing Images

To transform your Illustrator images into a bitmap or raster image, you must execute the Rasterize command. Here's how to do it.

1. **Select the image that you want to Rasterize.**

2. **Choose Object⇨Rasterize.**

3. **Choose a color model from the Color Model pop-up menu.**

   - Choose RGB to create a color image created by mixing Red, Green, and Blue color components. Choose this option if you are outputting images to slides or for screen presentations.

   - Choose CMYK to create color images that will be printed using cyan, magenta, yellow, and black inks.

   - Choose Grayscale for noncolor images that must display shades of gray.

   - Choose Bitmap for black and white images.

4. **Choose a Resolution. An image's resolution specifies how many pixels per inch (sometimes measured in dots per inch) make up the image.**

   - Choose Screen for images that will be seen only on computer screens. For print production, choose Medium or High. Medium rasterizes images at 150 dpi. High rasterizes images at 300 dpi.

   - Choose Other to enter a custom resolution, and enter the number into the Other field.

5. **Select the Anti-Alias check box to smooth the edges of your image.**

6. **Select the Create Mask check box to create a mask. This option creates a transparent background for your image.**

   If you don't choose this option, Illustrator creates a bounding box around your image filled with white.

Third-Party Filters

If you just can't get enough of using filters, you'll be happy to know that several companies sell Illustrator-compatible filters. Like Illustrator's own filters, the third-party filters can help you create special effects and speed up tedious path-creation chores. Some of the better-known third-party filters are MetaTools KPT Vector Effects, Letraset Envelopes, and BeInfinite FX.

The KPT Vector Effects package includes over a dozen filters that can create some dynamic effects. For instance, the KPT 3D Transform filter changes paths into 3-D objects. The KPT ShatterBox makes your path look as though it were created out of shattered glass. KPT Flare creates lens flare effects, and KPT Shadow creates a variety of shadow effects, including Halos and Zooming shadows. Figure 16-19 shows the dialog boxes and related effects for the ShatterBox, Neon, and 3D Transform filters.

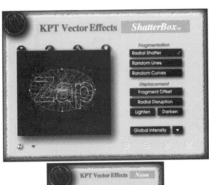

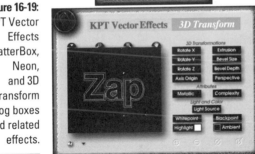

Figure 16-19:
KPT Vector Effects ShatterBox, Neon, and 3D Transform dialog boxes and related effects.

Letraset's Envelopes have nothing to do with mailing letters or even mailing labels. These filters alter a path. They are especially helpful when working with type. Figure 16-20 shows two dialog boxes and related filter effects.

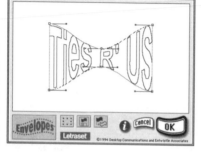

Figure 16-20:
Letraset's
Envelopes
dialog boxes
and effects.

BeInfinite FX allows you to rotate paths and create shears, bends, twists, and tapers in your paths. Figure 16-21 shows a star being transformed using BeInfinite FX's TCB filter.

Now that you've seen all the powerful things that filters can do for you, take some time to experiment with the different options that they provide. You'll soon find that they open up a new world of artistic possibilities for you.

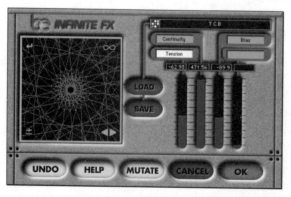

Figure 16-21:
Altering a
star by using
BeInfinite
FX's TCB
filter.

Chapter 17

The Perfect Blend

- -

In This Chapter

▶ Working with blends

▶ Blending two lines

▶ Calculating blend steps

▶ Blending two shapes

▶ Editing blends

▶ Morphing objects

- -

*W*ith Illustrator, it's easy to generate "ooh"s and "aah"s without breaking into a sweat. Pretty soon, everyone thinks that you're a genius. Little do these folks know that some intricate-looking effects are actually simple to perform. One Illustrator tool that can help you get started in the important realm of impressing your friends and colleagues is the Blend tool. Using the Blend tool, you can create objects that look quite intricate. People will ask, "How did you do that?" Only you'll know that, with the help of the Blend tool, the great effect took just a few clicks of the mouse.

Putting It into the Blender

The Blend tool creates effects by gradually transforming one path into another. This feature lets you create smooth transitions between the colors and shapes of two different paths. If you want to create a transitional effect that not only changes color but also changes shape, use the Blend tool.

For example, you can use the Blend tool to create the flower and the collar area below the flower, as shown in Figure 17-1. The flower is the result of blending dark and light spirals. The stems and leaves are later additions. Creating this spiral blend effect is covered later in the chapter.

Figure 17-1:
Flower
created with
the Blend
tool.

Creating simple blends

The simplest way to get started using the Blend tool is to create a transition between two paths that have the same size and shape. When you create a blend between two similar paths, the effect is comparable to that created by the Gradient Fill option in the Paint Style palette. Here are steps that you can use to create a simple blend:

1. **Use the Pen tool to create a line. Stroke the line, but don't fill it.**

   For more information about stroking objects, see Chapters 3 and 10.

2. **Activate the Selection tool; then press and hold down the Option key while you click and drag the line.**

   As you drag, a copy of the line appears (because you have the Option key pressed). Drag the line a few inches away from the first line. Stroke the second line with another color, but don't fill it, as shown at the top of Figure 17-2.

3. **Select the lines by clicking and dragging over both lines with the Selection tool — or select one line and then Shift+click to select the second.**

4. **Select the Blend tool in the Toolbox.**

5. **With the Blend tool, click one anchor point of the first line and then click the corresponding anchor point on the second line.**

   In other words, if you clicked the top anchor point of the first line, click the top anchor point of the second line.

6. **When the Blend dialog box appears, click OK.**

Don't worry about any of the dialog box settings; the section "Calculating blend steps" explains these later in the chapter. If you're in Preview mode, you see the blend on-screen, as shown in the middle of Figure 17-2. If you're in Artwork mode, press ⌘+Y to switch to Preview mode. While in Preview mode, you can get a better look at the blend by pressing ⌘+Shift+H to temporarily hide the selection edge lines and anchor points.

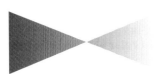

Figure 17-2:
Two lines
converted
into a blend.

What happens if you don't select two corresponding points when using the Blend tool? Your blend could look like the bow-tie shape shown at the bottom of Figure 17-2. This bottom blend is the result of clicking the left anchor point on the top of one line and the right anchor point on the bottom of the other line. If you don't want the bow-tie effect, click the corresponding anchor points (like the tops of both lines), as described in Step 5.

Now that you've created a simple blend, here are a few rules to remember when using blends:

✔ You can't blend more than two objects together. You can, however, create sophisticated effects by blending between two objects in a group, then two more objects in a group, and so on.

✔ The two paths that you blend must both be open or both be closed. You can't create a blend between an open and a closed path.

✔ You can't create a blend between two objects that have different patterns.

✔ If you create a blend between a path filled with a process color and one filled with a custom color, the blend is created with the process color.

Creating color gradations is handled best by Gradient fills, which are less complex than color transitions created with the Blend tool. (Gradient fills are discussed in Chapter 11.) However, if you need to create a spiral shape that exhibits color gradations around the spiral, use the Blend tool. When you work, the Blend tool can create gradations as it creates the spiral.

Performing blend tricks

The Blend tool is most valuable for creating shapes and color transitions. After you know the basics of using the Blend tool, you can start experimenting with different objects to create your own special, remarkable effects. Often, you can achieve exotic effects by simply creating two similarly shaped paths at different sizes. Try the following steps to create a vortex shape, as shown on the right of Figure 17-3, from two spiral shapes. The vortex is the basis of the flower in Figure 17-1.

1. **Use the Spiral plug-in tool in the Plug-ins palette to create a spiral shape, and then stroke the spiral with a light color — with no fill.**

2. **Double-click the Scale tool. In the Scale dialog box, shrink the spiral unproportionally and click Copy to copy it. Stroke the copied spiral with a dark color — with no fill.**

3. **Select and use the Rotate tool to align the two spirals, as shown on the left of Figure 17-3.**

   The Scale and Rotate tool are discussed in Chapter 8.

4. **Select both spiral paths.**

5. **Activate the Blend tool.**

6. **With the Blend tool active, click the center anchor point of the dark spiral and then click the center point of the light spiral.**

7. **When you see the Blend dialog box, leave the value that is in the Steps field or enter a larger value; then click OK.**

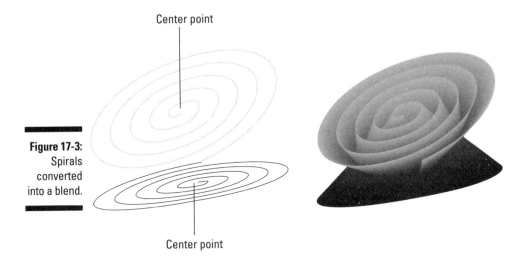

Center point

Figure 17-3:
Spirals
converted
into a blend.

Center point

Calculating blend steps

When Illustrator creates a blend, it gradually changes one path into another. The gradual transition is divided into segments called *steps*. After you begin to create a blend, Illustrator calculates the exact number of steps needed to create a good-looking blend. You see the calculated number of steps in the Blend dialog box. You may or may not need to change this setting. Read on for more information about the Blend dialog box, shown in Figure 17-4.

Figure 17-4:
The Blend
dialog box.

In the Blend dialog box, Illustrator suggests a number of steps for the transition between paths and displays the percentage change shown by the first and last steps. The numbers can be a bit confusing until you understand one important printing fact: The maximum number of gray levels between white and black is 256. On a high-resolution printer called an *imagesetter,* 256 is the highest possible number of gray levels.

Thus, if you start with pure white and end with pure black, the Steps field reads 254 (where 254, plus one for black and one for white, equals 256). If you start with 75 percent black and blend to 100 percent white, the Steps field shows 75 percent of 254; if you start with 50 percent black and blend to 100 percent white, the Steps field shows 50 percent of 254; if you start with 25 percent black — and so on.

If you decide to change the number of steps in a blend, Illustrator recalculates the percentages accordingly. For instance, if you are blending between 100% white and black, and change the number of steps to 1, Illustrator recalculates the First and Last fields each to 50 percent. When you produce the blend, Illustrator creates one object 50 percent black, halfway between the two original selected objects. If you had entered 9 in the Steps field in the Blend dialog box, Illustrator would have changed the First field to 10 percent and the Last field to 90 percent. When you produced the blend, Illustrator would have created nine steps, each step would appear as a separate object evenly distributed on-screen. There would be a 10 percent difference between the original selected object and the first step of the blend, and there would be a 10 percent difference between each subsequent step of the blend.

If you need to create several copies of the same object the same distance from one another, create a blend between the two objects. In the Blend dialog box, enter the number of new objects you want created into the Steps field.

If you print on a high-resolution printer, you have 256 possible shades of gray at your disposal. What if you aren't printing on a high-resolution printer? You can calculate the number of gray shades that your printer can handle with this complicated formula:

```
(dpi [dots per inch] ÷ screen frequency)²
```

Most 300 dpi lasers print at a screen frequency of 53 lines per inch. Thus, the number of gray shades output on most 300 dpi laser printers is 25 or $(300 ÷ 53)^2$.

Morphing Magic

One of the best tricks that Illustrator has up its blending sleeve is its capability to *morph* (or gradually change) one shape into another. Despite the morphing power of the Blend tool, don't expect your Illustrator handiwork to match the latest MTV rock video or Terminator movie. Illustrator's morphing capabilities are confined to transforming one simple, recognizable object into another.

Figure 17-5 shows examples of Illustrator's morphing capabilities: A duck blends into a sheep from left to right, and a camel morphs into a horse from right to left. Here's how you can use the Blend tool to morph one object into another:

Figure 17-5: Morph effects.

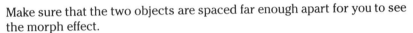

1. **Create the first object, and use it as the beginning of your morph effect.**

2. **Create the second object, which becomes the endpoint of your morph effect.**

   Make sure that the two objects are spaced far enough apart for you to see the morph effect.

3. **With the Selection tool, select both objects by clicking and dragging over them both or by selecting one and then Shift+clicking to select the other.**

4. **Click one point on the first object that is the base of the morph effect. Then click a corresponding point on the second object.**

   After your second click, Illustrator opens the Blend dialog box. For the examples shown in Figure 17-5, you can click the back leg of the camel and the back leg of the horse or the back part of the duck and the back part of the sheep.

5. **In the Steps field of the Blend dialog box, enter the number of transitional objects that you want to appear between your two shapes.**

6. **Click OK.**

If you want to try the effect again with a different number of steps, simply press Delete. Doing this deletes the transitional objects and leaves your original shapes on-screen.

The Blend tool can help you create several copies of objects or shapes very quickly. Start by duplicating an object once and placing the duplicate some distance away from the original object. Select both objects, click the corresponding points, and enter the number of extra copies of the object that you want in the Steps field of the Blend dialog box.

The 5th Wave By Rich Tennant

"WE FIGURE THE EQUIPMENT MUST HAVE SCARED HER AWAY. A FEW DAYS AFTER SETTING UP, LITTLE 'SNOWBALL' JUST DISAPPEARED."

Chapter 18

What's behind That Mask

Suppose that you've been asked to create an advertisement for a chain of local flower shops. Your artistic brainstorm is to have each letter of the flower shop's name filled with a scanned image of flowers — a great idea, but how do you do it? How do you solve the problem of putting flowers into each letter of the flower shop's name? The answer is simple: You need to create a mask. Before you create a mask for each letter, though, you need to understand how to make a compound path. "What is a compound path?" you ask. Read on.

Working with Compound Paths

Compound paths help you create special effects with paths. A compound path is a group created from two or more paths. When you create a compound path, overlapping areas of separate paths become transparent, and the paint attributes of the compound path change to match the paint attributes of the path that is at the back of the stack. It sounds complicated, but it really isn't. The easiest way to understand exactly what a compound path can do for you is to create a few paths and see the effects after you change them into a compound path.

Creating compound paths

Figure 18-1 shows an example of a compound path. To create the figure, we used two compound paths: one for the piano keys (shown at the bottom of Figure 18-2) and the other for the text (shown at the top of Figure 18-2). Tips for creating compound paths from text appear later in the chapter.

Here are the general steps for creating a compound path:

1. **Select the objects that you want to include in your compound path.**

   Remember that overlapping areas become transparent after you create the compound path.

2. **Choose Object⇨Compound Path⇨Make.**

   The overlapping areas of the paths become transparent, and the paint attributes of the entire compound path change to the paint attributes of the path that is at the back of all other paths.

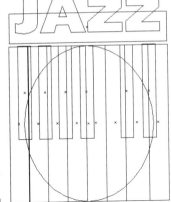

Figure 18-2:
The jazz
poster in
Artwork
mode.

Keep the following important facts in mind while working with compound paths:

✔ When you create compound paths, remember that the paint attributes of the entire compound path take on the attributes of the object (path) that is at the back of the object stack. Thus, if the back object is filled with a pattern, the entire compound path becomes filled with that pattern.

✔ After you create a compound path from separate objects, you can select and drag the compound path with the Selection tool. If you want, you can separate the objects in a compound path by clicking and dragging an individual object in the compound path with the Direct Selection or Group Selection tool. Even though you drag an object away, the overlapping areas remain transparent; therefore, by dragging with the Group Selection tool, you can change the size of the transparent area of the Compound path.

✔ If you click once on a compound path with the Group Selection tool, you select one of the paths in the compound path. Click again, and you add the next path or paths in the compound path to the selection.

Releasing a compound path

If you don't like the effect that your compound path creates, you can undo the transparent effects of the compound path by choosing Objects⇨Compound Paths⇨Release. After you release the compound path, that path is no longer a group, meaning Illustrator views each path as a separate object. However, the paint attributes do not return to their original state; that is, the paint attributes for all objects remain the paint attributes for the path at the back of the stack.

You may want to undo the transparent effects of a compound path and to return all objects to their original paint attributes. Choose Edit⇨Undo after you create the compound path to achieve this.

Reversing your path

When you create a compound path, you may find that Illustrator doesn't always create transparent areas where you want them to be. The reason for this relates to the direction in which you created the paths originally. For example, when you create a compound path out of text (as we did in Figure 18-1), all letters do not always become transparent with the initial application of the Object⇨ Compound Paths⇨Make command. When you create a compound path out of text outlines, the paths of the individual letters can go in different directions. Now, you're probably wondering, "How do I know and keep track of whether I created a path going to the right or to the left?" The answer is that you don't. All you need to do is reverse the direction of the paths that you want to be transparent. Fortunately, reversing is a very simple procedure.

To reverse the direction of a path, use the Direct Selection tool to select the path that you want to alter. Next, choose Objects⇨Attributes. In the Attributes dialog box, select the Reverse Path Direction check box. Click OK to close the dialog box. If you'd like to see how simple it is to reverse the direction of a path to create transparent effects, try the short exercise in the next section.

Creating compound paths with text

If you want to create transparent effects with text, you often need to reverse the direction of some of the text outlines. Reversing directions helped to create the word *JAZZ* as it appears in Figure 18-1. The following steps describe how to create a similar compound path and use the Reverse Path command:

1. **Activate the Type tool, and then type some text on-screen.**

2. **Click and drag over the text with the Type tool to select it; then choose Type⇨Size, and select a large font size (such as 72) from the submenu.**

   If you want to change the typeface, choose a different typeface from the Font menu.

3. **To convert the text into a path, click at the base of the text with the Selection tool and choose Type⇨Create Outlines.**

4. **Create a rectangle (or other object) that you want to include in the compound path.**

5. **Drag your object over the text, and send it to the back of the stack by choosing Arrange⇨Send to Back.**

6. **Select both the text and the object. (To select the objects, click and drag over them with the Selection tool.) To create the compound path, choose Object⇨Compound Paths⇨Make.**

Depending on the letters in your text, you may see that some overlapping areas of the letters are not transparent. To make these areas transparent, you need to select the non-transparent letters and reverse the direction of the paths.

7. **Select the Group Selection tool, and then press and hold Shift while you select each letter that is not transparent in overlapping areas.**

8. **With the letters selected, choose Object⇨Attributes; then click the Reverse path check box in the Attributes dialog box, and click OK.**

   After you click OK, the dialog box closes and the selected letters become transparent in the overlapping areas.

Creating Masks

Most people — at least the honest ones — generally wear masks around Halloween time. At Halloween, you can use a mask to hide your face, sometimes creating startling effects. Following that same concept, Illustrator lets you create some intriguing effects with electronic masks.

The easiest way to conceptualize an electronic mask is to think of it as a magical cookie cutter. This magical cookie cutter, or mask, is a path that cuts a shape out of another path. Figure 18-3 shows a photograph (from the *America Remembered* CD-ROM collection) before creating a mask. Figure 18-4 shows the photo after applying a mask in the shape of a heart. In this image, the heart path cut out (like a cookie cutter) a section of the old photograph.

You can find the specific steps for creating the heart-shaped path in Chapter 7.

Here are the steps for creating a mask:

1. **With the Freehand or Pen tool, create a shape that you want to use as the outline for your image (your mask).**

   This path becomes your electronic cookie cutter that creates the masking shape.

2. **With the Brush, Freehand, or Pen tool, create the object that you want to appear through the mask.**

   Or, you may want to use a photograph. If you use a scanned image, save it in EPS format and choose Place Art from the File menu to place the photograph into the document you are working on.

3. **Place the image to appear through the mask in back of the mask (cookie cutter path) by selecting it with the Selection tool and choosing Arrange⇨ Send to Back.**

Figure 18-3:
A photo-
graph
before being
masked.
Photograph
courtesy of
Boraventures
publishing,
(Fairfield,
Conn.).

Figure 18-4:
A holiday
sentiment
created by
masking
an old
photograph
into a heart-
shaped
path.

4. **Select both objects (the object being used as the mask and the object to appear in the mask); then choose Object⇨Mask⇨Make.**

   Instantly, Illustrator masks the image.

5. **If you'd like, you can add text and other items to your image. Figure 18-4 shows an added border, arrow, and text.**

To undo the effects of a mask, select the masked object on-screen and then choose Object⇨Mask⇨Release.

Here are a few tips for using masks:

- ✔ To quickly select all masks in a document and deselect all objects that are not masks, choose Filter⇨Select⇨Select Masks.

- ✔ To see if an image is a mask, select it and choose Object⇨Attributes. At the bottom of the dialog box, you'll see this message: The current selection is affected by a mask.

- ✔ If you are creating a mask out of text, you do not have to turn the text into paths (by using the Type⇨Convert to Outlines command).

- ✔ A mask can be used to crop an image. When you crop an image, it's like cutting around the image edges with a pair of scissors to make the image smaller. To crop an image using a mask, simply create a rectangle (with no fill or stroke) inside an image. Select the image and the rectangle. After you choose Object⇨Mask⇨Make, only the image areas within the rectangle appear on-screen.

- ✔ If you want to fill and/or stroke a mask, first set the fill or stroke option in the Paint Style palette and make sure that the Auto check box is selected. Next, choose Filter⇨Create⇨Fill & Stroke for Mask. After the command is executed, Illustrator places the stroked object in front of the mask and the filled object behind the mask.

Creating Masks Using Compounds

Many times, you may need to mask more than one item. For example, if you want to create a mask out of letters, as shown in Figure 18-5, you need to create a compound path and then execute the Object⇨Make⇨Mask command.

You can create the sunglasses shown in Figure 18-6 with a compound path, too. You first convert the two ovals (lenses) in the sunglasses into a compound path and then use them as masks for the landscape photograph (shown in Figure 18-7). You can add the bridge and stem of the sunglasses later.

Following are the steps for creating a mask from text or several objects with compound paths:

1. **Create the text or object paths that you want to use as your mask.**

2. **Select your paths, and choose Object⇨Compound Paths⇨Make.**

3. **Use the File⇨Place Art command to place an EPS digitized photograph on-screen for use inside the mask.**

   If you don't want to use a digitized photograph, you can create an object using Illustrator's drawing tools.

MAINE FLOWERS

Step 1

Step 2

MAINE FLOWERS

Step 3

Figure 18-5:
Using text
as a mask.

Figure 18-6:
Two compound ovals with a photograph masked inside.

Figure 18-7:
The photograph used in Figure 18-6.

 4. **Send the photograph or object created in Illustrator behind the compound path by selecting it and choosing Arrange⇨Send to Back.**

 5. **To create the mask, select the photograph or object and the compound path; then choose Object⇨Mask⇨Make.**

That's it. As you can see, creating masks can be quite easy, once you get the hang of it.

Chapter 19
It Even Draws Graphs

● ●

In This Chapter

▶ Creating graphs

▶ Choosing a graph style

▶ Entering data

▶ Importing data

▶ Adjusting a graph

▶ Creating and applying graph designs

● ●

*L*et's face it — numbers are boring. Numbers make most people cringe. No one wants to wade through page after page of bewildering and baffling statistics. The artistic antidote to row after row and column after column of never-ending numbers is to create a visual representation of the numbers — in other words, a graph.

Graphs can help your readers quickly analyze and understand mathematical information rather than force them to spend hours puzzling over a pile of numbers. Graphs can show the relationships between numbers or the periodic rise and fall of numeric data. A creative graph may even evoke a smile from an appreciative audience that admires the cleverness used to convey the information.

Topping the Charts with Illustrator's Graphs

Adobe Illustrator's graphing capabilities are tremendous. You can choose a graph style (such as a column, line, or pie graph) and enter data for your graph directly in Illustrator or import the data from a spreadsheet program, such as Microsoft Excel. After you enter your data, one little click of the mouse triggers your graph to be magically drawn on-screen. You can add some pizzazz to your graphs by integrating digitized images and illustrations into the presentation. Illustrator even enables you to make the bars of a graph from any object that you can draw. This feature means that you can create graph bars out of oil wells, automobiles, animals — or whatever it takes to make the graph more appealing.

If you still aren't convinced that you're better off creating graphs in Illustrator (as compared to by hand), consider this: If you change the numbers that the graph is based on, Illustrator automatically redraws the graph. If you were creating a chart traditionally, you may need to redraw the graph from scratch just to accommodate a change in data.

Getting a Graph off the Ground

Creating a graph in Illustrator is not complicated, but the process does involve several specific steps. This section presents the quick and easy steps for creating a graph. Later sections of the chapter cover the details on formatting, choosing the right graph style, and making your graph more attractive. To create a graph, follow these steps:

1. **Double-click the Graph tool in the Toolbox.**

2. **In the Graph Style dialog box (as shown in Figure 19-1), choose the type of graph that you want to create and click OK.**

Figure 19-1:
The Graph
Style dialog
box.

Graph Style

Graph type
- ● Grouped column
- ○ Stacked column
- ○ Line
- ○ Pie
- ○ Area
- ○ Scatter

Column graph options
Column width: 90 %
Cluster width: 100 %

Axis
- ● Use left axis
- ○ Use right axis
- ☐ Same axis both sides

[Left] Style [Right]
[Category]

- ☐ Drop shadow
- ☐ Legends across top
- ☐ First row in front
- ☒ First column in front

[Cancel] [OK]

The choices include Grouped column, Stacked column, Line, Pie, Area, and Scatter. (If you don't know what type of graph to use, don't worry — each choice is explained in the next section.)

3. **With the Graph tool still active, click and drag diagonally to create a rectangular shape in the area where you want the graph to appear.**

The size of the rectangle defines how large the graph is; its position defines where the graph appears in your document. After you release the mouse, the Graph data dialog box appears.

Before you click and drag to create the area to hold your graph, you may want to use Illustrator's rulers to help you set guides to position the graph exactly where you want it. The guides can also help you make sure the graph is the right size.

If you click in your document with the Graph tool activated, the Graph dialog box appears. In this dialog box, you can specify the size of the graph that you want to create. Then click OK to open the Graph data dialog box.

4. In the Graph data dialog box, enter the values that you want to graph into the cells area of the data sheet.

Figure 19-2 gives you an idea of how you enter data in the Graph data dialog box; Figure 19-3 shows a line graph created from the data.

In Figure 19-3, we created the background image by dragging and dropping an image from Adobe Photoshop into Illustrator. The background image courtesy of Digital Stock™'s *Food Signature* CD-ROM (photographs by Joshua Ets-Hokin).

5. Click OK to see your graph on-screen.

Figure 19-2:
Values
entered in
the Graph
data dialog
box.

	East Coast	West Coast	
"1993"	350.00	300.00	
"1994"	250.00	200.00	
"1995"	200.00	150.00	
"1996"	100.00	75.00	

Figure 19-3:
A candy
consumption
graph
generated
from data in
the Graph
data dialog
box.

6. Edit the completed graph's values or style, as you want.

Here are some suggestions for editing your graph after you create it:

- To reopen the Graph data dialog box so that you can edit the graph's values, select your graph with the Selection tool and choose Object⇨Graph⇨Data. The Graph data dialog box for your graph opens and appears on-screen. Now you can edit the values that Illustrator used to generate your graph. Click OK, and your graph is automatically updated.

- You may want to change your graph's style; for example, suppose that you created a line graph and want to change it to a pie graph. First select the graph. Then choose Object⇨Graph⇨Styles and select a new graph style from the resulting Graph Style dialog box.

Have we got a graph for you

Suppose that a client asks you to create a graph that compares the number of computer users who prefer computer manuals to the number of computer users who prefer . . .*For Dummies* books. Your client faxes you pages of statistics and surveys of computer users taken over the past ten years. Now you must decide exactly what type of graph to use to best present your findings. To pick the appropriate graph style, you need a basic understanding of each Illustrator graph style. Here's a brief review of the different types of graphs that you can create in Illustrator:

✔ **Grouped column:** Many people refer to grouped column graphs as *bar graphs* because the style uses vertical bars. Illustrator's grouped column graphs show separate vertical columns that represent different numerical values. This style is helpful when you want to depict differences between groups of data over a specific time period. The term *grouped column* refers to the fact that columns are grouped into sections.

For example, suppose that you want to compare the consumption of junk food (specifically, candy, potato chips, and pretzels) from the years 1996 and 1997. The grouped column graph can group the 1996 statistics in a column alongside a column for 1997. Illustrator would create one pair of bars (one for 1996 and one for 1997) for each of the junk food categories. Before using a grouped column graph, be aware that too many columns can be confusing. If you have lots of data to graph, you may be better off with a line graph.

✔ **Stacked:** The stacked graph plots values in different sections within a column or within several columns. Stacked graphs can help your audience visualize the proportional differences of data groups as they relate to the whole. For example, to compare the consumption of junk food by category for 1996 and 1997, you can create a graph with two stacked columns: one stacked column for 1996 and one for 1997. Each column can contain a section for each junk food category — candy, potato chips, and pretzels.

✔ **Line:** Line graphs can be especially useful for depicting data trends over a specified time period. Have you ever seen one of those old cartoons showing a patient in a hospital? Attached to the bed is a graph with one red line that slopes up or down and that (no doubt) displays the trend in the patient's fever. By using a line graph, you can also easily show the trend in sales of desktop publishing software and hardware over the past few years. The same graph can also feature a second line that shows a drop in sales of traditional typesetting equipment.

 ✔ **Pie:** Pie graphs depict proportional relationships of data. This graph style presents a simple and clear picture of exactly who's getting the largest and smallest pieces of the pie and how these pieces relate to the whole pie. Pie graphs, by their very nature, show relationships in percentages. For example, you can divide a single pie graph into pieces to show the percentage of pizza lovers who prefer pepperoni compared to the percentage that prefer sausage or extra cheese. When you add up all of the percentages, you get 100 percent — and hopefully, no heartburn.

 ✔ **Area:** Area graphs often look like the cutaway of a mountain sliced up into different sections. An area graph looks like a line graph that has the area under each line filled in with a pattern or color. As does a line graph, the area graph provides a visual representation of data trends over a specific period of time. Area graphs can be good for approximating volumes (such as inventory or amount of time). Unlike a line graph, the data of one data set appears directly above other data sets, and each data set is represented by a different color or shade.

 ✔ **Scatter:** A scatter graph can look like a bunch of confetti floating in the air. Scatter graphs show how two groups of discrete data are clustered or scattered over a specific period. Usually one group depends on the other group. For example, a graph of mosquito activity compared to sales of Raid would probably show sales growth when mosquito activity is at its highest and most annoying.

Getting the data in so that you can get the graph out

After you've chosen your graph type, you need to ensure that you enter your data correctly into Illustrator's Graph data dialog box. This dialog box contains a grid of columns and rows, or *datasheet,* into which you type the words and numbers that you want Illustrator to put on your graph. To reach the Graph data dialog box, you start by double-clicking the Graph tool to open the Graph Style dialog box. After you pick your graph style and click OK, the Graph data dialog box appears.

 If you already have a graph on-screen, you can open the Graph data dialog box by selecting the graph and choosing Object➪Graph➪Data.

TIP

Here are some tips for entering or editing data in the Graph data dialog box:

✔ To enter data, simply click the cell where you want to put the data, and then type the data. Next press the Tab key to move to the right or Return to move down. You can also use the directional arrow keys to move out of a cell in any direction after you type data. If you press Enter, the data appears in the cell you're in and the dialog box closes. You can also enter data by typing and then clicking the cell that you want to move to.

✔ If you want to change data that you entered already, first click the cell containing the data that needs to be changed. Type the new data, and then press Tab, Return, or a directional arrow key. Alternatively, you can edit the data by clicking the Entry line area, as shown in Figure 19-4. You can then click and drag over data in the entry line and type over the data. This deletes the previous entry and replaces it with whatever you type. After you're done, press Return, Tab, or a directional arrow key.

✔ Words that appear in your graph are called *labels*. To create labels for the (horizontal) x-axis of the graph, enter the appropriate words in the first column of the data sheet, as shown in Figure 19-4. Notice that the city names, LA, NYC, and SF, appear in the first column of the data sheet. The Graph created from this data sheet has the city names along the x-axis, as shown in Figure 19-5. Notice that the numbers in the row next to each city name are the data points on the y-axis that correspond to the city on the x-axis.

✔ To create labels for a legend, enter the labels in the first row of the graph (for most graphs that you create, you do not need to enter a label in the top cell of the first column because the first column contains x-axis labels). Entries in this first row are called *category labels*. In Figure 19-4, the words *Espresso* and *Cappuccino* appear at the top of the data columns. Notice that the legend in Figure 19-5 includes the words *Espresso* and *Cappuccino*.

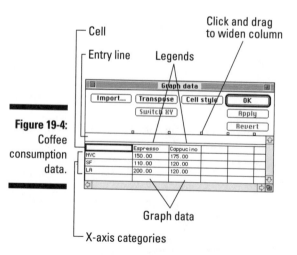

Figure 19-4:
Coffee
consumption
data.

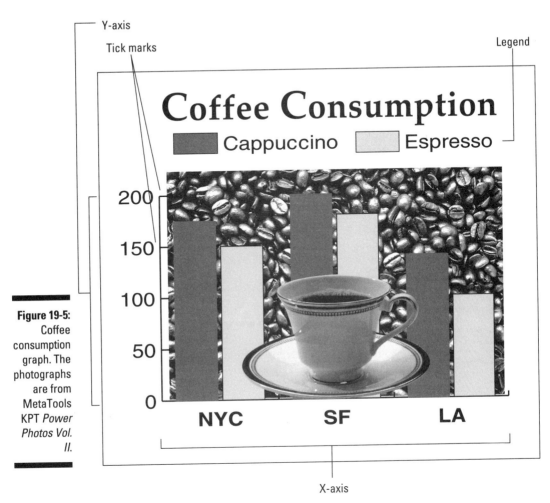

Y-axis

Tick marks

Legend

Figure 19-5:
Coffee
consumption
graph. The
photographs
are from
MetaTools
KPT *Power
Photos Vol.
II.*

X-axis

✔ If you need to create category labels using numbers, enter them with quotes, such as in the following example:

```
"1996"
```

If you don't enter them with quotes, Illustrator assumes that these numbers are supposed to be graphed.

✔ If you need to create a line break in the label, enter the vertical bar symbol (|) at the point where you want to break the line. For example, if your heading is *Western States* and you want the word *States* to drop down to the next line, type **Western | States**.

✔ When creating a pie graph with legends, enter the legend labels starting at the top of the column in the data sheet. Enter the data beneath the columns in the second row of the data sheet. If you enter more than one row of data, a pie graph is created for each row.

Changing cell column widths

As you enter data in the Graph data dialog box, you may need to adjust the size of the cells. The easiest way to change widths is with the mouse, as follows:

1. **Position the mouse pointer on the tiny column separator box that is above the entry line and over the right vertical bar of the column that you want to adjust.**

   When you place the cursor over the tiny box at the top of the column, the pointer changes to a double arrow.

2. **After you see the double-arrow pointer on-screen, click and drag the column separator box to adjust the column width.**

   As you drag, the column's right vertical boundary moves in the direction you drag the mouse. Drag the column separator to the right to widen the column; drag it to the left to decrease the column width.

3. **Release the mouse button after you reach the desired column width.**

You can also adjust the column width through the Cell Style dialog box. First, click Cell Style in the Graph data dialog box to access the Cell Style dialog box, as shown in Figure 19-6. In the Column width field, enter the number of digits that you want to fit in the currently selected column. This technique works for all columns that you haven't adjusted by clicking and dragging.

Getting your decimal points right

If you need to see your numbers more precisely, you can change the number of decimal places that appears in the data sheet section of the Graph data dialog box. From the Graph data dialog box, click Cell Style to reach the Cell Style dialog box, as shown in Figure 19-6. Enter the number of decimal digits for your data sheet numbers in the Number of decimals field; then click OK. Although this change affects all the numbers displayed in the Graph data dialog box, it does not affect the display of your graph.

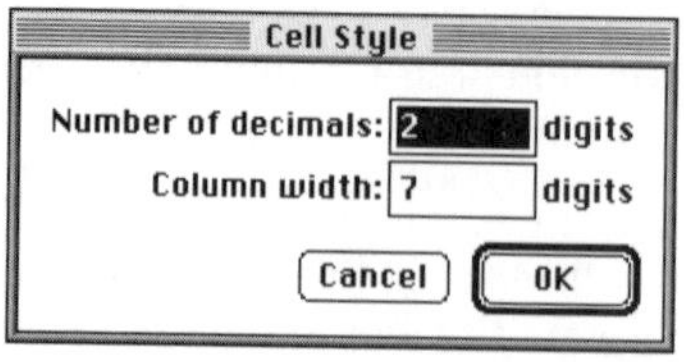

Figure 19-6:
The Cell
Style dialog
box.

```
╔══════════ Cell Style ══════════╗
║                                 ║
║  Number of decimals: [2     ] digits  ║
║      Column width: [7    ] digits  ║
║                                 ║
║       (Cancel)    (  OK  )      ║
╚═════════════════════════════════╝
```

Don't type if you can import

Typing numbers into tiny little boxes in the Graph data dialog box is no fun. You can avoid the chore of entering data by importing data that already exists in a word processing, spreadsheet, or database program. So that Illustrator can read the data from another program correctly, you must save the data in a text format commonly known as *tab delimited.*

Here are some hints for saving data in tab delimited format in Microsoft Excel and Microsoft Word:

✔ If the data is entered in Microsoft Excel (Mac or PC), you can save it in tab delimited format by using Excel's Save As command. Choose File⇨Save As and pick Text (Tab delimited) from the Save File as Type pop-up menu in the Save As dialog box. When you save a file this way, Excel inserts a tab character between each number and a carriage return between each line of data in the text file.

✔ If your data comes from Microsoft Word (Mac or PC), enter the data into a table and then choose File⇨Save As. In the Save As dialog box, choose Text Only from the Save File as Type pop-up menu.

After you save your data in text format, you can import it into Illustrator by following these steps:

1. **Select a graph that you have already created, and then open the Graph data dialog box by choosing Object⇨Graphs⇨Data.**

2. **To create a new graph for the data, double-click the Graph tool, select a graph type, and click OK; then open the Graph data dialog box by clicking and dragging in your document to create the rectangular area where you want your graph to appear.**

3. **Select the data sheet cell where you want the imported data to start.**

   For example, if you want imported data to begin at the top-left cell of the data sheet, select the first cell in the data sheet. If you want to leave space for labels and legends, you may want to select the second cell in column two.

4. **Click Import in the Graph data dialog box and, after the Open dialog box appears, select the file that you want to import; then click Open.**

5. **After you see the imported data, click OK.**

   The graph on-screen changes to reflect this data.

You can also copy your data from another computer application and paste it into the Graph data dialog box by choosing Edit⇨Copy in the other application and Edit⇨Paste in Illustrator.

I want my x-axis where my y-axis is

One annoying problem that can arise when your computer creates graphs is having your x-axis appear where you want your y-axis to be. Why does this problem occur? Usually, it occurs because you typed data in columns rather than in rows. Fortunately, the solution isn't to retype the data. Instead, you can have Illustrator *transpose* the data by following these steps:

1. **Open the Graph data dialog box by selecting your graph and then choosing Object⇨Graph⇨Data.**

2. **Click Transpose in the Graph data dialog box.**

   After you click Transpose, Illustrator reverses the data in the Graph data dialog box. That is, rows become columns, and columns become rows.

3. **Click OK, and Illustrator redraws the graph.**

To transpose data for scatter graphs, click the Switch XY button in the Graph data dialog box.

Editing and customizing a graph

After you create a graph, you may want to jazz it up or simply change its style (for example, change a line graph to a bar graph). To change graph styles, you need to open the Graph Style dialog box: First select your graph, and then choose Object⇨Graphs⇨Style. Options in the Graph Style dialog box enable you to select the Graph Type, specify Axis use, add elements such as drop shadows, and so on. Here are some handy options provided by the Graph Style dialog box:

✔ To change line widths for line graphs, select the Fill Line check box and enter a line width value in points in the Fill line width field. You can also select a line in a graph with the Direct Selection tool. With the line selected, you can change its width by adjusting the Stroke Weight field in the Paint Style palette.

✔ To place the label legends in the wedges of a pie graph, select the Labels in wedges option in the Graph Style dialog box.

✔ To add dollar signs or other formatting symbols to your graph's y-axis, click Use left axis or Use right axis (not necessary for Scatter charts) to choose the left or right y-axis. Next click the Left or Right Style button (the Right button is not available for Scatter graphs) to open the Graph Axis Style dialog box. In the Graph Axis Style dialog box, enter the symbol to appear on the graph in the Labels before field or the After field. If you enter the symbol in the Labels before field, the symbol appears before the label; if you enter the symbol in the After field, the symbol appears after the label.

✔ To change the spacing between columns in a grouped column graph, enter percentage values in the Column width and Cluster width fields. The Column width setting determines the amount of allotted space that is covered by the column group, and the Cluster width determines the space between the columns in a group.

The columns in a group of a Grouped column graph are the graphed representation of the values from one row of the data sheet.

✔ When you select the Grouped column, Line, or a Scatter graph style, you can specify the minimum and maximum numbers that appear on the y-axis. To change the left vertical axis, simply click the Left button in the Graph Style dialog box. This opens the Graph Axis Style dialog box, as shown in Figure 19-7. Next click the Use manual axis values check box. In the Maximum label value, Minimum label value, and Value between labels fields, you can enter the minimum and maximum values to appear on the y-axis, and you can specify the increment between the values. For example, if you set the Minimum label value to 0, set the Maximum label value to 200, and enter 50 into the Value between labels field, the resulting labels on the y-axis are 0, 50, 100, 150, and 200.

How to get properly ticked off

When creating graphs, you can often make the graph look more organized by adding vertical and horizontal grid lines and tick marks. Tick marks appear as tiny lines on the x- or y-axis and can help show the divisions between values on the y-axis or categories along the x-axis.

To add tick marks or vertical and horizontal grid lines on a graph, first select your graph and then choose Object⇨Graphs⇨Style. In the Graph Style dialog box, choose your axis or axes. If you want to add tick marks to both the left and right axes, click the Same axis both sides check box; otherwise, choose Use left axis or Use right axis. Next, click Left to add tick marks to the left axis, Right to add tick marks to the right axis, or Category to add tick marks to the x-axis.

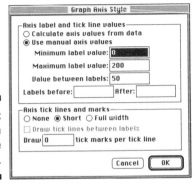

Figure 19-7:
The Graph Axis Style dialog box.

After you click Left, Right, or Category, the Graph Axis Style dialog box opens, as shown in Figure 19-7. (The word Bottom appears instead of Category if you're working with a Scatter graph.) In the Graph Axis Style dialog box, click the Short option to create small tick marks. Click the Full width option to create vertical or horizontal lines (the grid lines) that overlay the entire graph. If you want vertical lines to be placed between the x-axis labels, click the Draw tick lines between labels check box. If you want to control the number of tick marks that appear in your graph, enter a value in the Draw tick marks per tick line field.

The fine art of graph selecting

The graphs that Illustrator creates are very similar to the graphic objects that you create from scratch. You can change a graph's colors and its stroke weight. You can also scale, rotate, and shear graphs by using the same techniques that you use for editing other graphic objects. If you want to start customizing your graphs, you must remember that a graph is a group of objects. The trick in editing graphs is to keep the graph *grouped.* If you don't, you can't change the data in the Graph data dialog box so that Illustrator automatically updates the graph. In other words, if you ungroup a graph and make changes to the data, Illustrator doesn't automatically update the graph to reflect your changes.

If you need to select individual graph items from within the graph group, you should use the Group Selection or Direct Selection tool. For example, if you click the legend once with the Group Selection tool, you select only the legend. If you click the legend twice, you select the legend and one of the categories in the graph. As you continue to click the legend with the Group Selection tool, you continue to select more items in the graph — until you select everything.

Instead of the Group Selection tool, you can use the Direct Selection tool, with the Option key pressed, to select individual items. Or you can continue clicking to select the entire graph. Using the Direct Selection tool without the Option key pressed enables you to select individual points in a path.

After you select an individual object in a graph, you can change the object's color or you can move, scale, rotate, reflect, and/or shear it. You also can change the typeface and the size of the fonts in the graph and the legend.

For example, suppose that you create a grouped column graph and then want to place a pattern in the columns representing the years 1995 and 1996. To change the columns, you don't want to select each one individually but the group of columns representing the data series for 1995 and 1996. Fortunately, Illustrator graphs are grouped objects. By using the Group Selection tool or the Direct Selection tool with the Option key pressed, you can select exactly what you want.

The following steps show you how to use the Group selection tool to select different groups. The selection "trick" is to click the legend first and then to keep on clicking the legend until you select all items that you want. Follow these steps:

1. **Click the Group Selection tool.**

   The Group Selection tool is the Arrow icon with the plus next to it. If it doesn't appear in the Toolbox, click the Direct Selection tool and keep the mouse button pressed. When the Group Selection tool appears, drag the mouse over it; then release the mouse button.

2. **Move the mouse pointer over the legend symbol (the square) of the data series that you want to select, and click once.**

   The first click selects the legend.

3. **Click the legend once more to select the columns, lines, or other graph elements that are associated with the selected legend.**

   When you click again, you select all associated graph elements.

If you want to deselect an object from a selected group, first activate the Group Selection tool. Next, press and hold down Shift while you click the object (path) that you want to deselect.

To select type (text), click the base line of the type with the Group Selection tool. Click twice to select all text.

Creating Combination Graphs

When you create graphs, you may find that combining two types of graphs is sometimes beneficial. For example, Figure 19-8 shows a combination in which a grouped column graph represents time spent watching TV and a line graph represents time spent exercising. The figure shows the graph with a pattern added to the bars and a television in the background. The television in the graph was created mostly with the Rectangle, Rounded Rectangle, and Oval tools.

The following steps show you how to combine a grouped column graph with a line graph. You can use this same technique to combine any two types of graphs. You first create a grouped column graph and then change one of the columns to a line. Follow these steps:

1. **Create a grouped column graph.**

2. **With the Group Selection tool, click twice on the legend category that you want to change to a line graph.**

   Doing this selects the bar that you're changing to a line.

3. **Choose Objects⇨Graphs⇨Style, and select Line from the Graph Style dialog box.**

4. **To move the line in front of the columns in your graph, select the line by clicking the appropriate legend category twice with the Group Selection tool, and then choose Arrange⇨Bring to Front.**

Changing graph styles may remove previous formatting.

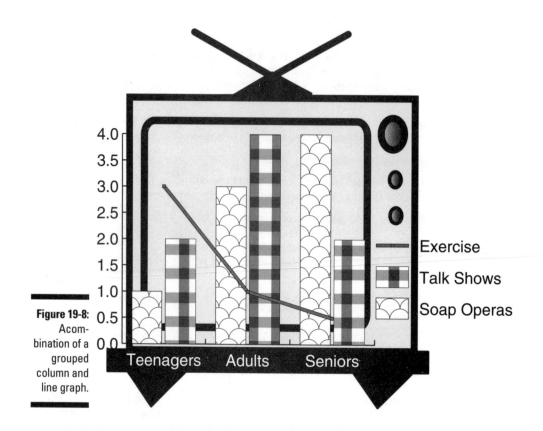

Figure 19-8:
A combination of a grouped column and line graph.

Creating and Applying Column and Marker Designs

If you want to create a graph that really attracts attention and drives home a point, you may want to present the graph information with pictures and objects, as shown in Figure 19-9. In this graph, the car, train, and airplane object are used instead of lines or grouped columns.

For another example, suppose that you want to graph the number of artists who own computers. You could start by creating a small image of a computer; then use Illustrator's Column Design feature to replace the column (which contains the number of artists information) with a stack of computer images. Likewise, if you wanted to graph the number of mosquito bites per camper over the past ten summers, you could create your graph columns from pictures of the tiny pests.

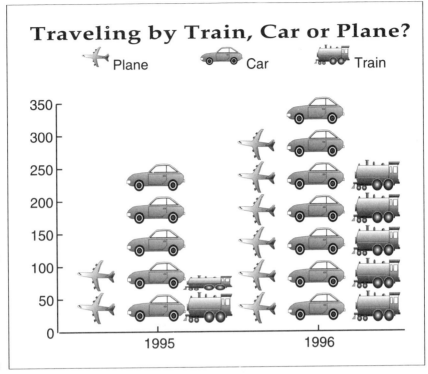

Figure 19-9:
A graph
created
by using
Column
Designs.

To make a graph that jumps off the page and really illustrates a point, you can apply Column or Marker Designs. Creating Column and Marker Designs is similar to creating a pattern. The following steps show you how:

1. **Use any of Illustrator's tools and commands to create a design.**

   We used the Pen tool to create the train, car, and plane that appear in the graph in Figure 19-9.

2. **With the design on-screen, use the Rectangle tool to create a rectangle around the design; then send the rectangle behind the design by choosing Arrange⇨Send to Back.**

3. **Select both the rectangle and the design, and then choose Object⇨ Graph⇨Design.**

4. **With the selected design appearing in the window at the right of the Design dialog box (as shown in Figure 19-10), choose New.**

5. **In the Change name to field, rename your design (if you want to) and click OK to save the design and close the dialog box.**

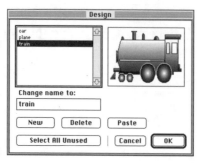

Figure 19-10:
The Design
dialog box
with the
train design
showing.

Whether you use a Column or Marker design depends on the style of graph that you are creating. When you work with a grouped column or stacked column graph, you use a Column design. When you work with a line or scatter graph, you use a Marker design.

The following steps show you how to apply a Column design to a graph:

1. **With a grouped column or stacked column graph on-screen, use the Group Selection tool to select the legend category for the columns that you want to replace; click again to select the columns representing the legend.**

   At this point you should have the legend and the columns representing it selected.

2. **Choose Object⇔Graphs⇔Column.**

3. **In the Graph Column Design dialog box (as shown in Figure 19-11), click a Column design name; then choose a Column design type: Vertically scaled, Uniformly scaled, Repeating, or Sliding.**

   • If you choose Vertically scaled, your column design grows or shrinks vertically, and the width does not change.

   • If you choose Uniformly scaled, your column design grows or shrinks both vertically and horizontally.

   • If you choose a Repeating design, copies of your column design appear on top of each other, repeated until the column is filled.

   • If you choose a Sliding design, you can choose a point on your design where you want it to grow or shrink vertically.

   • As you click each option, you see a preview of the design in the bottom-right corner of the dialog box. If you choose Repeating, you must enter a value in the Each design represents field. This enables you to control how many designs fit in a column. For example, if you enter 100, and the value for the column in the data sheet is 200, two designs appear in the column.

- You must click the Chop design fraction or Scale design fraction option. If you choose the Chop option, the last repeated image that doesn't fit in the column is cut off at its top. If you choose Scale design fraction, Illustrator scales the last repeated design to fit in the column.

Figure 19-11: Choosing a Column design name and a design type in the Graph Column Design dialog box.

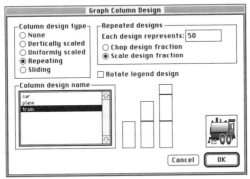

4. **Click OK to apply the Column design to your graph on-screen.**

The following steps show you how to apply a Marker design to a graph:

1. **With a line or scatter graph on-screen, use the Direct Selection or Group Selection tool to select at least one marker in your graph.**

2. **Choose Object⇨Graphs⇨Marker.**

3. **In the Graph Marker Design dialog box, as shown in Figure 19-12, click the On data point option in the Marker design type section; then click a Marker design name.**

4. **Click OK to apply the Marker design to your graph on-screen.**

Figure 19-12: The Graph Marker Design dialog box.

Part V
Advanced Topics

The 5th Wave   By Rich Tennant

"WAAIT A MINUTE—NO WONDER IT'S NOT WORKING. YOU BOUGHT ADOBE SOFTWARE! WE DON'T WORK IN AN ADOBE ENVIRONMENT!"

In this part . . .

*E*ven though this part deals with advanced Illustrator topics, you'll find useful techniques to impress your colleagues and help you get the job done right. You'll see how professional artists integrate their Illustrator work into image-editing programs, such as Photoshop, and 3-D programs, such as Strata StudioPro. The final chapter in this part deals with advanced outputting techniques for color publishing. If you've ever heard designers talking about *trapping, spreads,* and *chokes (*and thought that they were talking about wrestling) — you probably should read this chapter.

Chapter 20
Working with Different Programs

· ·

In This Chapter

▶ Using Illustrator and Photoshop

▶ Using Illustrator and Fractal Design Painter

▶ Using Illustrator and page layout programs

▶ Importing Macromedia Freehand files

▶ Using Illustrator and 3-D programs

▶ Using Illustrator and multimedia programs

▶ Using Illustrator and Adobe Acrobat

· ·

Sometimes you need more than one tool to get the job done correctly. When you create images for publication, for multimedia presentations, or for viewing on the Internet's World Wide Web, you often need to use Adobe Illustrator along with other graphics programs. For example, if you plan to design a newsletter or magazine layout, you need a page layout program such as Adobe PageMaker, QuarkXPress, or Adobe FrameMaker. If you're creating a book or CD-ROM cover, you may need to use an image-editing program such as Adobe Photoshop, which enables you to digitize photographs, color-correct, and create special effects. This chapter reviews some of the programs that graphics professionals frequently use with Illustrator.

Working with Photoshop

If you're an Illustrator user who likes to take photographs, you may want to integrate your Illustrator art or type effects into an image-editing program such as Adobe Photoshop.

Adobe Photoshop enables you not only to digitize photographs through a scanner but also to capture images from a digital camera or videotape (as long as you have a video board in your computer). After you digitize an image, you can use Photoshop to remove scratches and other flaws in the image, correct the colors in the image, or create amazing special effects.

After you use Photoshop to digitize, create, or enhance an image, you can import it easily into Illustrator by dragging and dropping the image directly from Photoshop. Dragging and dropping files between Illustrator and Photoshop is covered in Chapter 3.

When you copy and paste a path from Illustrator into Photoshop, a dialog box appears enabling you to choose whether you want to paste the path as pixels or as paths. If you choose to paste as paths, you can work with the path in Photoshop by using Photoshop's Pen tool.

If you need to load Illustrator files into Photoshop, you can drag and drop, or you can use Photoshop's standard File⇨Open command to open your Illustrator image. If you want to open your Illustrator image into a pre-existing Photoshop file, choose Photoshop's File⇨Place command.

After you choose File⇨Open and select your Illustrator file, Photoshop opens the Rasterize Adobe Illustrator Format dialog box. This dialog box contains controls for converting the Adobe Illustrator *vector* file to a *bitmap* (or raster) image — in other words, the image changes from a mathematical representation of an image to one composed of tiny individual image elements called *pixels*. For more information about the differences between raster and vector images, see Chapter 1.

In the Rasterize Adobe Illustrator Format dialog box, you can enter values for the image's height, width, resolution, and color mode. After you enter these values, click OK. You see a prompt that says `Rasterize Adobe Illustrator Format`. For more information on rasterizing images, see Chapter 16. When you use the File⇨Place command, Photoshop automatically sizes and rasterizes the Illustrator file.

When you import an Illustrator file with a pattern in it into Photoshop, the Parser dialog box appears. Adobe Photoshop's Illustrator Parser does not support patterns: When you import an Illustrator file with a pattern into Photoshop, the image appears in Photoshop without the pattern.

If you need to import Illustrator files with patterns into Photoshop, you must first apply Illustrator's Object⇨Expand command to the patterns, save your files, and then import them into Photoshop.

Figure 20-1 shows an example of an image created by using both Illustrator and Photoshop. To re-create the image shown, we followed these steps: we first loaded a digitized stock photograph of a smiling man into Adobe Photoshop. (This photo is from the *America Remembered* CD-ROM collection.) Using Photoshop, we resized the image and saved it in EPS format. Next, we imported the image into Illustrator by executing the File⇨Place command. In Illustrator, we created the curved text. (Most painting and image-editing programs do not enable you to create text along a curve.)

Figure 20-1:
A book cover created with Illustrator and Photoshop. Photograph courtesy of Boraventures Publishing (Fairfield, Connecticut).

Figuring out outputting

If you use Adobe Photoshop or a painting program such as Fractal Design's Painter, it's important to realize that the image quality of painting and image-editing programs is based upon the image's resolution — usually measured in the number of pixels per inch. In Illustrator, quality is based upon the output resolution. If you output an image to a 2,450 dots per inch (dpi) imagesetter, the image quality is better than if you print it on a 300 dpi laser printer. When outputting images in programs such as Painter and Photoshop, using a high resolution does not necessarily result in better quality.

For printed output, the general rule is to create your image-editing and painting files at 1½ to 2 times the screen frequency (measured in lines per inch). A common screen frequency used in color publishing is 133 to 150 lines per inch. Screen frequency for newspapers is often 80 to 90 lines per inch. Thus, if you are working in an image-editing program on an image to be printed in a newspaper, an acceptable image resolution for the printed output is 160 to 180 pixels per inch.

Figure 20-2 shows another image created by using both Illustrator and Photoshop. Artist Stacey Lewis created this image of a telephone that was commissioned by Drextec (in Mount Laurel, NJ). The image was created for an interactive multimedia background. The silhouettes of the keys were drawn in Illustrator. The Illustrator file was then imported into Photoshop where it was used as a mask when airbrushing the keys. Stacey scanned and retouched a photograph in Photoshop to create the wood texture underneath the telephone.

Figure 20-2:
Stacey Lewis
created this
image by
using both
Illustrator
and
Photoshop.

You can import Photoshop files into Illustrator by copying and pasting, dragging and dropping, or using Illustrator's File⇨Place Art command. For more information about dragging and dropping and copying and pasting, see Chapter 3. For more information about using Illustrator's File⇨Place Art command, see Chapter 9.

Working with Painter

If you're an Illustrator user who likes to paint, you may want to integrate your Illustrator art or type effects into a painting program such as Fractal Design's Painter. Painter enables you to create endless painterly effects. It features a Brushes palette with 18 different brushes, including oil brushes, water color brushes, pastels, and charcoal. Painter Version 4 also enables you to create mosaics and alter lighting effects. You can even warp images, create animation, and change an image into a series of weird looking blobs with the image in the blobs.

You can easily import Illustrator art or text that was converted to outlines into Painter Version 4 by choosing Painter's File⇨Acquire⇨Adobe Illustrator Format command. If you import an Illustrator file with gradations, Painter notifies you that Painter 4 may not import gradients correctly for some paths. Incorrect importing sometimes occurs because Painter creates colors from combinations of Red, Green, and Blue (RGB colors), whereas Illustrator creates them from percentages of Cyan, Magenta, Yellow, and Black (CMYK colors).

After you import your Illustrator art into Painter, you can use any of the program's painting or special effects features. If you want, after merging your Illustrator art or text with Painter, you can save your Painter file in Photoshop 3.0 format and import the file into Photoshop to take advantage of all of Photoshop's features.

Using Adobe Streamline

If you need to trace over and redraw scanned images, Adobe Streamline is one of the best software packages that you can buy. Streamline enables you to trace over digitized photographs or artwork in a variety of file formats such as PICT, TIFF, and Photoshop. Streamline provides more sophisticated controls for autotracing than does Illustrator's own Auto Trace tool. The program even enables you to do some simple editing of images before you trace them.

Figure 20-3 shows a jukebox created by artist Daniel Pelavin for a *New York Times Entertainment* cover (Art Director, Richard Aloisio). Daniel created the image with Illustrator, Photoshop, and Streamline. A scanned photograph of wood grain produced the wood texture for the jukebox. In Photoshop, Daniel saved the scanned photograph in TIFF file format so that he could import the file into Streamline. After opening the digitized photograph in Streamline, he chose the File⇨Convert command. Then Streamline autotraced the digitized photograph, and Daniel saved the image as a color Illustrator file. (**Note:** In Streamline you can also save the image in Freehand file format for use in Freehand. For more information about Freehand, turn to the "Working with Macromedia Freehand" section.) Next, Daniel opened the autotraced wood file in Illustrator and created the rest of the jukebox.

Figure 20-4 was created by using Adobe Photoshop, Streamline, and Illustrator. This image was created by Daniel Pelavin for *PC World* (Art Director, Barbara Adamson). To produce this image, Daniel first created a sketch of the disks and background, as shown at the top of Figure 20-4. He scanned the sketch and

Figure 20-3:
A jukebox created by Daniel Pelavin by using Photoshop, Streamline, and Illustrator.

saved it in PICT format by using Adobe Photoshop. Next he loaded the PICT image into Streamline, where he converted the digital sketch into paths. The Streamline image was opened in Illustrator, where the image was edited and filled with colors and gradations, as shown at the bottom.

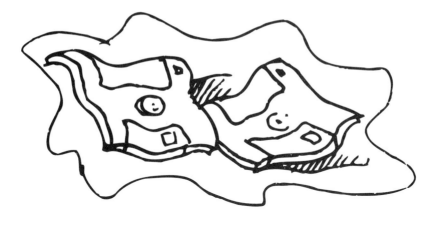

Figure 20-4:
Sketch (top);
image
created by
Daniel
Pelavin after
using Adobe
Photoshop,
Streamline
and
Illustrator
(bottom).

Working with Page Layout Programs

If you're designing a booklet, a newsletter, a magazine, or even a computer manual, you're probably laying out your pages in a page layout program such as Adobe PageMaker, Adobe FrameMaker, or QuarkXPress. You need to save your Illustrator files in Illustrator EPS format to load them into these programs. EPS is a standard format read by most page layout and many image-editing programs. To save your Illustrator file in EPS format, simply choose File⇨Save As. In Illustrator's Save As dialog box, click the Format pop-up menu and select Illustrator EPS from the list of choices.

When you save an image in Illustrator EPS format, a dialog box appears enabling you to create a *preview*. The preview enables you to see the Illustrator image in the page layout program. If you choose an 8-bit preview in the EPS dialog box, the image appears in color in the page layout program. If you choose 1-bit, the image appears in black and white.

Working with Macromedia Freehand Files

If you are a Macromedia Freehand user and want to import your Freehand files into Illustrator, you can save your Freehand files in Illustrator format. After you do so, you can open the file and edit it with any of Illustrator's tools and commands, just as if you had created the image in Illustrator. Figure 20-5 is an image that was created by Art Director Ron Coddington (Researcher, Roy Gallop) at Knight-Ridder Tribune Graphics (Washington, D.C.). To produce this image, Ron went back and forth from Illustrator to Freehand and back to Illustrator. Ron started this image by creating the swimmers with the Pen tool in Illustrator. Next, he imported the Illustrator file into Freehand where he added the gradations to the swimmers. Finally, he imported the Freehand file into Illustrator for the finishing touches.

Working with 3-D Programs

You can create two-dimensional images in Illustrator and convert them into three-dimensional images in 3-D programs such as Adobe Dimensions, Strata Vision 3D, Strata StudioPro, Specular Infini-D, Alias Sketch, and RayDream Designer. Most of these programs load files saved in Illustrator EPS format. Saving in Illustrator EPS format is discussed in the Working with Page Layout Programs section of this chapter and in Chapter 9.

If you've never used a 3-D program, you may want to get started with Adobe Dimensions, which you can install from the CD-ROM included with Illustrator 6. Adobe Dimensions not only enables you to convert Illustrator two-dimensional images into three-dimensional ones, but also enables you to create simple 3-D shapes. The Dimensions toolbox contains tools that help you to automatically create spheres, cylinders, cubes, and pyramids.

Figure 20-5:
An image
created by
Knight-
Ridder
Tribune
Graphics,
using both
Illustrator
and
Freehand.

Figure 20-6 shows an image created with Illustrator, Dimensions, Photoshop, and Xaos Tools Paint Alchemy filters. We created the image for a multimedia presentation. The Dimensions Pen tool helped us to create the separate three-dimensional elements of the 3-D characters. We later extruded (stretched the wire frame) or revolved the two-dimensional shapes to make them 3-D shapes. To create the balloons, we used the Sphere primitive tool and, after creating an element, applied lighting effects.

For the female character, we created flowers with the Pen tool in the Dimensions Map Artwork dialog box and then mapped the flowers onto the character's hat and dress. We also created the stripes on one balloon (with the Pen tool in this same dialog box) and then applied them to the balloon. All the separate 3-D elements were composited in Illustrator. After we composed the 3-D elements, we imported the Illustrator file into Photoshop, where we applied the background that we created by using a Xaos Tools Paint Alchemy filter.

Figure 20-6:
Image
created
using
Dimensions,
Illustrator,
and
Photoshop.

Figure 20-7 was created by John Ryan for Micro Biomedics while John worked at MCA Graphic Services (Stamford, Conn.). John used Adobe Photoshop, Dimensions, and Illustrator. He created various 3-D elements, such as the CD-ROM, modem, and packages, in Dimensions. To create the textures on the packages, he scanned photographs of paper into Photoshop and saved the images as EPS files. Next, John imported the EPS files into Illustrator and applied them to the packages. He created most of the other elements in Illustrator.

You can't wrap scanned images onto three-dimensional shapes in Dimensions. You need to use another 3-D program, such as Strata Vision 3D, Strata Studio Pro, Infini-D, Alias Sketch, and RayDream Designer to do this.

Using Dimensions, you can wrap text around three-dimensional shapes, as shown in Figure 20-8. Use the following steps to wrap text around a three-dimensional shape:

1. **Use one of the Dimensions primitive tools to create a simple 3-D wireframe shape.**

   Figure 20-8 shows the use of the Cylinder tool.

2. **With a 3-D wireframe shape on-screen, use the Direct Selection tool to select the front of the shape.**

3. **With the front of the 3-D wireframe shape selected on-screen, choose Appearance➪Map Artwork.**

Figure 20-7:
Image
created by
John Ryan,
using
Dimension,
Illustrator,
and
Photoshop.

Figure 20-8:
Text
wrapped
around a
glass.
Courtesy
Digital
Stock™'s
Food Stock
CD-ROM.
Photograph
by Joshua
Ets-Hokin.

4. **In the Mapped Artwork dialog box, use the Type tool to create your text; then click Apply to wrap the text onto the 3-D wireframe shape.**

If you want the text to appear on a diagonal as shown in Figure 20-8, use the Rotate tool to rotate the text. If you want your text to be a specific color, make sure that you change colors before you click the Apply button.

5. **With the text wrapped around the 3-D wireframe shape (as shown in Figure 20-9), set the Fill and Stroke of the 3-D wireframe shape to None in the Surface Properties palette.**

Figure 20-9: A wireframe view of the text wrapping around the cylinder.

6. **Choose View⇨Shaded Render to see the results.**

7. **If you want to edit this file in Dimensions at some time in the future, choose File⇨Save to save the file in Dimensions 2.0 format.**

To later import this file into Illustrator, Photoshop, or Painter, choose File⇨Export to save the file in Illustrator 5 format.

Figure 20-10 (at the bottom) shows "Pillar of Stars" created by George Krauter for the February 1996 cover of *Analog Science Fiction & Fact.* To create the image, George started by drawing all basic shapes of the spaceship with the Pen tool in Adobe Illustrator. George then imported the shapes into Strata StudioPro, where he used StudioPro's lathing, extruding, and revolving commands to turn the 2-D shapes into 3-D. Figure 20-10 (at the top) shows the 3-D wireframe model of the spaceship in Strata StudioPro.

To create the textures on the spaceship, George used Illustrator for the initial images, rasterized them in Photoshop, and saved them in PICT file format. He then loaded the texture images into Strata StudioPro, where he "mapped" them onto the surfaces of the spaceship. To complete his creation, George placed the final spaceship image into a Photoshop file containing the background planet and stars.

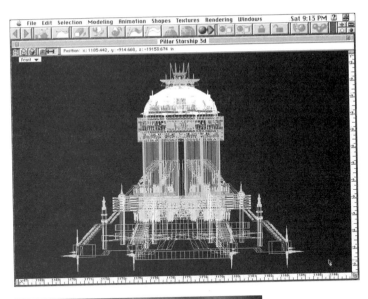

Figure 20-10:
At the top is a 3-D wireframe model in Strata StudioPro. Below is the final image created by George Krauter using Illustrator, Strata StudioPro, and Photoshop.

Figure 20-11 shows an image entitled "Caliper." Rob Mageira created it for *PC Magazine* by using Illustrator, Photoshop, and Alias Sketch. Rob started this image by scanning a caliper into Photoshop and saving it in EPS file format so that he could place the image in Illustrator to use it as a guide to create the two-dimensional shape. Rob created the two-dimensional shape in Illustrator with the Pen tool. In Figure 20-12, the image on the top shows both the scanned image and two-dimensional image created in Illustrator. He then imported the 2-D Illustrator file into Alias Sketch, where the *Bézier curve* information from the file changed to sophisticated 3-D curves called *NURBS*. To make this 2-D to 3-D transformation, Rob used the Revolve (Lathe) feature of Alias Sketch. The Revolve (Lathe) dialog box is shown in the center image of Figure 20-12. In Figure 20-12, the image on the bottom shows the Illustrator file converted into a three-dimensional wireframe model before applying textures to it.

Figure 20-11:
Image created by Rob Mageira by using Illustrator, Photoshop, and Alias Sketch.

To complete the image, Rob applied textures (that he created by using Illustrator and Photoshop) to the 3-D shapes in Alias Sketch.

Another feature that many 3-D programs provide is 3-D animation. Some of the programs that provide 3-D animation are Strata Vision 3D, Strata StudioPro, Specular Infini-D, and RayDream Designer.

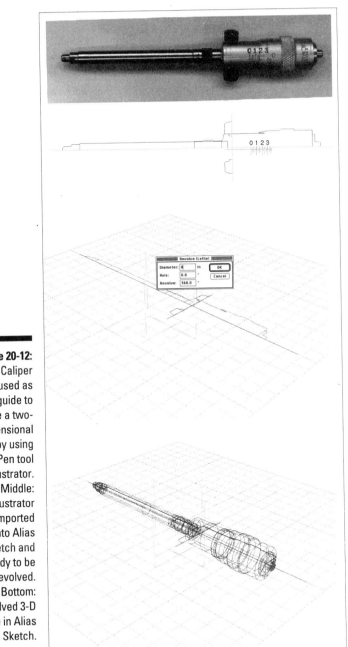

Figure 20-12:
Top: Caliper
photo used as
a guide to
create a two-
dimensional
path by using
the Pen tool
in Illustrator.
Middle:
Illustrator
path imported
into Alias
Sketch and
ready to be
revolved.
Bottom:
Revolved 3-D
image in Alias
Sketch.

Working with Multimedia Programs

Illustrator is often useful for creating titles and type effects in multimedia programs, such as Macromedia Director — one of the most popular animation and multimedia tools in the country. Director is frequently used to create interactive CD-ROM presentations and CD-ROM games.

If you want to use Illustrator to create objects (such as beveled buttons or images) to appear in multimedia productions, you must save your Illustrator files in PICT file format. PICT is a common file format used by many Macintosh graphics programs. Unfortunately, you cannot save an Illustrator file in PICT format from within Illustrator. To convert an image to PICT format, you first save your Illustrator file in Illustrator EPS format and use a program such as Adobe ScreenReady (which comes on the Illustrator CD-ROM), Equilibrium DeBabelizer, Adobe Photoshop, or Fractal Design Painter. After you convert the Illustrator file to PICT format, you can load it into most Macintosh multimedia programs. To load a PICT file into Macromedia Director, simply choose Director's File⇔Import command.

Figure 20-13 shows a screen from a Director presentation. We used Illustrator, Specular Infini-D, and Photoshop to create the screen. We first created the curtains, the sax player, and the sax itself in Illustrator. We then imported the Illustrator files into Specular Infini-D, where we extruded the images into three-dimensional shapes. Using Kai's Power Tools 3, we created textures in Photoshop, saved them in PICT format, and imported them into Specular Infini-D so that they could be mapped onto the three-dimensional shapes. All the separate elements — the curtains, the sax person, and the sax — were composited by using Photoshop. We saved the final Photoshop file in PICT format and imported it into Director.

If you're going to create digital video presentations, you're likely to use Adobe Premiere, Avid Videoshop, or Adobe After Effects. Importing your Illustrator art or text into these programs is easier when you save your Illustrator files in PICT format. (Saving an Illustrator file in PICT format is discussed in the previous section.) To import a PICT image into Premiere, you simply choose File⇔Import⇔ File. However, you can open an Illustrator file (saved in Illustrator format) by choosing File⇔Open. This opens a dialog box alerting you that your file must be rasterized into Filmstrip format. If you need to import several Illustrator files, you probably want to convert them to PICT format to avoid this dialog box.

To import an Illustrator image into Adobe After Effects, choose File⇔Import⇔ Footage File. In the dialog box that appears, locate and double-click the Illustrator file you want to open.

Figure 20-13:
A screen
from a
Director
presentation
created by
using
Illustrator,
Specular
Infini-D, and
Photoshop.

Working with Acrobat

You can use Illustrator to save a file in Adobe Acrobat's Portable Document
Format (PDF) file. PDF files can be used for output on the Internet's World Wide
Web. PDF files can also be used by computer users who do not have Adobe
Illustrator. All these users need is an Acrobat Reader, and they can view your
Illustrator files on a Mac or PC.

To save a file in PDF format, choose File➪Save As. In the Format pop-up menu,
choose Acrobat (PDF 1.1). Name your file; then click OK.

Chapter 21

Outputting Like the Pros

- Checking out the separation process
- Understanding calibration
- Understanding overprinting
- Using traps
- Using the Separation Setup dialog box
- Outputting tips

*O*ne of the most satisfying aspects of being an Illustrator artist is seeing your final artwork reproduced in a book, magazine, or newspaper. Undoubtedly, after you've spent hours fine-tuning and perfecting your work on-screen, you want the printed version to look as good as possible. Fortunately, most Illustrator artists don't need to be experts on all facets of print production. Many artists rely on professionals that work at service bureaus and prepress houses to handle the more complicated parts of the output process. However, if you want your color artwork to print properly, a little extra knowledge may come in handy.

If you have a general understanding of printing and color separation processes, you can communicate intelligently with the professionals who take your Illustrator files and output them on the printed page. A little extra knowledge about these processes can also help you save money — which almost everyone likes to do.

As you read through the following sections, don't be concerned if you find the subject matter complicated — to some degree, it is. You might think of this chapter as a helpful, get-acquainted chapter. You certainly don't need to memorize how to do everything discussed here, but at least you know that the information is here if you want to know more about the outputting process.

An Overview of the Separation Process

Getting your Illustrator art out the door and onto a printing press involves many steps. To understand the process, remember the basic concepts involved in creating colors. Chapter 10 describes how you can create colors by combining different percentages of cyan, magenta, yellow, and black (these colors are called *process colors*). When working in Illustrator, you can also use custom (or *spot*) colors, which often come from color libraries created by companies such as PANTONE and TRUMATCH.

Before you can output your artwork on a printing press, its colors must be separated into their basic components. That is, the image is first output not as one composite image on a piece of paper, but often as a series of separate filmed negatives: one for each process color or one for each custom color.

You create these separations by specifying options in Illustrator's Separation Setup dialog box and outputting your Illustrator files to a device called an *imagesetter*. During the output process, the imagesetter produces one negative for each process color or one for each custom color. A commercial printer then uses these negatives to create printing plates: one plate for each process color or one for each custom color.

If you are using more than four custom colors, you can save money by converting them to process colors — because the printer can print the print job with a total of four plates.

Understanding Resolution and Screen Frequency

As an Illustrator artist, you can benefit not only from understanding the basic steps involved in print production, but also from knowing what determines print quality. When an imagesetter outputs your file, it outputs at a specific *resolution,* which is usually measured in dots per inch (dpi). The more dots per inch used to reproduce your file, the better the color reproduction (usually). High quality color files are often output at 2,450 dpi.

Another factor related to print quality is the *screen frequency* used to output your Illustrator file. When an imagesetter outputs your file, the dots that it creates go into larger, specific patterns of dots. These tiny dot patterns are called *halftones.* The combination of halftones on the different CMYK printer plates have the responsibility of properly recreating your artwork and color.

The higher the screen frequency, the tighter the dots, and the sharper the images. Color printing often uses screen frequencies of 150, whereas newsprint uses screen frequencies of 80 to 90. The quality of the paper and the printing press used to output the image also affect the choice of screen frequencies.

Fortunately, you don't need to be an expert at resolution and screen frequency. But as you work more with Illustrator, you may need to discuss these subjects with the prepress house or service bureau that outputs your files.

When you print spot colors, inks are mixed together to produce a specific color and are output on a different plate. Therefore, if you print with less than four spot colors, your print job costs less than if you use a four-color print process (with cyan, magenta, yellow, and black inks, one per plate). Occasionally, to get the job done, you need to use the four process colors and a *fifth* color (for a fluorescent color, metallic color, or varnish). Printing both four-color process inks and a fifth color obviously costs more than printing just a four-color process file.

If you don't know (or forgot) whether spot or process colors make up an image, you can use the Eyedropper tool to click on the different colors in the image and watch for the corresponding colors to appear in the Paint Style palette. For more information on using the Eyedropper tool, see Chapter 10.

If you are printing on a black and white or color printer (not on a commercial printing press), you'll probably be printing composites. For more information about printing composites, see Chapter 5.

Color Separation Overview

The following steps give you a summary of the color separation output process in Illustrator. The information in each step is reviewed in greater detail throughout this chapter.

1. **Calibrate your monitor if you have not already done so.**

   For more information on calibrating your monitor, see the section, "Getting Calibrated," later in the chapter.

2. **Apply colors to your Illustrator artwork.**

3. **Set the Overprint option in the Paint Style palette, if needed.**

   You find the discussion of Overprinting later in the chapter.

4. **Complete any necessary *trapping*.**

   Trapping is also a topic for discussion later in the chapter.

5. **Set crop marks on the image that you want to separate.**

   See Chapter 5 for more information on using crop marks.

6. **Choose File⇨Separation Setup to open the Separation Setup dialog box, and specify separation options.**

7. **Output the Separations on an imagesetter, or save them to disk.**

If you output your work in Adobe PageMaker, Adobe FrameMaker, or QuarkXPress, you can create separations in these programs instead of in Illustrator.

Getting Calibrated

When you choose colors on your computer, you might naturally assume that the green you see on your computer screen will match the green that is printed. Unfortunately, this isn't always the case. Your monitor forms the colors that you see on-screen from different components of red, green, and blue light emissions. In most color print jobs, colors represent mixtures of cyan, magenta, yellow, and black inks. When you see your color artwork on the printed page, you see the colors because light is reflected from and absorbed by the ink on the page.

The difference between the way the monitor and the print process reproduce the colors often means that the colors on-screen don't always match the printed page. To avoid these problems, Illustrator lets you calibrate your monitor. When you calibrate your monitor, Illustrator helps you match the screen to the printed page, as closely as possible.

If you are creating artwork to display on-screen only, you don't need to calibrate your monitor.

Illustrator's Paint Style palette allows you to create millions of colors. Unfortunately, many computers can display only 256 colors (unless they have an extra video card or extra video memory). Many newer Macintoshes let you add video memory so that you can view millions of colors — often called *24-bit color*. If you can't see millions of colors, your monitor may only give you an approximate idea of the true colors that you are using or creating.

Following are the steps for calibrating your monitor. Before you begin, you should obtain a progressive color bar. This bar is a strip of colors showing the different combinations of cyan, magenta, yellow, and black. You'll use the color bar to match the colors on-screen to the colors on the color bar. If you don't have a progressive color bar, you can find one in the *Adobe Illustrator User Guide*.

1. **Choose File⇨Preferences⇨Color Matching.**

2. **If you work with both Adobe Illustrator and Adobe Photoshop, select the CIE calibration check box in the Color Matching dialog box. If not, proceed to step 4.**

   If you're wondering what CIE stands for, here it is: Centre International d'Eclairage. CIE developed color standards that Adobe Photoshop uses when converting a file from red, green, and blue colors (RGB) to cyan, magenta, yellow, and black colors (CMYK). When you choose the CIE choice, Illustrator can use the same settings as those specified in Photoshop.

3. **If you choose the CIE settings, set the Ink, Monitor, and Gamma settings to match those you've set up in Adobe Photoshop's Monitor Setup and Printing Inks Setup dialog boxes.**

4. **Compare the colors in the Color Matching dialog box to the progressive color bar; if needed, click a color swatch in the dialog box.**

   If the colors look pretty much the same, you don't need to calibrate. If the colors are not the same, click a color swatch (that doesn't match the printed sample) in the dialog box.

5. **When you click a color swatch in the Color Matching dialog box, the Apple Color picker opens. In this dialog box, try to match the color by clicking in the Color Circle and/or clicking and dragging the color slider. Click OK after you've matched the color as closely as possible.**

6. **Repeat steps 4 and 5 for each color that needs to be matched.**

 When picking colors for use in your artwork, you may want to use a swatchbook (color swatches printed on paper) to get a better idea of how the color looks when printed on the kind of paper that you want to use. PANTONE, TRUMATCH, FOCOLTONE, and Toyo are companies that sell color swatch books.

It's a Knockout: Understanding Overprinting

Before you start assigning colors in Illustrator, you should understand how Illustrator treats colors that appear over one another. When you place one color over another, Illustrator doesn't mix the colors together. Instead, you see one color over another, as if one color cuts out the area beneath it. Printing professionals call this a *knockout* because one color knocks out whatever is beneath it. If you want to make overlapping colors appear transparent when printing, you must *overprint* the colors. When you overprint colors that overlap, a new color may result.

If you want to overprint colors in Illustrator, you should realize that you cannot see overprinting on-screen. Overprinting is visible only after you separate and output your artwork on filmed negatives.

If you want to overprint colors in Illustrator, follow these steps:

1. **Select the object that you want to overprint.**

2. **In the Paint Style palette, click the Overprint Fill option in the right panel of the palette.**

Before you begin to use Illustrator's overprint option, you may want to consult your prepress house or printer to make sure that you get the results you expect.

Using the Overprint Black Filter

You can also add or remove overprinting for colors that contain black using the Overprint black filter. Overprinting black can be used as a form of *trapping* to help prevent *misregistration* problems. (See the next section for more information about trapping and misregistration.)

These steps show you how to use the Overprint Black filter:

1. **Select the objects that you want to filter by adding or removing overprinting for black.**

2. **Choose Filter⇨Colors⇨Overprint Black.**

3. **In the Overprint Black dialog box, select the Add option to add overprinting or the Remove option to remove overprinting.**

4. **In the Percentage black field, enter a percentage of black to specify at what point you want overprinting added or removed.**

   For example, if you enter **70%**, the settings in the dialog box affect objects containing a minimum of 70 percent black

5. **Choose Include Blacks with CMY to apply the dialog box settings to objects painted with cyan, magenta, and yellow, only if the object contains black at the minimum percentage of black specified in step 3.**

6. **Choose Include Custom Blacks to apply the dialog box settings to custom colors that contain the minimum percentage of black specified in step 3.**

Trapped!

When colors print on a commercial printing press, the final color output comes from different colors printing on different printing plates. For example, when a color image has many colors, individual cyan, magenta, yellow, and black plates combine to produce the countless colors in the final image. Unfortunately, if your image is not properly trapped, *misregistration* can occur. Misregistration, as shown in Figure 21-1, produces a small gap where one color overlaps or adjoins another due to misalignment between plates on the printing press. One technique used to compensate for misregistration is called *trapping*. When you trap, colors expand so that they overlap. Overlapping the colors helps to eliminate the gaps that occur in the printing process. *Spread traps* and *choke traps* are the primary trapping methods used to cure misregistration problems.

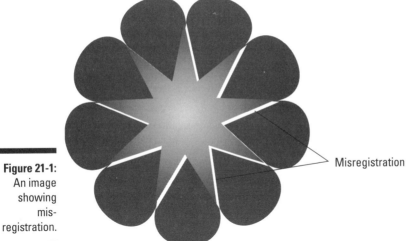

Misregistration

Figure 21-1:
An image
showing
mis-
registration.

In a spread trap, shown on the left of Figure 21-2, lighter areas overlap darker areas. The technique is called *spread* because the lighter areas appear to expand over their background.

A choke trap, shown on the right of Figure 21-2, is often applied when darker areas overlap lighter backgrounds. In a choke trap, the lighter background appears to squeeze in and *choke* the foreground object.

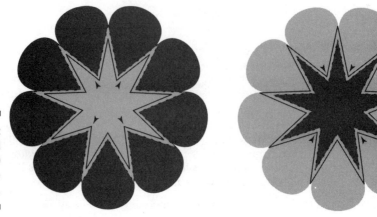

Figure 21-2:
A spread trap (left) and a choke trap (right).

You don't have to worry about trapping if the overlapping object is white or black. When working with process colors, you can avoid trapping if overlapping colors in your artwork share 10 percent of the other color's CMYK color components. See Chapter 10 for more information about working with process colors (cyan, magenta, yellow, and black).

Trapping artwork can be quite time consuming. If your artwork is complex, you'll probably want to pay a service bureau to do the work for you. Using a service bureau costs you more than doing the work yourself, but (chances are) the work will be done correctly.

The following sections describe how to create traps with Illustrator.

Using a Spread trap

You use Spread traps most frequently when the background of an object is darker than the overlapping object. You create the trap by adding a stroke to the overlapping object and setting the overprint option in the Paint Style palette. These actions essentially spread the lighter object over the darker one.

1. **Select the lighter object that is on top of the darker background object.**

2. **In the Paint Style palette, set the stroke color to be the same color as the Fill.**

3. **Set the Stroke Weight field to a value between .6 and 2.0.**

   If you are unsure of how high to set the stroke weight value, contact your commercial printer or service bureau.

4. **In the Paint Style palette, select the Overprint Stroke option. You can find this check box in the right panel of the Paint Style palette.**

Using a Choke trap

You use Choke traps most frequently when the background is lighter than the object that overlaps it. You create the trap by adding a stroke to the overlapping object that matches the fill color of the background object. By stroking the topmost object with the fill color of the background object, you can prevent a color gap between the two objects that you are trapping. Use the following steps:

1. **Select the darker object that is on top of the lighter background object.**

2. **In the Paint Style palette, set the stroke color of the foreground object to be the exact same color as the fill of the object in back of it.**

3. **Set the Stroke Weight field to a value between .6 and 2.0.**

   If you are unsure of how high to set the stroke weight value, contact your commercial printer or service bureau.

4. **In the Paint Style palette, select the Overprint Stroke option. You can find this check box in the right panel of the Paint Style palette.**

Trapping a line

A straight or curved line may require trapping, as follows:

1. **Select the line that you wish to trap.**

2. **Choose Edit⇨Copy and then Edit⇨Paste in front.**

   You use the copied line to create a Spread trap.

   Instead of copying and pasting the line, you can use the Filter⇨Objects⇨ Outline Path command to stroke the line. Then you use the stroke on the line to create a Spread trap.

3. **In the Paint Style palette, set the Stroke color of the copied line to be the same color as the original line's color.**

4. **In the Paint Style palette, set the Stroke weight to a weight larger than the original line.**

5. **With the copied line still selected, select the Overprint Stroke check box in the Paint Style dialog box.**

Trapping by using filters

To make the trapper's life a little easier, Adobe created filters that speed up the process.

Filters that help you trap include Filter⇨Pathfinder⇨Trap and Filter⇨Objects⇨ Outline path. These filters work well in trapping simple graphics, but we don't recommend using them for complex artwork.

Using the Trap filter

The following steps show how to use the Trap filter:

1. **Select the object that you want to trap; then choose Filter⇨ Pathfinder⇨ Trap.**

2. **In the Pathfinder Trap dialog box, enter the stroke width that you want to use in the Thickness field.**

   Adobe recommends entering values between .3 and 1 point.

3. **In the Height/Width field, enter the trap value for horizontal lines; this value is a percentage of the trap value in the Thickness fields.**

   In other words, if you enter **100%** here, the horizontal thickness and vertical thickness are the same. If you enter **200%**, the horizontal thickness is twice the vertical thickness. Changing the Height/Width field changes the horizontal thickness without changing the vertical thickness.

4. **Enter a value in the Tint reduction field to lighten the color values of the lighter color being trapped.**

5. **If you are trapping custom colors, you may want to select the Convert custom colors to process colors option.**

   Doing this creates a process color for the new path created from the trap, instead of creating a new custom color.

6. **If you want to trap darker colors over lighter colors, click the Reverse Traps check box.**

   This doesn't work with blacks containing cyan, magenta, and yellow values.

7. **Click OK.**

Using the Outline Path filter

The Outline Path command can be very helpful when trapping lines because the filter creates closed paths from open paths. (It is easier to trap a line that is a closed path because you can put a stroke and a fill on the line.)

When you apply the Filter⇨Objects⇨Outline Path command to a line that is an open path (that is stroked, but not filled), the line becomes a closed path based upon the size of the stroke weight.

After you execute the filter, the stroke color becomes the fill color. The line (formerly an open path) becomes a closed path with a fill, not an open path with a stroke (and no fill). After the line is a closed path, you can fill and stroke the path with its fill color or the fill color of the object behind it. In other words, you can easily use the object created by the filter to create a Spread or Choke trap. (See "Using a Choke trap" and "Using a Spread trap," in this chapter, for more information.)

Using the Separation Setup Dialog Box

To output color separated files in Illustrator, you need to execute Illustrator's File⇨Separation Setup command. The following is an overview of the options in the Separation Setup dialog box:

1. **To open the Separation Setup dialog box, choose File⇨Separation Setup.**

2. **If you want to see a preview of your art on-screen, leave the Preview check box selected.**

3. **In the Separation Setup dialog box (shown in Figure 21-3), click the Open PPD file to choose a PostScript Printer Description (PPD) that matches your printer or imagesetter.**

   Choosing a PPD file tells Illustrator what type of printer you have and what its capabilities are.

4. **Choose the layers in your document that you want to create separations for by selecting from the Layer pop-up menu.**

5. **Choose the colors that you want to create separations for.**

   The Separation Setup dialog box shows a dot next to the colors that it will create separations for. If you don't want to create a separation for a specific color, click in the crossed-out printer column next to that color. To turn the separation back on for that color, click in the printer column next to the color. (These columns appear in the section below the Image pop-up menu.)

6. **If you want to convert all custom colors to process colors, click the color and select the Convert to Process. To convert individual custom colors to process colors, select the Convert to Color check box.**

   In the Process color column, click next to each custom color that you want converted to a process color. The process color column is the column to the right of the printer column.

Crossed out printer column icon

Printer column icon

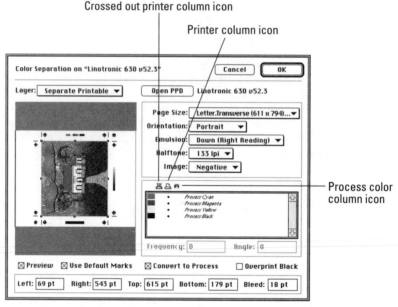

Process color
column icon

Figure 21-3:
The
Separation
Setup dialog
box allows
you to print
color
separations.

7. **Set the halftone screen ruling using the Halftone pop-up menu.**

If you are uncertain what halftone screen ruling to pick, ask your commercial printer or prepress house for advice. Halftone screen ruling is determined by the printing press and paper used to output images.

8. **Choose a page size from the Page Size pop-up menu.**

9. **Choose Portrait or Landscape from the Orientation pop-up menu. Choose Portrait to print vertically or Landscape to print horizontally.**

10. **Choose Up or Down in the Emulsion pop-up menu setting.**

The emulsion deals with the photosensitive side of film or paper that the separations are output to.

11. **Choose Positive or Negative from the Image pop-up menu.**

Most commercial printers in the United States make printing plates from negative film. In Europe and Japan, they commonly use positive film.

12. **Choose the Overprint Black check box, if you want.**

Discuss this option with your commercial printer; it may save you money.

13. **If desired, change the bleed setting in the Bleed field. Entering a bleed value helps ensure that ink prints to the edge of the page.**

The *bleed* figure is the distance in points that the artwork extends beyond the crop marks.

14. **If desired, click and drag the bounding box to reposition it on-screen.**

    The bounding box is the gray rectangle around the artwork.

15. **To print crop marks (at the edge of the bounding box) and registration marks, leave the Use Default Marks setting on.**

    Commercial printers use registration marks to help line up the separations in preparation for printing. The registration marks appear next to the crop marks in Figure 21-3.

16. **After completing these steps, you can print the separations by choosing File⇨Print. In the Print dialog box, select Separation in the pop-up menu.**

    If you want to save your separations to disk, set the Destination option to File and make sure that Separations appears in the pop-up menu.

Printing Tips

When you are printing complicated artwork, you may experience printing problems that prevent you from being successful. Following are things you can try to get your file to print:

- ✔ Whenever possible, use the Pen tool instead of the Freehand tool. The Pen tool usually creates fewer anchor points than the Freehand tool. Unnecessary anchor points can cause problems when printing.

- ✔ If your artwork has too many anchor points you may want to use the Delete Anchor Point tool to delete anchor points. For more information on using the Delete Anchor Point tool, see Chapter 7. You can also delete stray anchor points by choosing Filter⇨Objects⇨Cleanup.

- ✔ If you have complex paths in your artwork, you can choose Split long paths in the Document Setup dialog box. (You can find the Document Setup dialog box in the File menu.) Before choosing this option, you should back up your artwork because Illustrator edits your path when it executes this option.

- ✔ Lower the output resolution in the Document Setup dialog. You must change this setting *before* you create your objects.

- ✔ Lower the resolution for an object that won't print by selecting the object and then choosing Object⇨Attributes. In the Attributes dialog box, Adobe recommends entering resolutions from 100 to 300 (when printing at 300 dpi) or 240 to 300 (when outputting at 2,400 dpi).

✔ If you *placed* any images in your artwork, make sure that you save them and don't remove them from your hard disk. If you are sending your artwork to a service bureau or prepress house to print, make sure that you provide them with the Illustrator file *and* the placed image file.

✔ Also, save your Illustrator file in EPS format. When you save your file in this format, you can click the Include Placed EPS Files option in the EPS Format dialog box. Doing this causes an alert message to the operator who opens your file for printing. The alert message tells the operator to locate the placed EPS file.

Part VI
The Part of Tens

THE GREAT THING ABOUT ILLUSTRATOR IS THAT IT'S MADE GRAPHIC DESIGN AS EASY AS PUTTING ONE FOOT IN FRONT OF THE OTHER.

In this part . . .

You know the great thing about the chapters in this part? They're straightforward! The information is easy to find and easy to read. This part provides you with the ten best path and ten best type keyboard shortcuts. To conclude the part, we put you on the path to success with the ten best drawing and type tips.

Chapter 22

The Top Ten Path and Type Keyboard Shortcuts — and a Few Others

● ●

*F*or your reviewing pleasure, I compiled a listing of the most commonly used and helpful keyboard shortcuts.

Helpful Path Keyboard Shortcuts

Using Illustrator tools together with particular keys from your keyboard can be quite helpful.

Key and tool combination	*Does the following*
⌘ (with any tool selected)	Activates a Selection tool
Ctrl (with the Pen tool selected)	Activates the Add Anchor Point tool
Option (with the Add Anchor Point tool selected)	Activates the Delete Anchor Point tool
Option (with the Delete Anchor Point tool selected)	Activates the Add Anchor Point tool
Option (with the Scissors tool selected)	Activates the Add Anchor Point tool
Ctrl+Option (with the Pen tool selected)	Activates the Convert Direction Point tool
Ctrl (with any Selection tool selected)	Activates the Convert Direction Point tool
Ctrl (with the Freehand tool selected)	Activates the Pen tool
⌘+drag (while drawing with the Freehand tool)	Erases a path
Option+drag a path (with the Selection tool activated)	Duplicates a path

Helpful Type Keyboard Shortcuts

Try these key combinations for quick Type shortcuts.

Key combination	Does the following
⌘+Shift+>	Increases point size
⌘+Shift+<	Decreases point size
Option+Down-arrow key	Increases leading
Option+Up-arrow key	Decreases leading
Option+Right-arrow key	Increases tracking/kerning
Option+Left-arrow key	Decreases tracking/kerning

(If you press the ⌘ key while pressing one of the last two key combinations above, you increase or decrease the tracking/kerning by five times the amount in the Tracking field in the General Preferences dialog box.)

Key combination	Does the following
Option+Shift+Up-arrow key	Increases baseline shift
Option+Shift+Down-arrow key	Decreases baseline shift
⌘+Shift+Right-arrow key	Increases a selection to the next word on the right
⌘+Shift+Left-arrow key	Decreases a selection to the next word on the left

See the Cheat Sheet at the beginning of this book for even more keyboard shortcuts.

Chapter 23
The Top Ten Path and Type Tips

• •

*I*nstead of throwing in all those Tip icons, we'll just tell you up front that this chapter is full of general tips and specific references for working with paths and type. Enjoy!

Use the Pen Tool and Few Anchor Points

Try not to use too many anchor points when working with paths. Also, try to use the Pen tool rather than the Freehand tool to create paths. That way, you don't have too many anchor points, your artwork isn't very complex, and you can probably avoid printing problems. See Chapter 6 for more information about using the Freehand tool. See Chapter 7 for more information about using the Pen tool. See Chapters 5 and 21 for the scoop on printing.

Use the Convert Direction Point Tool

If you have a hard time creating curved paths, you may want to use the Convert Direction Point tool to convert corner points to curves (or vice versa). See Chapter 7 for more information about the Convert Direction Point tool.

Jazz Up Your Artwork

To jazz up your artwork, you may want to place photographs into your images, use custom patterns and/or gradients, or use compounds or masks. See Chapters 3 and 9 for more information about placing images, Chapter 12 for working with patterns, Chapter 11 for more about gradients, and Chapter 18 for the goods on compounds and masks.

Add Depth to Your Work

To add depth to your work, you may want to apply drop shadows, use gradients, or use a 3-D program such as Adobe Dimensions. See Chapter 16 for more information about making drop shadows. See Chapters 15 and 20 for tips on using Adobe Dimensions.

Snazz Up Your Graphs

To snazz up your graphs, you may want to use photographs or create art to use as column or marker designs. See Chapter 19 for more information about exciting graphs.

Use Cool Filters

You may want to use Illustrator's own filters or third-party filters to quickly and easily alter your paths. See Chapter 16 for more information on finding and using filters.

Morph and Blend

You can use the Blend tool to morph (or change) one object into another. See Chapter 17 for tips on morphing by using the Blend tool.

Convert Your Text for Editing Ease

When working with text, you may want to convert your text to paths so that you can easily edit it and apply filters to it. Also by converting to paths, you turn your text into art and it no longer prints as a font. However, if you are using small type and convert it to paths, it may become hard to read.

Before you convert your text to paths, you may want to duplicate the text and place it in another file or in the scratch area (where you can get it back). When you do this, you can always edit the font, size, or text using a Type tool. See Chapter 15 for more information on converting text to paths.

Check Your Spelling

This one's really important. If you are working with a lot of type, it's a good idea to run the spell checker. Nothing says amateur like misspellings. See Chapter 14 to find out how to use this feature.

Show Your True Colors

If you are going to output your work to a printing press, don't rely on how colors look on-screen — calibrate your monitor and use swatch books for precision. For more information, look at Chapter 21 (or talk to your pre-press house or printer).

Index

• **E** •